PLANT PHYSIOLOGY

STRESS, DISEASES AND MANAGEMENT

ENV BOOKS SERIES

PLANT PHYSIOLOGY

STRESS, DISEASES AND MANAGEMENT

Editors

Mr. Prasann Kumar

Assistant Professor

Department of Agronomy, School of Agriculture

Lovely Professional University, Jalandhar - 144 411

(Punjab) (India)

&

Dr. Pawan Kumar 'Bharti'

Society for Environment, Health

Awareness of Nutrition & Toxicology (SEHAT)

B-225/5D, Top Floor, Subhash Gali, Road No. 7, Block B

Ashok Nagar, Shahdara

Delhi-110 093

(India)

Foreword by

M.S. Swaminathan

Founder Chairman

Ex-Member of Parliament (Rajya Sabha)

DPH

DISCOVERY PUBLISHING HOUSE PVT. LTD.

INDIA

Published by:
Namit Wasan
DISCOVERY PUBLISHING HOUSE PVT. LTD.
4383/4B, Ansari Road, Darya Ganj
New Delhi-110 002 (India)
Phone : +91-11-23279245; 23253475; 43596065
E-mail : discoverybooksindia@gmail.com
discoverypublishinghouse@gmail.com
namitwasan9@gmail.com
web : www.discoverypublishinggroup.com

First Edition: **2019**

ISBN: 978-93-88854-00-9

Plant Physiology: ***Stress, Diseases and Management***

Printed at:
Infinity Imaging Systems
Delhi

FOREWORD

M.S. Swaminathan
Founder Chairman
Ex-Member of Parliament (Rajya Sabha)

I am very glad to know that a several books are being edited under the aegis of ENVBOOKS series Delhi, India on various sub-themes of Agriculture and environment like:

- Heavy Metals and Pesticides in Environment
- Heavy conservation and renewable sources Climate Change and Agriculture Production
- Geospatial Technology and Ecosystem Assessment
- Food Technology and Agriculture Advancement
- Vermicompost and Vermitechnology
- Pest Control and Management
- Plant Response to Environmental Stress
- Bioremediation and Biotechnology
- Noise and Air Pollution
- Risk and Disaster Management
- Agro-ecology and Environmental Biotechnology
- Water and Wastewater Management
- Soil Pollution and Lithosphere
- Earth Ecosystem and Pollution
- Microbial Ecology
- Waste Recycling and Product Development

I am very happy to learn that a number of editors and authors from different institutions and university of different nations are involved in editing these books. The books are the compendium of screened-in manuscripts received from different countries like UK, Canada, Egypt, Nigeria, Ghana, Ethiopia, China, South Africa, Japan, Guyana, PNG, Nepal, South America and various parts of India. I am feeling delighted in writing forward to these books and congratulate to Dr. Pawan Kumar 'Bharti', Editor-in-Chief and founder of ENVBOOKs series and of course his team for their tenacity and hard work in compiling these valuable compendiums.

I hope these books will be beneficial for academician, researchers, industrialist policy makes and students as study material and will work as reference for further research work.

M.S. Swaminathan

PREFACE

Plant physiology is a subdiscipline of botany concerned with the functioning, or physiology, of plants. Closely related fields include plant morphology (structure of plants), plant ecology (interactions with the environment), phytochemistry (biochemistry of plants), cell biology, genetics, biophysics and molecular biology.

Fundamental processes such as photosynthesis, respiration, plant nutrition, plant hormone functions, tropisms, nastic movements, photoperiodism, photomorphogenesis, circadian rhythms, environmental stress physiology, seed germination, dormancy and stomata function and transpiration, both parts of plant water relations, are studied by plant physiologists.

The field of plant physiology includes the study of all the internal activities of plants—those chemical and physical processes associated with life as they occur in plants. This includes study at many levels of scale of size and time. At the smallest scale are molecular interactions of photosynthesis and internal diffusion of water, minerals and nutrients. At the largest scale are the processes of plant development, seasonality, dormancy and reproductive control. Major subdisciplines of plant physiology include phytochemistry and phytopathology. The scope of plant physiology as a discipline may be divided into several major areas of research.

The present book updates the subject content of agriculture crops, plant physiology, environmental stress, plant tolerance, plant disease, crop plant treatment, agriculture management.

Thanks are due to publisher and contributors from various institutions and universities.

The book will be helpful for the researchers, academia working in the field of agriculture crops, plant physiology, environmental stress, plant tolerance, plant disease, crop plant treatment, agriculture management.

Editors
(envbooks@gmail.com)

CONTENTS

Plant Physiology : *Stress, Diseases and Management* Pages 1-8
Edited by: Mr. Prasann Kumar; Dr. Pawan Kumar 'Bharti'
ISBN: 978-93-88854-00-9
Edition: 2019
Published by: Discovery Publishing House Pvt. Ltd., New Delhi (India)

1 Introduction

Plant physiology is a branch of botany concerned with the functioning, or physiology, of plants. Closely related fields include plant morphology (structure of plants), plant ecology (interactions with the environment), phytochemistry (biochemistry of plants), cell biology, genetics, biophysics and molecular biology.

Fundamental processes such as photosynthesis, respiration, plant nutrition, plant hormone functions, tropisms, nastic movements, photoperiodism, photomorphogenesis, circadian rhythms, environmental stress physiology, seed germination, dormancy and stomata function and transpiration, both parts of plant water relations, are studied by plant physiologists.

The field of plant physiology includes the study of all the internal activities of plants—those chemical and physical processes associated with life as they occur in plants. This includes study at many levels of scale of size and time. At the smallest scale are molecular interactions of photosynthesis and internal diffusion of water, minerals, and nutrients. At the largest scale are the processes of plant development, seasonality, dormancy, and reproductive control. Major subdisciplines of plant physiology include phytochemistry (the study of the biochemistry of plants) and phytopathology (the study of disease in plants). The scope of plant physiology as a discipline may be divided into several major areas of research.

First, the study of phytochemistry (plant chemistry) is included within the domain of plant physiology. To function and survive, plants produce a wide array of chemical compounds not found in other organisms. Photosynthesis requires a large array of pigments, enzymes, and other compounds to function. Because they cannot move, plants must also defend themselves chemically from herbivores, pathogens and competition from other plants. They do this by producing toxins and foul-tasting or smelling chemicals. Other compounds defend plants against disease, permit survival during drought, and prepare plants for dormancy, while other compounds are used to attract pollinators or herbivores to spread ripe seeds.

Secondly, plant physiology includes the study of biological and chemical processes of individual plant cells. Plant cells have a number of features that distinguish them from cells of animals, and which lead to major differences in the way that plant life behaves and responds differently from animal life. For example, plant cells have a cell wall which restricts the shape of plant cells and thereby limits the flexibility and mobility of plants. Plant cells also contain chlorophyll, a chemical compound that interacts with light in a way that enables plants to manufacture their own nutrients rather than consuming other living things as animals do.

Thirdly, plant physiology deals with interactions between cells, tissues, and organs within a plant. Different cells and tissues are physically and chemically specialized to perform different functions. Roots and rhizoids function to anchor the plant and acquire minerals in the soil. Leaves catch light in order to manufacture nutrients. For both of these organs to remain living, minerals that the roots acquire must be transported to the leaves, and the nutrients manufactured in the leaves must be transported to the roots. Plants have developed a number of ways to achieve this transport, such as vascular tissue, and the functioning of the various modes of transport is studied by plant physiologists.

Fourthly, plant physiologists study the ways that plants control or regulate internal functions. Like animals, plants produce chemicals called hormones which are produced in one part of the plant to signal cells in another part of the plant to respond. Many flowering plants bloom at the appropriate time because of light-sensitive compounds that respond to the length of the night, a phenomenon known as photoperiodism. The ripening of fruit and loss of leaves in the winter are controlled in part by the production of the gas ethylene by the plant.

Finally, plant physiology includes the study of plant response to environmental conditions and their variation, a field known as environmental physiology. Stress from water loss, changes in air chemistry, or crowding by other plants can lead to changes in the way a plant functions. These changes may be affected by genetic, chemical, and physical factors.

Plant Disease

Plant disease, an impairment of the normal state of a plant that interrupts or modifies its vital functions. All species of plants, wild and cultivated alike, are subject to disease. Although each species is susceptible to characteristic diseases, these are, in each case, relatively few in number. The occurrence and prevalence of plant diseases vary from season to season, depending on the presence of the pathogen, environmental conditions, and the crops and varieties grown. Some plant varieties are particularly subject to outbreaks of diseases while others are more resistant to them.

Control of plant diseases is crucial to the reliable production of food, and it provides significant reductions in agricultural use of land, water, fuel and other inputs. Plants in both natural and cultivated populations carry inherent disease resistance, but there are numerous examples of devastating plant disease impacts such as Irish potato famine and chestnut blight, as well as recurrent severe plant diseases like rice blast, soybean cyst nematode, and citrus canker. However, disease control is reasonably successful for most crops. Disease control is achieved by use of plants that have been bred for good resistance to many diseases, and by plant cultivation approaches such as crop rotation, use of pathogen-free seed, appropriate planting date and plant density, control of field moisture, and pesticide use. Across large regions and many crop species, it is estimated that diseases typically reduce plant yields by 10% every year in more developed settings, but yield loss to diseases often exceeds 20% in less developed settings. Continuing advances in the science of plant pathology are needed to improve disease control, and to keep up with changes in disease pressure caused by the ongoing evolution and movement of plant pathogens and by changes in agricultural practices. Plant diseases cause major economic losses for farmers worldwide. The Food and Agriculture Organization estimates indeed that pests and diseases are responsible for about 25% of crop loss. To solve this issue, new methods are needed to detect diseases and pests early, such as novel sensors that detect plant odours and spectroscopy and biophotonics that are able to diagnose plant health and metabolism.

Plant pathology (also phytopathology) is the scientific study of diseases in plants caused by pathogens (infectious organisms) and environmental conditions (physiological factors). Organisms that cause infectious disease include fungi, oomycetes, bacteria, viruses, viroids, virus-like organisms, phytoplasmas, protozoa, nematodes and parasitic plants. Not included are ectoparasites like insects, mites, vertebrate, or other pests that affect plant health by consumption of plant tissues. Plant pathology also involves the study of pathogen identification, disease etiology, disease cycles, economic impact, plant disease epidemiology, plant disease resistance, how plant diseases affect humans and animals, pathosystem genetics, and management of plant diseases.

Plant Pathogens

Fungi

Most phytopathogenic fungi belong to the Ascomycetes and the Basidiomycetes. The fungi reproduce both sexually and asexually via the production of spores and other structures. Spores may be spread long distances by air or water, or they may be soilborne. Many soil inhabiting fungi are capable of living saprotrophically, carrying out the part of their life cycle in the soil. These are facultative saprotrophs. Fungal diseases may be controlled through the use of fungicides and other agriculture practices. However, new races of fungi often evolve that are resistant to various fungicides. Biotrophic fungal pathogens colonize living plant tissue and obtain nutrients from living host cells. Necrotrophic fungal pathogens infect and kill host tissue and extract nutrients from the dead host cells. Significant fungal plant pathogens include:

Ascomycetes

Fusarium spp. (Fusarium wilt disease)

Thielaviopsis spp. (canker rot, black root rot, Thielaviopsis root rot)

Verticillium spp.

Magnaporthe grisea (rice blast)

Sclerotinia sclerotiorum (cottony rot)

Basidiomycetes

Ustilago spp. (smuts)

Rhizoctonia spp.

Phakospora pachyrhizi (soybean rust)

Puccinia spp. (severe rusts of cereals and grasses)

Armillaria spp. (honey fungus species, virulent pathogens of trees)

Fungus-like organisms

Oomycetes

The oomycetes are fungus-like organisms. They include some of the most destructive plant pathogens including the genus Phytophthora, which includes the causal agents of potato late blight and sudden oak death. Particular species of oomycetes are responsible for root rot.

Despite not being closely related to the fungi, the oomycetes have developed similar infection strategies. Oomycetes are capable of using effector proteins to turn off a plant's defenses in its infection process. Plant pathologists commonly group them with fungal pathogens.

Significant oomycete plant pathogens include:

Pythium spp.

Phytophthora spp., including the potato blight of the Great Irish Famine (1845–1849)

Phytomyxea

Some slime molds in Phytomyxea cause important diseases, including club root in cabbage and its relatives and powdery scab in potatoes. These are caused by species of Plasmodiophora and Spongospora, respectively.

Bacteria

Most bacteria that are associated with plants are actually saprotrophic and do no harm to the plant itself. However, a small number, around 100 known species, are able to cause disease. Bacterial diseases are much more prevalent in subtropical and tropical regions of the world.

Most plant pathogenic bacteria are rod-shaped (bacilli). In order to be able to colonize the plant they have specific pathogenicity factors. Five main types of bacterial pathogenicity factors are known: uses of cell wall–degrading enzymes, toxins, effector proteins, phytohormones and exopolysaccharides.

Pathogens such as Erwinia species use cell wall–degrading enzymes to cause soft rot. Agrobacterium species change the level of auxins to cause tumours with phytohormones. Exopolysaccharides are produced by bacteria and block xylem vessels, often leading to the death of the plant.

Bacteria control the production of pathogenicity factors via quorum sensing.

Significant bacterial plant pathogens:

- Burkholderia
- Proteobacteria
    - Xanthomonas spp.
    - Pseudomonas spp.

Pseudomonas syringae pv. tomato causes tomato plants to produce less fruit, and it "continues to adapt to the tomato by minimizing its recognition by the tomato immune system."

Phytoplasmas and Spiroplasmas

Phytoplasma and Spiroplasma are genera of bacteria that lack cell walls and are related to the mycoplasmas, which are human pathogens. Together they are referred to as the mollicutes. They also tend to have smaller genomes than most other bacteria. They are normally transmitted by sap-sucking insects, being transferred into the plant's phloem where it reproduces.

Viruses, Viroids and Virus-like Organisms

There are many types of plant virus, and some are even asymptomatic. Under normal circumstances, plant viruses cause only a loss of crop yield. Therefore, it is not economically viable to try to control them, the exception being when they infect perennial species, such as fruit trees.

Most plant viruses have small, single-stranded RNA genomes. However some plant viruses also have double stranded RNA or single or double stranded DNA genomes. These genomes may encode only three or four proteins: a replicase, a coat protein, a movement protein, in order to allow cell to cell movement through plasmodesmata, and sometimes a protein that allows transmission by a vector. Plant viruses can have several more proteins and employ many different molecular translation methods.

Plant viruses are generally transmitted from plant to plant by a vector, but mechanical and seed transmission also occur. Vector transmission is often by an insect (for example, aphids), but some fungi, nematodes, and protozoa have been shown to be viral vectors. In many cases, the insect and virus are specific for virus transmission such as the beet leafhopper that transmits the curly top virus causing disease in several crop plants.

Nematodes

Nematodes are small, multicellular wormlike animals. Many live freely in the soil, but there are some species that parasitize plant roots. They are a problem in tropical and subtropical regions of the world, where they may infect crops. Potato cyst nematodes (Globodera pallida and G. rostochiensis) are widely distributed in Europe and North and South America and cause $300 million worth of damage in Europe every year. Root knot nematodes have quite a large host range, they parasitize plant root systems and thus directly affect the uptake of water and nutrients needed for normal plant growth and reproduction, whereas cyst nematodes tend to be able to infect only a few species. Nematodes are able to cause radical changes in root cells in order to facilitate their lifestyle.

Protozoa and Algae

There are a few examples of plant diseases caused by protozoa (e.g., Phytomonas, a kinetoplastid). They are transmitted as durable zoospores that may be able to survive in a resting state in the soil for many years. Further, they can transmit plant viruses. When the motile zoospores come into contact with a root hair they produce a plasmodium which invades the roots.

Some colourless parasitic algae (e.g., Cephaleuros) also cause plant diseases.

Parasitic Plants

Parasitic plants such as mistletoe and dodder are included in the study of phytopathology. Dodder, for example, is used as a conduit either for the transmission of viruses or virus-like agents from a host plant to a plant that is not typically a host or for an agent that is not graft-transmissible.

Management

Quarantine

A diseased patch of vegetation or individual plants can be isolated from other, healthy growth. Specimens may be destroyed or relocated into a greenhouse for treatment or study. Another option is to avoid the introduction of harmful nonnative organisms by controlling all human traffic and activity (e.g., AQIS), although legislation and enforcement are crucial in order to ensure lasting effectiveness.

Cultural

Farming in some societies is kept on a small scale, tended by peoples whose culture includes farming traditions going back to ancient times. (An example of such traditions would be lifelong training in techniques of plot terracing, weather anticipation and response, fertilization, grafting, seed care, and dedicated gardening.) Plants that are intently monitored often benefit from not only active external protection but also a greater overall vigor. While primitive in the sense of being the most labor-intensive solution by far, where practical or necessary it is more than adequate.

Plant Resistance

Sophisticated agricultural developments now allow growers to choose from among systematically cross-bred species to ensure the greatest hardiness in their crops, as suited for a particular region's pathological profile. Breeding practices have been perfected over centuries, but with the advent of genetic manipulation even finer control of a crop's immunity traits is possible. The engineering of food plants may be less rewarding, however, as higher output is frequently offset by popular suspicion and negative opinion about this "tampering" with nature.

Chemical

(See: pesticide application) Many natural and synthetic compounds can be employed to combat the above threats. This method works by directly eliminating disease-causing organisms or curbing their spread; however, it has been shown to have too broad an effect, typically, to be good for the local ecosystem. From an economic standpoint, all but the simplest natural additives may disqualify a product from "organic" status, potentially reducing the value of the yield.

Biological

Crop rotation may be an effective means to prevent a parasitic population from becoming well-established, as an organism affecting leaves would be starved when the leafy crop is replaced by a tuberous type, etc. Other means to undermine parasites without attacking them directly may exist.

Integrated

The use of two or more of these methods in combination offers a higher chance of effectiveness.

REFERENCES

Agrios, George N. (1972). Plant Pathology (3rd ed.). Academic Press.

Martinelli, F., Scalenghe, R., Davino, S., Panno, S., Scuderi, G., Ruisi, P., Villa, P., Stroppiana, D., Boschetti, M., Goulart, L.R., Davis, C.E., Dandekar, A.M. (2014). "Advanced Methods of Plant Disease Detection. A Review". Agronomy for Sustainable Development. 35: 1–25. doi:10.1007/s13593-014-0246-1.

Nicole Davis (September 9, 2009). "Genome of Irish Potato Famine Pathogen Decoded". Haas *et al.* Broad Institute of MIT and Harvard. Retrieved 24 July 2012.

Kamoun, S.; Furzer, O.; Jones, J. D. G.; Judelson, H. S.; Ali, G. S.; Dalio, R. J. D.; Roy, S. G.; Schena, L.; Zambounis, A.; Panabières, F.; Cahill, D.; Ruocco, M.; Figueiredo, A.; Chen, X. R.; Hulvey, J.; Stam, R.; Lamour, K.; Gijzen, M.; Tyler, B. M.; Grünwald, N. J.; Mukhtar, M. S.; Tomé, D. F. A.; Tör, M.; Van Den Ackerveken, G.; McDowell, J.; Daayf, F.; Fry, W. E.; Lindqvist-Kreuze, H.; Meijer, H. J. G.; *et al.* (2015). "The Top 10 Oomycete Pathogens in Molecular Plant Pathology" (PDF). Molecular Plant Pathology. 16: 413–434. doi:10.1111/mpp.12190.

Grünwald, N. J.; Goss, E. M.; Press, C. M. (2008). "Phytophthora ramorum: A Pathogen with a Remarkably Wide Host Range Causing Sudden Oak Death on Oaks and Ramorum Blight on Woody Ornamentals". Molecular Plant Pathology. 9 (6): 729–40. doi:10.1111/J.1364-3703.2008.00500.X. PMID 19019002.

"Scientists Discover How Deadly Fungal Microbes Enter Host Cells". (VBI) at Virginia Tech Affiliates. Physorg. July 22, 2010. Retrieved July 31, 2012.

Jackson RW (editor). (2009). Plant Pathogenic Bacteria: Genomics and Molecular Biology. Caister Academic Press. ISBN 978-1-904455-37-0.

Burkholder (October 1948). "Bacteria as Plant Pathogens". Annual Review of Microbiology. Cornell University. 2: 389–412. doi:10.1146/annurev.mi.02.100148.002133. PMID 18104350.

"Research Team Unravels Tomato Pathogen's Tricks of the Trade". Virginia Tech. 2011.

Creamer, Rebecca; H. Hubble; A. Lewis (May 2005). "Curtovirus Infection of Chile Pepper in New Mexico". Plant Diseases. 89 (5): 480–486. doi:10.1094/PD-89-0480.

Huynh, Bao-Lam; Matthews, William C.; Ehlers, Jeffrey D.; Lucas, Mitchell R.; Santos, Jansen R. P.; Ndeve, Arsenio; Close, Timothy J.; Roberts, Philip A. (2015-10-08). "A major QTL Corresponding to the Rk Locus for Resistance to Root-knot Nematodes in Cowpea (Vigna unguiculata L. Walp.)". Theoretical and Applied Genetics. 129 (1): 87–95. doi:10.1007/s00122-015-2611-0. ISSN 0040-5752. PMC 4703619/Freely Accessible. PMID 26450274.

Jankevicius, J.V. *et al.* Ciclo biológico de Phytomonas / Biological Cycle of Phytomonas. Memórias do Instituto Oswaldo Cruz, Rio de Janeiro, v. 83, supl. 1, 1988.

Ma, Winbo (March 28, 2011). "How Do Plants Fight Disease? Breakthrough Research by UC Riverside Plant Pathologist Offers a clue". UC Riverside.

"1st Large-scale Map of a Plant's Protein Network Addresses Evolution, Disease Process". Dana-Farber Cancer Institute. July 29, 2011. Archived from the Original on 12 May 2012. Retrieved 24 July 2012.

Aisnworth, G.C. (1981). Introduction to the History of Plant Pathology. Cambridge University Press. ISBN 0-521-23032-2.

https://www.goodhousekeeping.com/home/gardening/a20705625/common-plant-diseases/

https://www.britannica.com/science/plant-disease

https://en.wikipedia.org/wiki/Plant_physiology

Plant Physiology : *Stress, Diseases and Management* **Pages 9-26**
***Edited by:* Mr. Prasann Kumar; Dr. Pawan Kumar 'Bharti'**
ISBN: 978-93-88854-00-9
***Edition:* 2019**
***Published by:* Discovery Publishing House Pvt. Ltd., New Delhi (India)**

2

Absorption of Water by Plants with Special Reference to Physiology of Cells

[1]Prasann Kumar and [2]Shweta Pathak

ABSTRACT

Soil is the major source of water for plants. The plants absorb water through root hairs from the soil. There are four types of water, but all of them are not available to the plants. Water is said to be the liquid of life. Because, life is originated in organs, environmental and in the course of evolution, it became fully dependent upon water in a number of ways. Water is one of the most plentiful chemicals available in the earth and the chemical formula is H_2O. It is a tiny V-shaped molecule contains three atoms do not stay together as the hydrogen atoms are constantly exchanging between water molecules. The water molecule consists of an oxygen atom covalently bonded to two hydrogen atoms. The two O—H bonds form an angle of 105°. Because the oxygen atom is more electronegative than hydrogen, it tends to attract the electrons of the covalent bond. This attraction results in a partial negative charge at the oxygen end of the molecule and a partial positive charge at each hydrogen.

Keywords: Agriculture, Biotic, Crop, Density, Environment, Forage

Introduction

Water has special properties that enable it to act as a solvent and to be readily transported through the body of the plant. These properties derive primarily from the polar structure of the water molecule.

- The Polarity of water molecules gives rise to hydrogen bonds.
- The Polarity of water makes an excellent solvent.
- The Thermal properties of water result from hydrogen bonding.
- The Cohesive and adhesive properties of water are due to hydrogen bonding.

Plants absorb water mostly from soil by their roots. As a general rule, a plant's root system is about as extensive as its shoot system. Water and minerals

[1] Department of Agronomy, School of Agriculture, Lovely Professional University, Jalandhar, Punjab, 144411, India

[2] Department of Plant Physiology, I.Ag. Sci., BHU., Varanasi, 221005, U.P., India

enter the plant from the soil through the surface of the fine branches of its roots. Several centimeters of the tip of each root are covered with numerous root hairs. Each root hair is a tubular projection of an epidermal cell. Root hairs provide the plant with an extensive surface area and maximum access to the water supply.

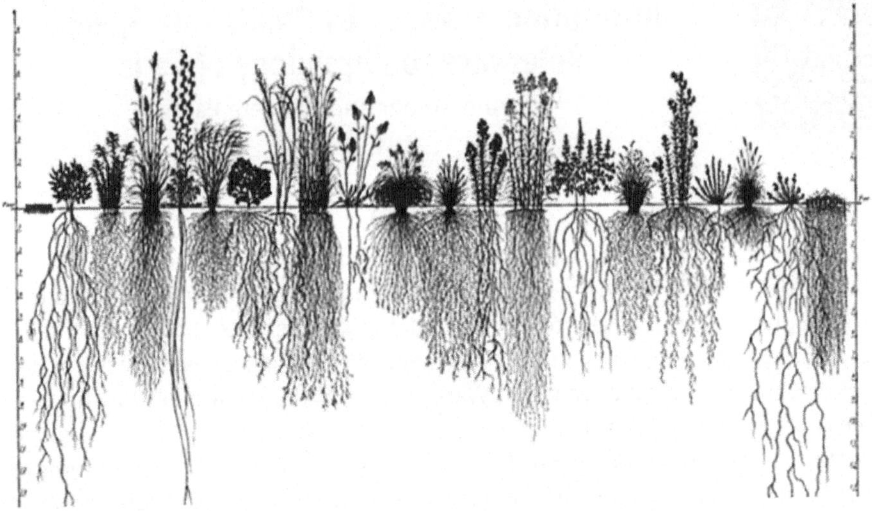

Fig. 2.1: Extensive root system of the plant to absorb water from soil

(**Source:** Based on Review literature, 2018)

Importance of Water to Plants

- Water typically constitutes 80 to 95% of the mass of growing plant tissues.
- Water is the main constituent of protoplasm comprising up to about 90-95 per cent of its total weight. In the absence of water, protoplasm becomes inactive and is even killed.
- Different organic constituents of plants such as carbohydrates, proteins, nucleic acid and enzymes etc. Lose their physical and chemical properties in the absence of water.
- Water participates directly in many metabolic processes. Inter conversion of carbohydrates and organic acids depend upon hydrolysis and condensation reaction.
- Water increases the rate of respiration. Seeds respire fast in the presence of water.
- Water is the source of hydrogen atom for the reduction of CO_2 in the reaction of photosynthesis.

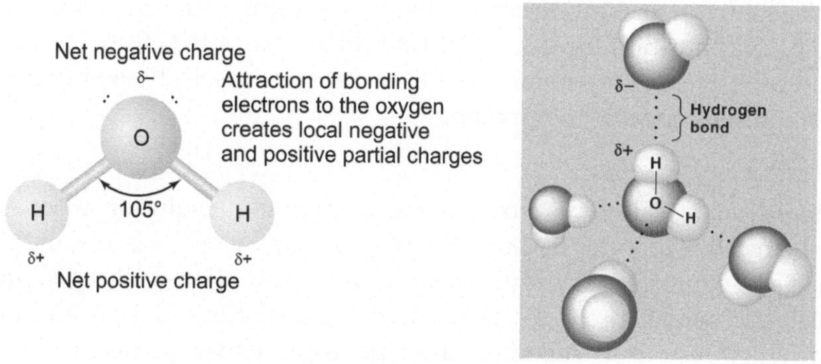

Fig. 2.2: Structure of water molecules

(**Source:** Review Literature, 2018)

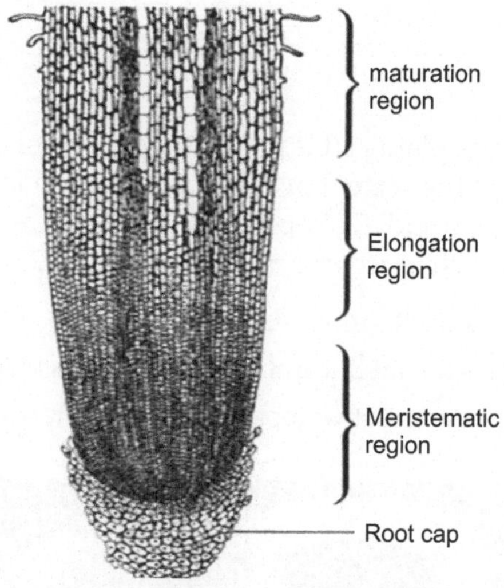

Fig. 2.3: Water absorption area root

(**Source:** Review Literature)

Osmotic Pressure

As a result of the separation of solution from its solvent (or) the two solutions by the semi permeable membrane, a pressure is developed in solution to the pressure by dissolved solutes in it. This is called as osmotic pressure (O.P). OP is measured interms of atmospheres and is directly proportional to the concentration of dissolved solutes in the solution. More concentration solution has higher O.P. O.P of a solution is always higher than its pure solvent. During osmosis, the movement of solvent molecules taken place form the solution whose osmotic pressure is lower (*i.e.,* less concentration as hypotonic) into the solution whose osmotic pressure is higher (*i.e.,* more concentrated as hypertonic). Osmotic diffusion of solvent molecules will not take place if the two solutions separated by the semipermeable membrane are of equal concentration having equal *Osmotic pressures* (*i.e.*, they are isotonic). In plant cells, plasma membrane and tonoplant act as selectively permeable or differentially permeable membrane.

End-osmosis

Of a living plant cell is placed in water or hypotonic solution whose O.P is lower than cell sap, water in-terms into the cell sap by osmosis and the process is called end osmosis. As a result of entry of water with the cell sap, a pressure is developed which press the protoplasm against the cell wall and become turgid. This pressure is called a turgor pressure. Consequence of the turgor pressure is the wall pressure which is exerted by the elastic cell wall against the expanding protoplasm. At a given time, turgor pressure (T.P) equals the wall pressure (W.P).

$$T.P = W.P$$

Exosmosis

If on the other hand, the plant cell is placed in hypertonic solution (whose O.P is higher than cell sap) the water cover out the cell sap into the outer solution and the cell becomes flaccid. This process is known as exosmosis. Cell (or) tissue will remain as such in isotonic solution (Figure 2.4 and 2.5).

Significance of Osmosis in Plants

1. Large quantities of water are absorbed by roots from the soil by osmosis.
2. Cell to cell movement of water and other substances dissolve is involves osmosis.

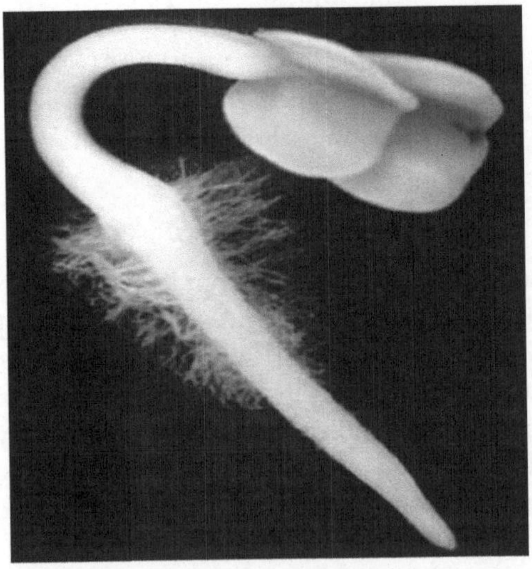

Fig. 2.4: Root hairs of crop plants

(**Source:** Review of Literature)

3. Opening and closing of stomata depend upon the turgor pressure of guard cells.
4. Due to osmosis, the turgidity of the cells and hence the shape or from of them organs is maintained.
5. The resistance of plants to drought and frost increases with increase in osmotic pressure to later cells.
6. Turgidity of the cells of the young seedling allows them to come out of the soil.

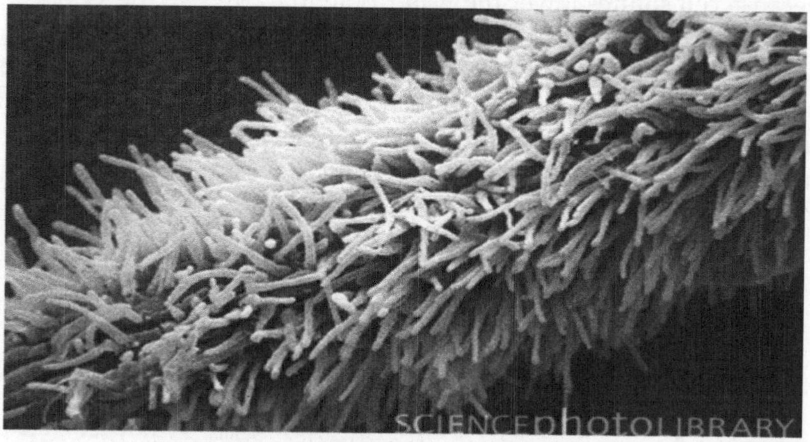

Fig. 2.5: Microscopic study of roots

(**Source:** Review Literature)

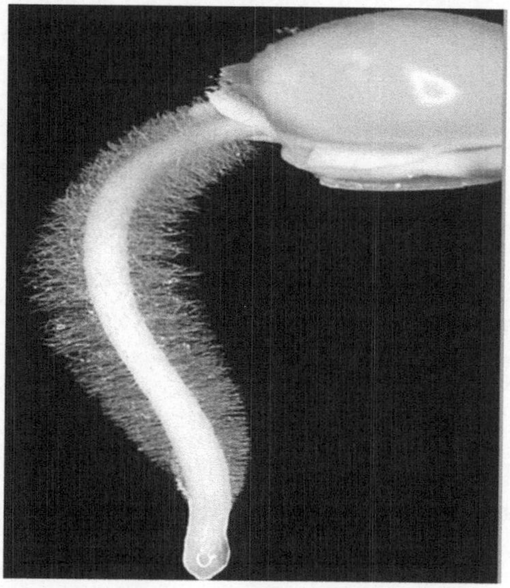

Fig. 2.6: Corn root with prolific growth of root hairs for uptake of water and nutrients from root hairs

(**Source:** Review of Literature)

As the root tip grows into the soil, new root hairs emerge behind it, and thus new reservoirs of water are continually being tapped. Meanwhile, older root hairs usually die. Plant physiologists discuss water relations in terms of water potential (ψw), an expression of the free energy of water in a system. In this concept, water moves from a high to a low water potential. The water potential of pure water is set arbitrarily at 0. In a solution or under tension, the water potential is lower, a negative value. Plant water transport is readily explained in terms of water potential. Water enters a root hair cell from the soil because cell solutes lower the water potential (ψw). In the xylem vessels, water is under tension and has a still lower ψw, and water is pulled from the endodermis and across the root. Up in the leaf, the bundle sheath cells contain solutes and have a low ψw; they pull water from the xylem. Photosynthetic cells in the leaf, with their high sugar content, have a still lower ψw and draw water from adjacent cells in a chain extending to the bundle sheath (Figure 2.7 and 2.8).

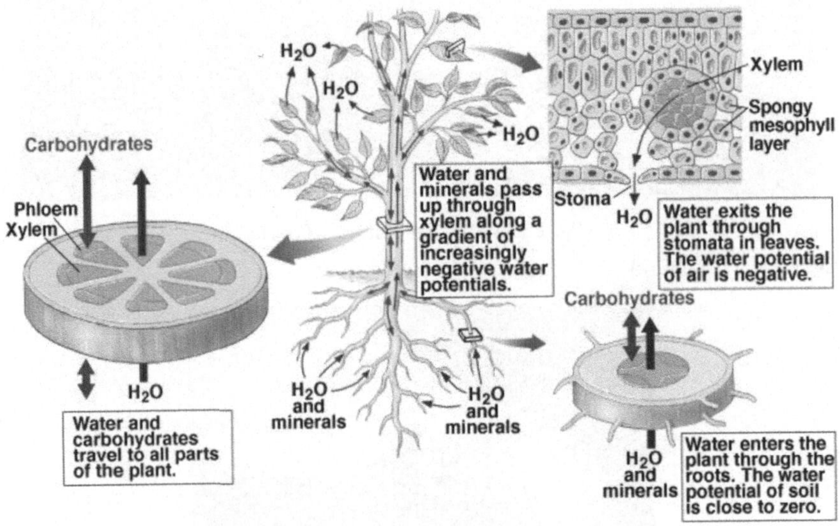

Fig. 2.7: Water movement through a plants

(**Source:** Review of Literature)

Mechanism of Water Absorption

Water is absorbed in plants by two methods:

1. Active absorption
2. Passive absorption

Active Absorption

Water is absorbed due to activities going on in roots. Absorption of water occurs with the help of energy in the form of ATP, which is released due to

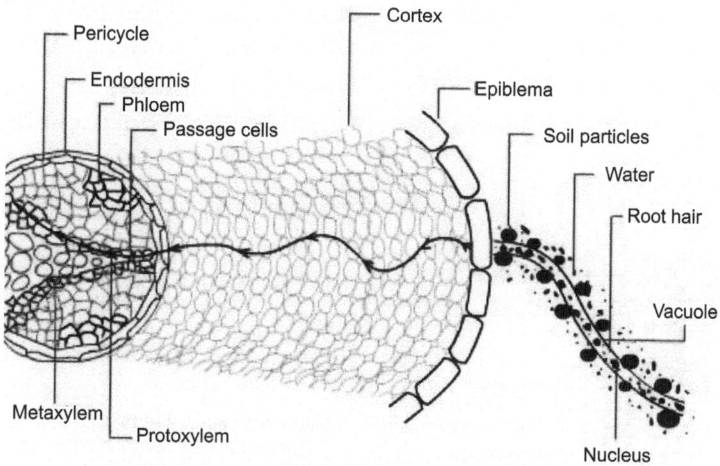

Fig. 2.8: Movement of water and minerals from the root hairs cells

(**Source:** Review of Literature)

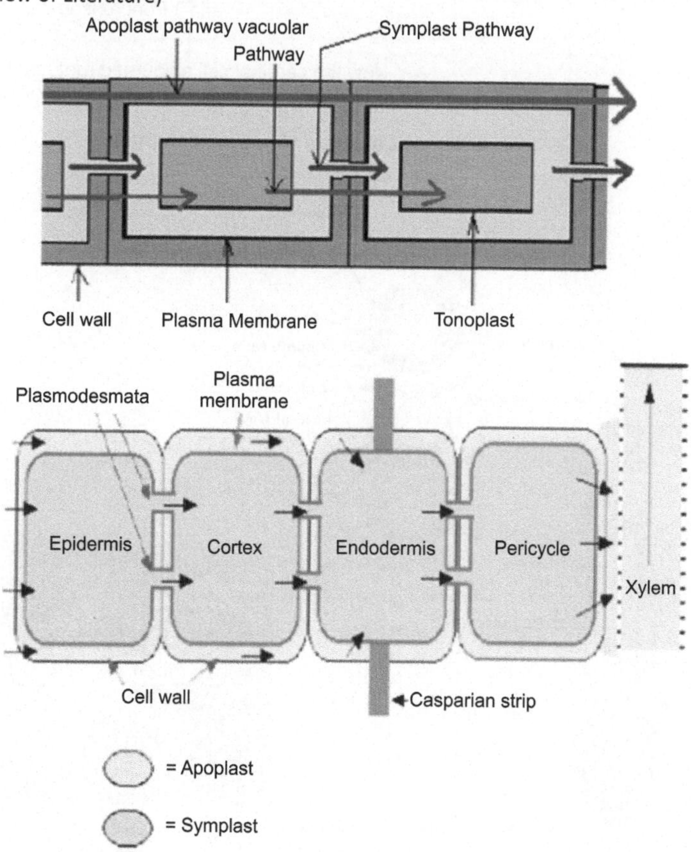

Fig. 2.9: Schematic diagram of apoplastic and symplastic movement of water

(**Source:** Review of Literature)

metabolic activities of root cells such as respiration. Absorption takes place against concentration gradient - even when the concentration of cell sap is lower than that of soil water (Figure 2.10, 2.11 and 2.12).

Water is absorbed from the soil into the xylem of the roots according to osmotic gradient

Oemoticabaorption

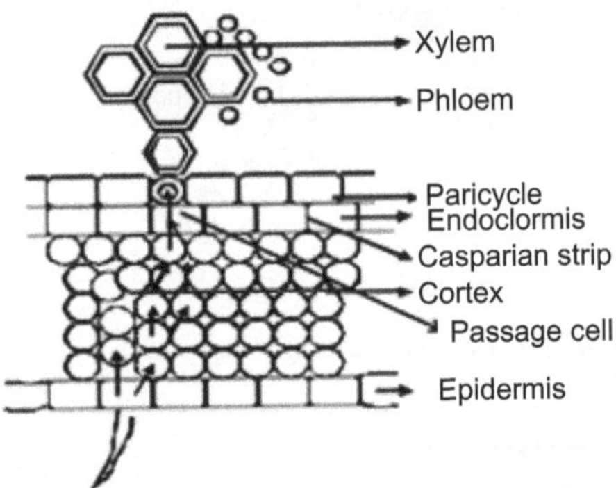

Steps involved

Im bibition of soil water by hydrophilic cell wall

↓

O.P. Cell sop > O.P Soil water

↓

DPD in root hair becomes higher

↓

Water from cell wall enter into them thro' membrane by osmotic diffusion

↓

As a result, O.P, DPD of root becomes lower and T.P increased

↓

Now the cardinal cell adjourned root hair have higher O.P, DPD in comparison to root hair by osmotic diffusion

Fig. 2.10: Schematic diagram of active absorption

(**Source:** Review of Literature)

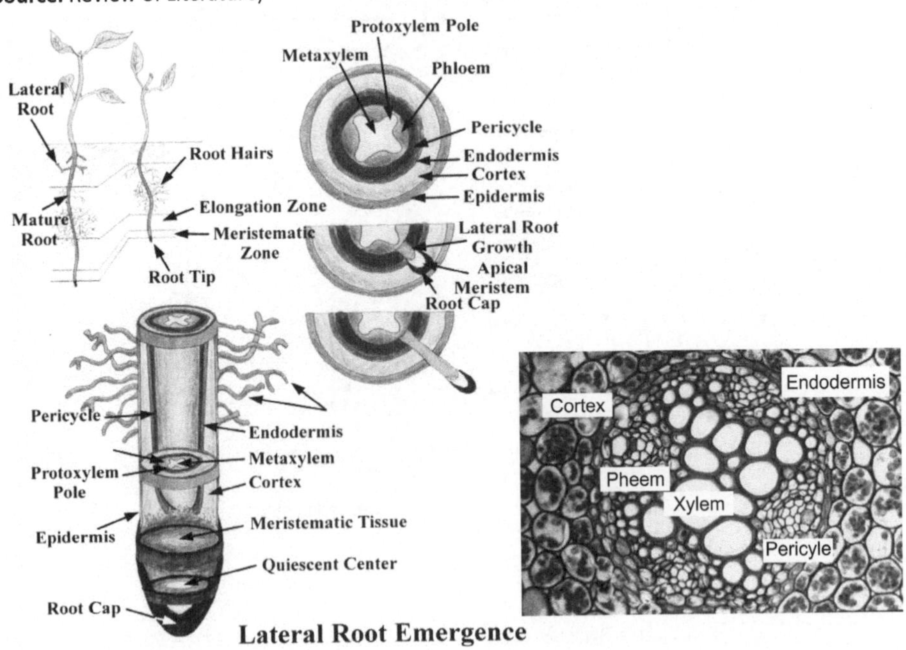

Fig. 2.11. Cross section of roots

(**Source:** Based on Review of Literature)

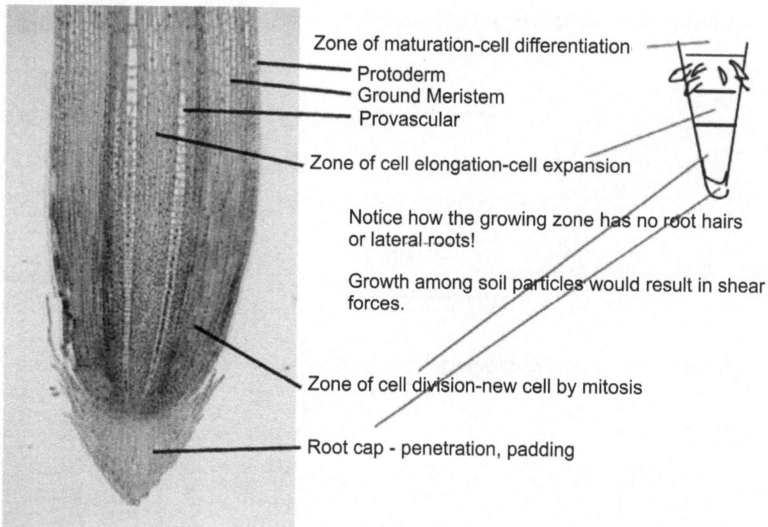

Fig. 2.12: Structure of root hairs

(**Source:** Review of Literature)

Plasmolysis

When a plant cell or tissue is placed in a hypertonic solution water cover out from the cell sap into the outer solution of exosmosis and the protoplasm begins to sprinkler or contract. The protoplasm separate from the cell wall and assures a spherical form and them phenomenon is called plasmolysis. Incipient plasmolysis is stage where protoplasm begins to contract from the cell wall. If a plasmolysed cell in tissue is placed in water, the process of endosmosis take place. Water enters into the cell sap, the cell becomes turgid and the protoplasm again assumes it normal shape and position. This phenomenon is called deplasmolysis (Figure 2.13).

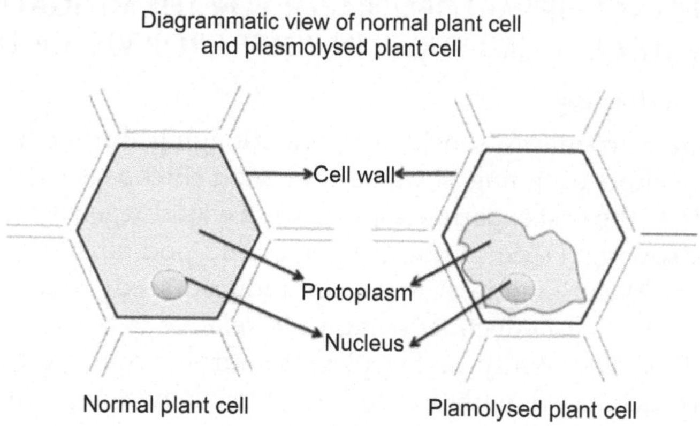

Fig. 2.13: Schematic diagram of normal plant cell and plasmolysed cell

(**Source:** Based on Review of Literature)

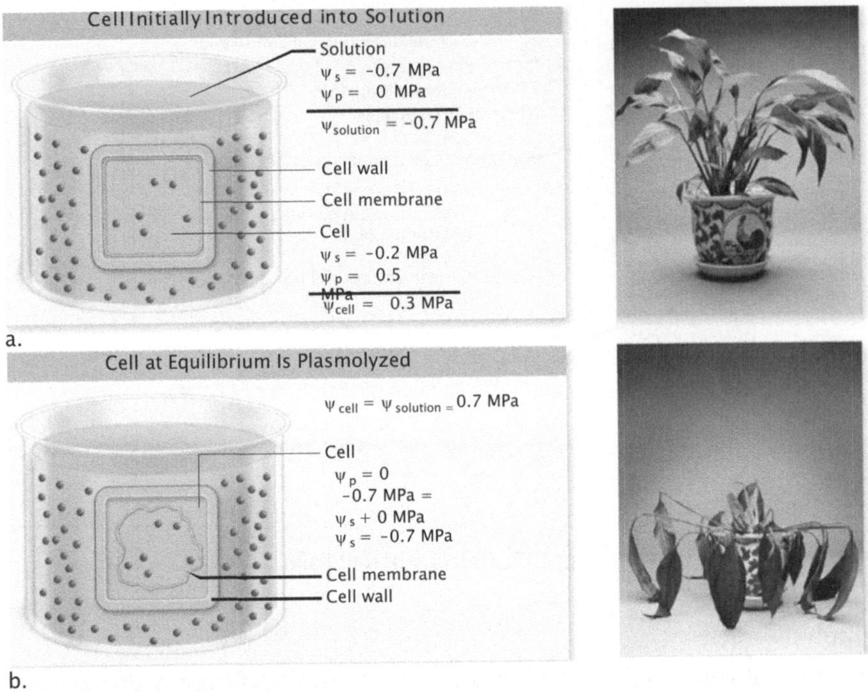

Fig. 2.14: Water potential as key driver for the movement of water

(**Source:** Review of Literature)

Passive Absorption

Passive absorption is by osmosis. Passive absorption takes place along the concentration gradient – when the concentration of cell sap is higher than that of soil water. Water is absorbed when transpiration rate is high or soil is dry.

SIGNIFICANCE OF PACLOBUTRAZOL FOR THE MITIGATION OF WATER LOGGED STRESS IN PULSE CROP VIZ. CICER

Effects of Waterlogging

Chickpeas are particularly sensitive to waterlogging during flowering and podding. The effect of timing of waterlogging on chickpeas was examined in two pot trials. In the first experiment pants were waterlogged for ten days from 21 days after sowing (DAS), at flowering or at mid-pod fill, plus combinations of these times. Waterlogging at any stage reduced seed yield; waterlogging at 21 DAS had the least effect, reducing yield relative to the non-waterlogged control by 35%. The ability of the plant to survive and regrow following waterlogging decreased with increasing physiological age: mortality rate averaged 0, 30 and 100% after waterlogging at 21 DAS, flowering and pod fill, respectively. Tolerance to waterlogging was not enhanced by previous exposure to waterlogging.In the second experiment, waterlogging was imposed at six different times shortly before or after flowering begins. Ability to survive waterlogging declined sharply as flowering commenced: mortality rate increased from 13% when waterlogging was imposed six days before flowering to 65% one day after flowering, and 100% when waterlogging began 7.5 days after flowering. Scientist suggests that survival and recovery after waterlogging may have been inhibited in flowering plants by an inadequate supply of nitrogen or carbohydrates.The experiments were conducted in a glasshouse with daily maximum/minimum temperatures limited to 28/15°C. Tyson was sown into 20 cm diameter pots containing 4.2 kg air-dry, cracking gray clay (TypicPellustert) which had been pasteurized in a steam steriliser for 16 hours. Phosphate fertilizer (50 kg ha -1 P as triple superphosphate) was incorporated before sowing inoculated seed. After emergence, plants were thinned to four per pot in Experiment 1 and five per pot in Experiments 2 and 3. Waterlogging was imposed by immersing pots in water-filled buckets and maintaining the water level at the soil surface for ten days, after which pots were allowed to drain:

Experiment 1

Five treatments were included in a randomized complete block design with five replicates:

(1) Control; (2) BA + GA: Benzyladenine + gibberellic acid (each 25 mg L-1, with 3 mL L^{-1} "Agra160"ionic surfactant, active ingredient nonyl phenol ethylene oxide, 600 g L-l), when the buds were just visible, at waterlogging, and on the fifth day of waterlogging; (3) Leaf: leaflets removed immediately before and during, but not after waterlogging; (4) Bud: buds removed when pedicels began to elongate, prior to and during, but not after waterlogging. All treatments were waterlogged. Waterlogging was imposed individually to each pots when the pedicel had begun to elongate at the most advanced apex of at least two plants in the pot.One additional pot of four plants was maintained as a non-waterlogged reference for measurements of leaf diffusive resistance, which was undertaken daily during waterlogging, between 1100 and 1400 hours, using a Delta-T diffusion porometer. The abaxial surface of the terminal leaflet of the youngest fully expanded leaf on the tallest branch was measured on each plant, and the result expressed relative to the average of the four non-waterlogged plants. Measurements were discontinued when the resistance of a leaf was eight times greater than the non-waterlogged plants. Height from soil surface to uppermost leaf node was measured before waterlogging and at harvest,30 days after the end of waterlogging. The number of green leaves on "new shoot" and mortality rate per pot were recorded before harvest. Plants were divided into root, nodules, "new shoots" and "old shoots" (see Cowie *et al.*, 1996 for definitions of "green leaf', "dead", "new shoots" and "old shoots"). Plant material was dried at 80° for 48 hours and weighed.

Experiment 2

The experiment comprised two sowing times, ten days apart, two bud treatments (retained and removed), and two waterlogging treatments (waterlogged and nonwaterlogged control), arranged in a complete factorial design, giving eight treatments. Treatments were replicated three times, and the whole experiment was duplicated to allow two complete harvests. Buds were removed when pedicels began to elongate. The waterlogging treatment was imposed on the two sowing times simultaneously, at a stage when older plants (Sowing 1) had been flowering, on average, for seven days and the most advanced younger plants. Chickpea (*Cicer arietinum* L.) is cultivated under marginal and rainfed areas. Therefore, drought is one of the major constraints in chickpea production. At present, the application of bioregulators attracts more attention to protect plants from biotic stresses. Paclobutrazol (PBZ) interferes with gibberellins biosynthesis and provides plant protection against water deficit stress.Thus, the present study was undertaken using two contrasting chickpea varieties viz. Desi (Pusan 362) and Kabuli (Pusa1108) for identifying optimum dose of paclobutrazol for foliar and drenching applications under water deficit condition and to analyze the physiological and biochemical alterations to gain insight into the mechanism of paclobutrazol induced water deficit stress tolerance.Initially, a preliminary experiment was conducted with varying dose of paclobutrazol for both floor and drenching applications and Water deficit stress was imposed by restricting water supply until severe symptoms of wilting were visible.Before the imposition of water stress, plants were treated exogenously with an identified optimum dose of paclobutrazol. Based on relative water content, membrane stability index, photosynthetic pigments and photosynthesis rate, optimum dose of PBZ for foliar spray (60 ppm) and drenching (120 ppm) were identified and used for main experiment. Main experiment was comprised two main treatments (*i.e.*, Sufficient watered and water deficit condition) and four sub-treatments (PBZ foliar spray (60 ppm), PBZ drenching (120 ppm), water spray and water drenching). Main results of the experiment showed decrease in RWC, MSI, rate of photosynthesis, stomatal conductance, transpiration rate, Fv/Fm ratio, water use efficiency, chlorophylls, carotenoids, growth parameters, harvest index, drought tolerance efficiency, yield and its attributes and disrupted chloroplast grana under imposed water deficit stress condition. Applications of paclobutrazol maintained higher values of all these parameters and maintained the integrity of chloroplast structureunder imposed water stress and also stimulated faster recovery after water deficit stress termination in both chickpea varieties.Biochemical analysis revealed that total soluble sugars, total free amino acids and proline content increased under imposed water deficit stress and paclobutrazol maintained these at a higher level and hence has a role in osmo-protection. Paclobutrazol reduced the rate of lipid peroxidation and hence provided reduced membrane leakage. It also enhanced the activity of antioxidant enzymes and provided stress tolerance ability to both chickpea varieties. Paclobutrazol increased the level of abscisic acid and thus contributed in stress tolerance. In general PBZ drenching in terms of physio-biochemical responses were found better over the foliar application of PBZ. From the present study it can be concluded that paclobutrazol maintained RWC, MSI, photosynthetic activity, photosynthetic pigments and protected the photosynthetic machinery by enhancing the level of osmolytes, antioxidant activities and level of endogenous hormones and thereby induced water deficit stress tolerance and enhanced the yield.Paclobutrazol reduce the rate of lipid peroxidation and hence provided reduced membrane leakage. It also enhanced the activity of antioxidant enzymes and provided stress tolerance ability to both chickpea varieties. Paclobutrazol increased the level of abscisic acid and thus contributed in stress tolerance. In general PBZ drenching in terms of physio-biochemical responses were found better over the foliar application of PBZ. From the present study it can be concluded that paclobutrazol maintained RWC, MSI, photosynthetic activity, photosynthetic pigments and protected the photosynthetic machinery by enhancing the level of osmolytes, antioxidant activities and level of endogenous hormones and thereby induced water deficit stress tolerance and enhanced the yield.

How Does Paclobutrazol Act?

Available evidence strongly suggests that flower initiation depends on the presence of an unknown flowerpromoting factor or factors synthesized in the leaves. At the same time, there are other factors in the shoots which work against the flowering factor or factors. It is believed that a group of plant hormones called gibberellins act as inhibitors to flowering. When paclobutrazol is applied to the soil, it moves up through the roots into the shoots and, due to its anti-gibberellin properties, blocks the synthesis of flowering inhibitors, thereby allowing the flower-promoting factor(s) to work (Figure 2.15).

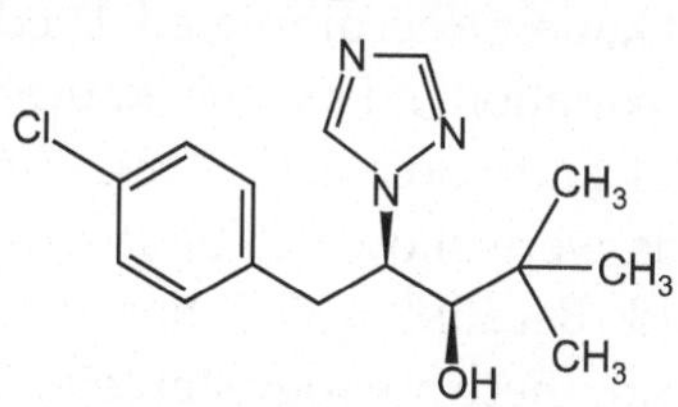

Fig. 2.15: Chemical structure of Paclobutrazol

(**Source:** Based on Review of Literature)

The growth behavior and yield formation of crop plants are governed by their genetic potential, climatic conditions, and the supply of nutrients. Specific control of these processes by the application of plant bioregulators of natural or synthetic origin is increasingly emerging in recent years. Because of their specific properties in regulating shoot growth, the plant growth retardants have become the most widely used groups of bioregulators in agricultural and horticultural practice. For detailed summaries of commercially realized and possible future applications of growth retardants the reader is referred to reviews by Davies *et al.* (1988), Rademacher (1991), and Hoffmann (this volume). When applied in appropriate concentrations, growth retardants modify plant architecture in a typical fashion. Number of internodes and leaves. Concomitantly, the green colour of the foliage is intensified and leaf thickness and epicuticular wax may increase. In contrast to the shoot, the growth retardants maintain or slightly enhance root formation. Therefore, the root-shoot ratio is clearly changed in favour of the root. The morphological effects of growth retardants are accompanied by alterations in the development and physiological behavior of treated plants. The most striking changes include reduction of water consumption, retardation of senescence, and improved resistance to environmental stresses. As a result of this bio-regulation, the economically most important use of growth retardants is in improving lodging resistance and yield formation, particularly in cereals (Bruinsma, 1982; Jung, 1984). Extremely effective compounds have been discovered and developed in recent years. These include substances with a nitrogen containing heterocycle, such as pyrimidine (e.g. in ancyrnidol), 4-pyridine (in inabenfide), triazole (e.g. in uniconazole, "paclobutrazol", triapenthenol, BAS 111, and norbomanodiazetine (in tetcyclacis), and compounds with a cyclohexanetrione (acylcyclohexanedione) structure as the chemical feature. (E)-1-(4-Chlorophenyl)-4,4-dimethyl-2-(1,2,4-triazol-1-yl)-1-penten-3-ol (S-3307), a new plant growth retardant, was investigated to determine the inhibitory sites in gibberellin biosynthesis and the comparative effects of its stereoisomers in a cell-free system from *Cucurbita maxima*. After treatment with S-3307, the incorporation of [^{14}C]mevalonic acid into GA_{12}-aldehyde and GA_{12} clearly was inhibited, and kaurene accumulated. Feeding experiments showed that S-3307 inhibited the oxidation of kaurene, kaurenol and kaurenal, but did not affect the oxidation of kaurenoic acid. Thus the reaction sites of S-3307 in gibberellin biosynthesis were shown to be the three oxidation steps from kaurene to kaurenoic acid. Because S-3307 has an asymmetric center and a tri-substituted double bond, there are four stereoisomers; two optical isomers and two geometrical isomers. The activities of these isomers as a growth retardant and gibberellin biosynthesis inhibitor were examined with a rice seedling assay and the cell-free system. The relative activity of these isomers was basically the same in the two assay methods. The (S)-(E) form was the most active, being 7-fold more active in the cell-free system and 70-fold more active in the bioassay than the (R)-(E) form. The (RS)-(Z) form showed no activity in the cell-free system, but weak dwarfing effects in the rice seedling assay.

Paclobutrazol (Pbz) Induces Morphological Adaptations that Enhance Tolerance to Deficit Irrigation

Water deficit or drought stress is diligently regulated *via* active participation of ABA, jasmonic acid, salicylic acid, auxins and brassinosteroids. Pbz application has shown a positive impact on drought tolerance potential of crop plants.Paclobutrazol application resulted in a reduction in plant height irrespective of growth conditions. Reduced size in Paclobutrazol-treated plants may be linked with its inhibitory action on the GAs, which are involved in cell division. Paclobutrazol application also increased stem width and leaf number in all the conditions tested. Paclobutrazol (at 1.6 ppm) significantly reduced leaf area (LA) (28% and 24%) in both irrigated and deficits irrigated conditions. Integrating leaf and root observations, Paclobutrazol application led to decreased LA/RA ratio in irrigated plants. The Pbz-induced change in LA under deficit irrigation may be linked to improved water use efficiency. Water use efficiency (WUE) increased in 0.8 I and 1.6 I plants as compared to irrigated control. However, in case of deficit irrigation, the WUE increased only in 0.8 DI plants. The 0.8 DI plants have WUE close to irrigated control plants, which suggest that the Pbz induced higher WUE in deficit irrigated plants affording them improved WUE as irrigated control plants (Figure 2.16).

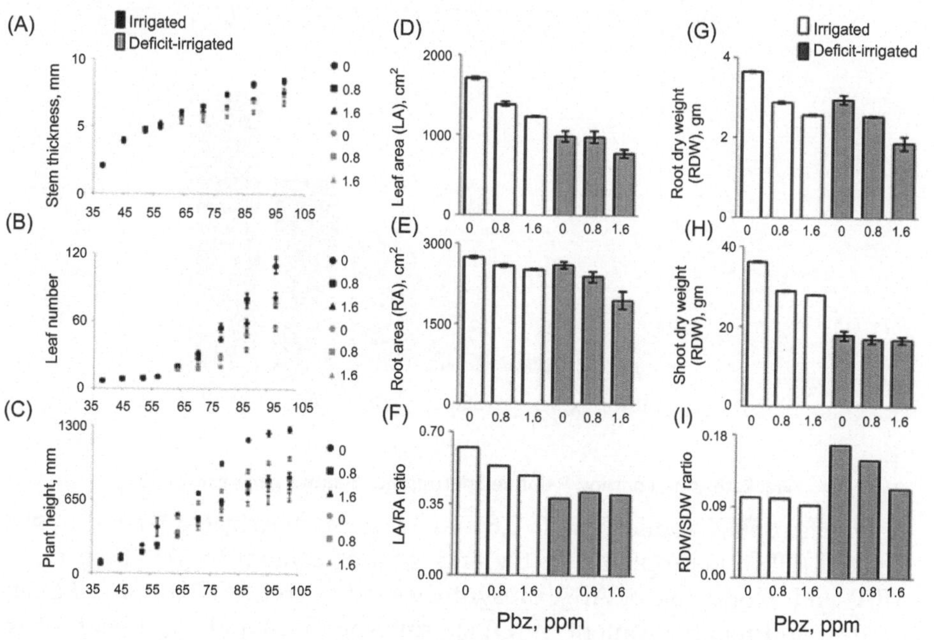

Fig. 2.15: Paclobutrazol induced morphological adaptations under deficit irrigation

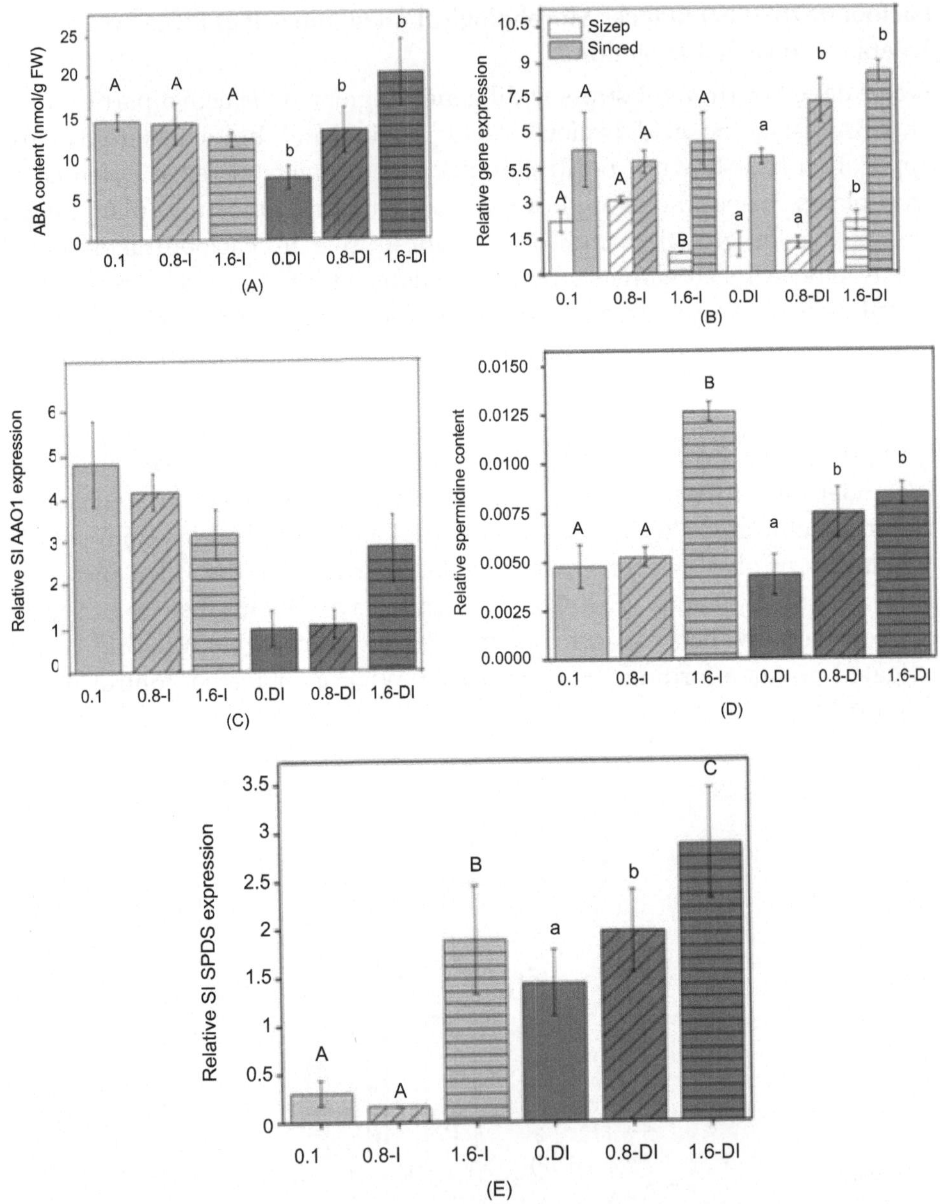

Fig. 2.16: ABA content, Relative Spermidine, Relative gene expression

Effects of PBZ application (0, 0.8 and 1.6 ppm) in irrigated (I) and deficit-irrigated (DI) tomato plants on the endogenous content of (A) abscisic acid (ABA) and expression of ABA biosynthesis genes (B,C) *SlZEP, SlNCED and SlAAO1*, and relative content of (D) spermidine (Spd) and expression of (E) spermidine synthase gene (*SlSPDS*) in the leaf tissue of 105-days old tomato plants. Letters (A, B and a,b,c) indicate significant differences (one way

ANOVA, $p<0.05$) from the control in irrigated and deficit-irrigated conditions, respectively.

Biosynthesis

Paclobutrazol and flurprimidol both significantly reduced growth compared to controls when applied at 0 .5 mg/plant, but XE-1019 was more effective. All three gibberellin (GA) biosynthesis inhibitors effective retarded growth at a dosage of I mg/plant. A number of commercially important plant growth regulators are retards or inhibitors (Nickell 1982, Steffens 1980) . Several are classed as giberellin (GA) biosynthesis inhibitors and have uses or potential uses in commercial agriculture. Examples include triazole compounds represented by palclobutrazol. Other new triazole compounds also have plant growth-regulating activity. A pyrimidine, has been shown to be a potent inhibitor of plant growth via the GA biosynthesis inhibition route. Other potent GA biosynthesis inhibitors include ancymidol. Several triazoles including triadimefon, inhibit ergosterol biosynthesis in fungi and have become commercially important fungicides. Triadimefon applied at 10 mg/plant had essentially no effect on growth, but at 50 and 100 mg/plant it caused significant but less dramatic growth retardation when compared with the GA inhibitors. Major differences in effectiveness among the triazole GA biosynthesis inhibitors may be due to longevity of effect as well as to the extent of inhibition.The plant growth retardants PBZ should be applied to the crops only once at the vegetative growth stage. One method to manipulate flowering is to use the plant growth regulator, paclobutrazol. The post-harvest application of a small amount of paclobutrazol to the soil significantly promotes flowering and fruiting in the following year. Trials over the last two years have shown the following benefits from the treatment: A significant increase in flowering leading to increased yields. The early flowering considerably enhanced fruit maturity. Treated trees flowered three to four weeks early, which reduced the time to fruit maturity by at least two weeks. Visually, the fruit developed a better external colour. The application of paclobutrazol to soil as a drench around the tree trunk (collar drench) is the most effective method, as it ensures proper uptake by the tree. The required quantity is mixed in approximately one litre of water and poured onto the soil around the trunk in a circular band. In the Top End, the ideal time to apply paclobutrazol is from soon after harvest to early January. In dry conditions, a light irrigation is recommended after application. Foliar sprays have been ineffective.

Conclusion

Plants absorb water mostly from soil by their roots. As a general rule, a plant's root system is about as extensive as its shoot system. Water and minerals enter the plant from the soil through the surface of the fine branches of its roots. Several centimeters of the tip of each root are covered with numerous root hairs. Each root hair is a tubular projection of an epidermal cell. Root hairs provide the plant with an extensive surface area and maximum access to the water supply.

REFERENCES

A.L. Cowie, R.S. Jessop and D.A. 1996.MacLeod Plant and Soil. 183(1): 97-103.

Biosynthesis, https://link.springer.com/article/10.1007/BF02054159.

Cubero, J.I. 1987. Morphology of chickpea. p. 35-66. In: M.C. Saxena and K.B. Singh (eds.), The Chickpea. CAB. International, Wallingford, Oxon, OX10 8DE, UK.

Grossi; *et al.* (2005). "Effects of Paclobutrazol on Growth and Fruiting Characteristics of Pitanga Ornamental Pepper". Acta Horticulturae. 683: 333–336.

http://krishikosh.egranth.ac.in/handle/1/5810018882.

http://www.icrisat.org/chickpea/taxonomy/frachc.htm.

https://www.harvesttotable.com/how_to_grow_chickpeas_garbanzo/

http://krishikosh.egranth.ac.in/bitstream/1/68048/1/T-83710.pdf.

https://www.nature.com/articles/srep39321#f1.

Mode of action,https://link.springer.com/chapter/10.1007/978-94-011-2458-4-97.

Pal, S. *et al.* 2016. Paclobutrazol Induces Tolerance in Tomato to Deficit Irrigation Through Diversified Effects on Plant Morphology, Physiology and Metabolism. Sci. Rep. 6, 39321.

Role of Paclobutrazol, http://krishikosh.egranth.ac.in/handle/1/5810018882.

The Plant List: A Working List of All Plant Species". Retrieved 22 October 2014.

Plant Physiology : *Stress, Diseases and Management* **Pages 27-50**
Edited by: **Mr. Prasann Kumar; Dr. Pawan Kumar 'Bharti'**
ISBN: 978-93-88854-00-9
Edition: **2019**
Published by: **Discovery Publishing House Pvt. Ltd., New Delhi (India)**

3

Seed Dormancy with Special Reference to Crop Growth Physiology-Functional Relationships

[1]Prasann Kumar and [2]Shweta Pathak

ABSTRACT

The inability of a seed to germinate physiologically even or doing under the condition which are favorable. This is called as seed dormancy. There are many different kinds and types of seeds those which can be germinated very soon after their maturation. And in some citrus species the seeds may germinate in the fruit itself. But in some of the most cases, these seed passes across the time period of rest stage or else the inactive stage or else the inactive stage before the germination. Such types of seeds even they have external favorable conditions they do not get germinated.

Keywords: Agriculture, Biotic, Crop, Density, Energy, Forage.

Introduction

There is something that which blocks this germination process which is seed dormancy. A dormant seed is one that is unable to germinate in a specified period of time under a combination of environmental factors that are normally suitable for the germination of the non-dormant seed. Dormancy is a mechanism to prevent germination during unsuitable ecological conditions, when the probability of seedling survival is low. One important function of most seeds is delayed germination, which allows time for dispersal and prevents germination of all the seeds at the same time. The staggering of germination safeguards some seeds and seedlings from suffering damage or death from short periods of bad weather or from transient herbivores; it also allows some seeds to germinate when competition from other plants for light and water might be less intense. Another form of delayed seed germination is seed quiescence, which is different from true seed dormancy and occurs when a seed fails to germinate because the external environmental conditions are too dry or warm or cold for germination. Many species of plants have seeds that

[1] Department of Agronomy, School of Agriculture, Lovely Professional University, Jalandhar, Punjab, 144411, India

[2] Department of Plant Physiology, I.Ag. Sci., BHU., Varanasi, 221005, U.P., India

delay germination for many months or years, and some seeds can remain in the soil seed bank for more than 50 years before germination. Some seeds have a very long viability period, and the oldest documented germinating seed was nearly 2000 years old based on radiocarbon dating (Figure 3.1).

Causes of Seed Dormancy

1. Hard seed coat
2. Immaturity of the embryo
3. After ripening
4. Light sensitive seeds
   (*a*) Positive photoblastic
   (*b*) Negative photoblastic
5. Chilling requirement
6. Dormancy due to germination inhibitors

Types of Dormancy

Ecologically depending upon them, how do each of them are raised.

1. Primary dormancy:

Its types

(*a*) Innate

(*b*) Enforced

(*c*) Induced

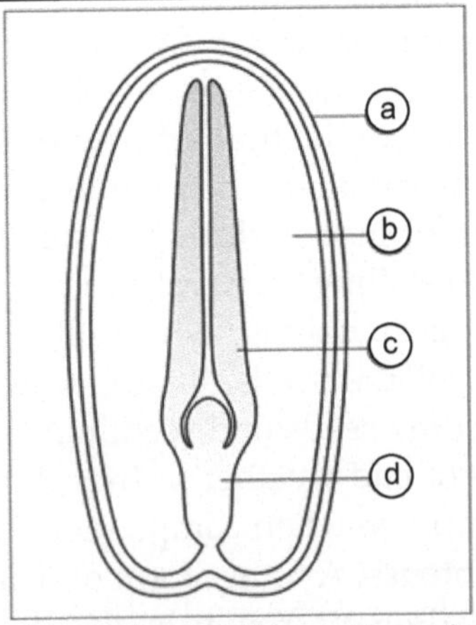

This simple seed diagram shows the
(a) seedcoat, (b) endosperm, (c) cotyledons, and (d) embryo.

Fig. 3.1: Schematic diagram of seed

(**Source:** Review of Literature)

(*a*) **Innate Dormancy:** It is also called true dormancy that which is caused by the conditions within the seed that which prevents the germination even during under the ideally normal conditions. Often based on what part of seed that produces dormancy by that the seed dormancy is been divided into two major different categories.

I. Exogenous dormancy

(*i*) Physical dormancy

(*ii*) Mechanical dormancy

(*iii*) Chemical dormancy

II. Endogenous Dormancy:

(*i*) Physiological dormancy

(*ii*) Drying

(*iii*) Photo dormancy

(*iv*) Thermo dormancy

II. Morphological dormancy

III. Combined dormancy

In the innate dormancy the seeds those which are not capable when dispersed freshly for the germination even in the favorable conditions are being supplied for the growth of the seedlings. This type of inability of the seeds to germinate might be due in the species which are certain for being an immature embryo at disperse time.

I. Exogenous dormancy: It is caused due to the outside conditions of the embryo and its been divided into three groups:

(*i*) Physical dormancy: This occurs when only the seeds are not permeable for the gas exchange and for water which is due to development of seed which is in the last stages e.g.: leguminous seeds.

- These seeds are having very low content of moisture in them and the seed coat prevents them from the water inhibition for this the cracking and chipping of seed coat are the methods for breaking of seed dormancy.
- Most probably the impermeability is caused often by the mucilaginous cell layer which is a composition of macrosclereid cells in the outer layer of the cells.
- Another cause for the impermeability in the seed is due to the endocarp which is hardened.

(*ii*) Mechanical dormancy: In this type of dormancy during the germination if when the seed coats or the other coverings which are very hard for allowing the expanding of embryo, at this situation the mechanical dormancy is been occurred. In the past times instated of this type of mechanisms of the dormancy which was ascribed to a number of species that has been formed to have endogenous factors for their dormancy, which are the factors that include low growth potential of embryo.

(*iii*) Chemical dormancy: Around the covering of the embryo there is presence of growth regulators, etc., those are included by the chemical dormancy. By soaking or washing of the seeds they might leach out of tissues or may be deactivated through other means. Due to the rainwater or the snow melt if there are other chemicals those are been washed out of seeds that which prevents the germination.

II. Endogenous dormancy: Due to the conditions caused within the embryo itself is called as endogenous dormancy.

(*i*) Physiological dormancy: Until and unless when the chemical changes are occurring this physiological dormancy prevents the germination of seeds and the growth of an embryo. The indication of physiological dormancy can be seen whenever the rate of germination takes place after the gibberellin acid (GA3) application or storage in the dry conditions after the dry or after the ripening. Physiological dormancy can be broken only when the inhibiting chemicals are no longer being produced are broken down in the seeds often by the period of cool moisture conditions, below 39F normally, are in case of many species.

(*ii*) Morphological dormancy: In this dormancy the embryo is being under development or undifferentiated. In some seeds they have the embryo which have differentiated fully before the germination of the seeds that should be grown more or the embryo are not differentiated into different tissues at fruits ripening time.

(*iii*) Combined dormancy: Those seeds which are having both physiological and morphological dormancy. These both dormancies occur combined only when the embryos are underdeveloped in the seeds and also have the components which are physiological to dormancy. These types of seeds are needed with the temperature for braking dormancy and also along with the time period for the embryo which are to be grown fully.

- Intermediate simple
- Deep simple
- Deep simple epicotyl
- Deep simple double
- Intermediate complex
- Deep complex

(*b*) Enforced dormancy: It's been occurring when only the seed, which is being simply to be deprived of its or by its requirements for the germination e.g., absence of the oxygen, light, moisture, which is to be sufficient and lack of temperature which is suitable. There is no involvement of any physiological mechanism in this, if the seeds which are being sown deep under the soil due to the absence or lack of the oxygen and sunlight are those which are probably being prevented from germination. Those seeds which fell on top surface of the soil are being exposed to the extreme temperature and irradiance. Those seeds which fell under the shade of other plants which might suffer dormancy which is enforced due to effects of inhibitory of the quality of leaf filtered light.

These are all the different cases in which the enforced dormancy occurred that which prevents the germination process even in the circumstances or the conditions which are unfavorable.

2. Combinational dormancy: This dormancy is caused where both the exogenous and endogenous conditions occur within the same seed.

- In exogenous (physical)
- In endogenous (physiological)

3. Secondary dormancy: These are the dormancy that occurs in some seeds which are post dormant and non-dormant, which are exposed to the non-favorable condition like high temperature for the germination. This dormancy based on the conditions which are occurring after the dispersal of the seeds. Actively the secondary dormancy mechanism which has not yet been fully understood but in the plasma membrane the sensitivity of loss might involve receptors.

Methods of Breaking Seed Dormancy

1. A Natural method of breaking seed dormancy automatically in the nature:

- By developing the growth hormones for the counter growth inhibitors.
- By leaching of the germination inhibitors.
- By the after ripening of embryo and the maturation of embryo.
- By weakening of the tough and the impermeable seed coats by the action of microbes, abrasion, passage through digestive animal's tact etc.

2. Artificially breaking of seed dormancy:

(*i*) Breaking dormancy for the hard seed coat.

Scarification: The hard seed coat which is impermeable, ruptured or weakened by the filling, hot water, chemicals and chipping.

Shaking and pressure: To weaken the seed coats we use the hydraulic pressure and vigorous shaking.

(*ii*) Breaking dormancy of light sensitive seeds:

Exposure to White Light

This process can be promoted by exposing to the light. Some of the seeds do respond at 30-40% moisture contents to a light that after imbibing only. The ineffectiveness of light is shown during the conditions which are dry. The ineffectiveness of light is shown during the conditions which are dry.

Exposure to Red and Far Red Light

For the germination process the red part in the white light of the wavelength 660u it is very effective. In the red part of the white light there are two forms, one is red radiations and the other is far red radiations. When the seed is being exposed to the far red the germination will be inhibited through it in any way. If the seed exposed to the red light as the last installing then the germination takes place in the seed. Normally the far red has been followed soon after the red light, so for this we have to expose the seed first to the far red and then to the red for a number of times and in finial exposure it should be the red light as the seed behavior depended on the radiations.

Roll of Phytochromes

In the U.S in an agricultural department, Handricks and Borthwick during their work they discover a newest pigment in plants and named it as phytochromes that which is responsible for the absorption of the radiation which are far red and red. These control the various phenomena of morphogenetic which are like flowering and seed germination etc.,

Use of Plant Hormones

In these the hormones had been applied. The hormones called kinetin and the gibberllic acid have the ability to replace the requirement of red light by that in the presence of darkness, these hormones then germinate the seeds.

Role of Darkness

By placing the seeds of negative photoblastic in the dark for more than critical period the dormancy can be broken. Because in the seeds of negative photoblastic the phytochromes and the reversibility of far red do not play any role.

(*iii*) Braking dormancy for chilling requiring seeds:

Stratification

For a variable time period the seed have been moistened and exposed to oxygen at low and high temperature.

Counteracting Inhibitors

Use of Gibberellin

By dipping the seeds in the gibberellin inhibitors are being is destroyed. The chilling requiring seed contains abscisic acid, which has an inhibitory hormone which disappears during the process of stratification by that in place gibberellin appeared which has promotes growth in seeds, so that the dormancy which is because of the chilling requirement is under the control of the promoter and inhibitor hormones. Therefore gibberellin acid application replaces the chilling requirement and so, in the presence of this hormone the seeds get germinated as they don't require any chilling temperature.

Use of Growth Promoting Substrates

Chemicals like thiourea, KNO_3 and ethylene chlorohydrin are those used as germination promoters which are mostly used in common. By dipping the seeds in these the inhibitors are destroyed.

APICAL DOMINANCE

In many plants, if the terminal bud is intact and growing, the growth of lateral buds just below it remains suppressed. Removal of the apical bud results in the rapid growth of lateral buds. This phenomenon in which the apical bud dominates over the lateral buds and does not allow the lateral buds to grow is known as *apical dominance*. Skoog and Thimmann (1948) pointed out that the apical dominance might be under the control of auxin produced at the terminal bud and which is transported downward through the stem to the lateral buds and hinders the growth. They removed the apical bud and replaced it with *agar* block. This resulted in rapid growth of lateral buds. But when they replaced the apical bud with agar block containing auxin, the lateral buds remained suppressed and did not grow (Figure 3.2).

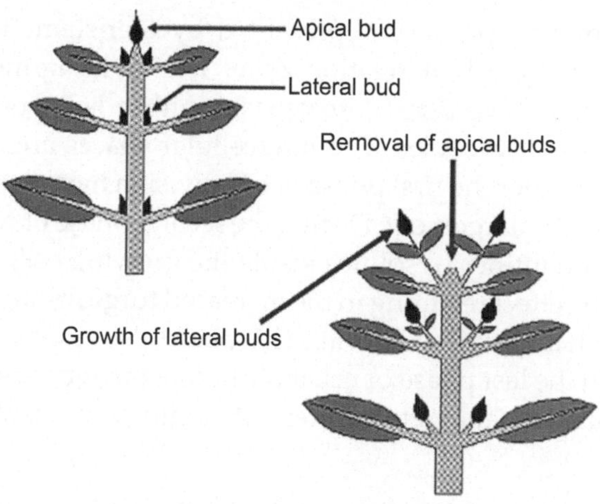

Fig. 3.2: Apical dominance

(**Source:** Review of Literature)

Growth is defined as a vital process that brings about a permanent and irreversible change in any plant or its part in respect to its size, form, weight and volume. Growth is restricted only to living cells and is accomplished by metabolic processes involving synthesize of macromolecules, such as nucleic acids, proteins, lipids and polysaccharides at the expense of metabolic energy. Growth at the cellular level is also accompanied by the organization of macromolecules into assemblages of membranes, plastids, mitochondria, ribosome and other cell organelles. Cells do not definitely increase in size, but divide, giving rise to daughter cells. An important process during cell division is a synthesis and replication of nuclear DNA in the chromosomes, which then passed into the daughter cells. Therefore, the term growth is used to denote an increase in size by cell division and cell enlargement, together with the synthesis of new cellulose materials and the organization of cellular organelles.

Growth Regions

Typical growth regions in plants are the apices of shoot and root. Such growing regions are known as apical meristems, primary meristems or regions of primary growth. These apical meristems are responsible for the increase in length, differentiation of various appendages and formation of plant tissues.

Phases of Growth

Growth is not a simple process. It occurs in meristematic regions where the meristematic cell has to pass through the following 3 phases.

1. Cell formation phase
2. Cell elongation phase
3. Cell differentiation (cell maturation)

The cell formation phase is represented by meristematic zone and cell enlargement phase by cell elongation zone. The dividing meristematic cells are thin walled and have dense protoplasm with a large nucleus and with or without very small vacuoles. The intercellular spaces are also absent. The newly formed cells after the first phase of cell division have to pass through the second phase of cell enlargement. During the second phase of cell elongation on account of large quantities of solutes inside the growing cell, water enters the cell due to osmotic effect resulting in the increased turgidity and expansion and dilation of the thin and elastic cell wall. This phase also results in appearance of large vacuoles. In the last phase or cell maturation, the secondary walls are laid down and cell matures and gets differentiated into permanent tissue.

Growth Curve

The growth curve is a graph obtained by plotting the growth rate of a plant against time factor. The growth rate of a cell, a plant organ, a whole plant or the whole life cycle of plant is measured in terms of length, size, area, volume or weight. It has been found that different growth phases result in 'S' shaped curve or sigmoid curve. In the initial stages during the phase of cell formation, the growth rate increases slowly while it increases rapidly during the phase of cell elongation or cell enlargement and again slows down during the phase of cell maturation (Figure 3.3).

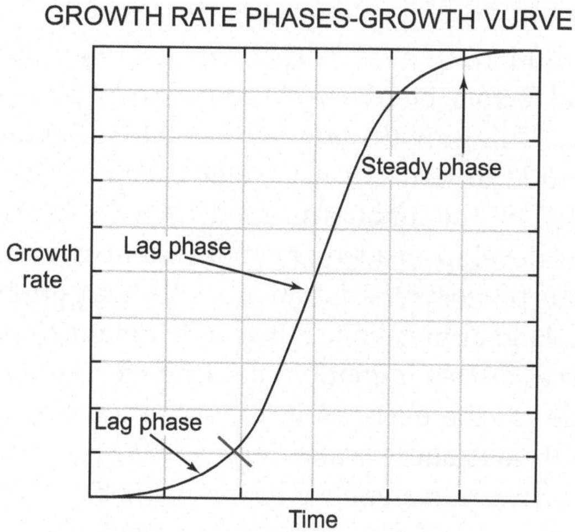

Fig. 3.3: Growth Phases of Plant

(**Source:** Based on Review of Literature)

The period during which the course of growth takes place is known as the grand period of growth. Thus, in a standard growth curve, three well marked regions can be observed, the initial growth stage (lag phase), the grand period

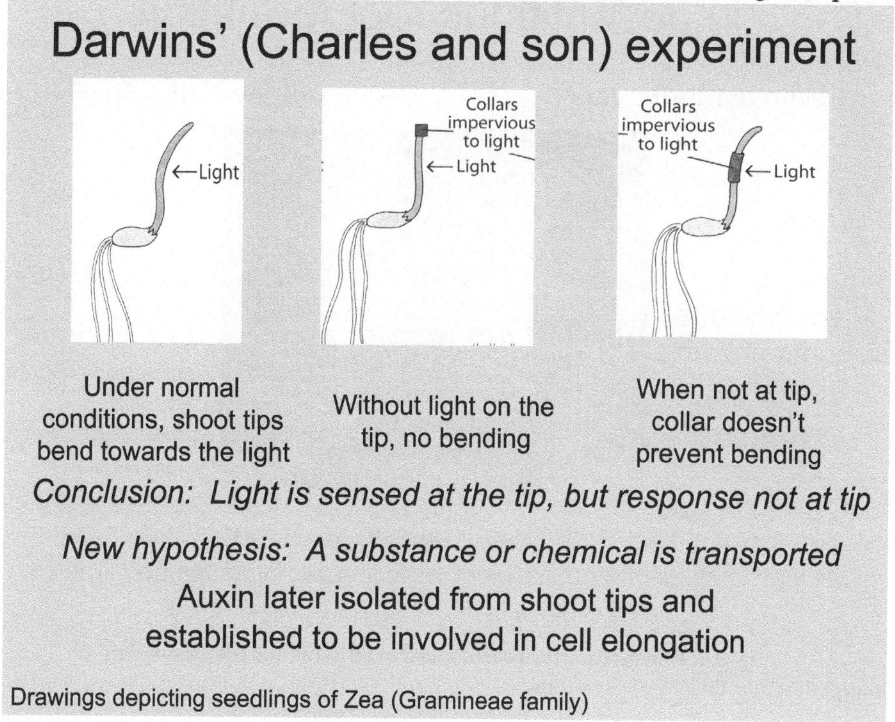

Fig. 3.4: Darwins's experiment

(**Source:** Based on Review of Literature)

of growth (exponential or log phase) and the steady stage (maturity stage or senescence or stationary phase). The overall growth may be affected by external or internal factors, but the S- shaped curve of grand period of growth is never influenced. This growth curve suits well to the entire life of an annual plant when measured in terms of dry weight against time. Early growth of the plant is limited by the amount of food reserves in the seed. When the emerged seedlings develop an adequate root system and enough leaf surfaces to support vigorous photosynthesis and anabolism, a period of rapid increase in size is possible. Higher metabolic rates are not maintained indefinitely and eventually processes are set in motion that leads to cessation of growth. The factors responsible for the decrease in growth are competition for essential metabolites, growth substances, water, light or the accumulation of inhibitors, toxic substances or waste materials (Figures 3.4, 3.5, 3.6, 3.7, 3.8, 3.9, 3.10 & 3.11).

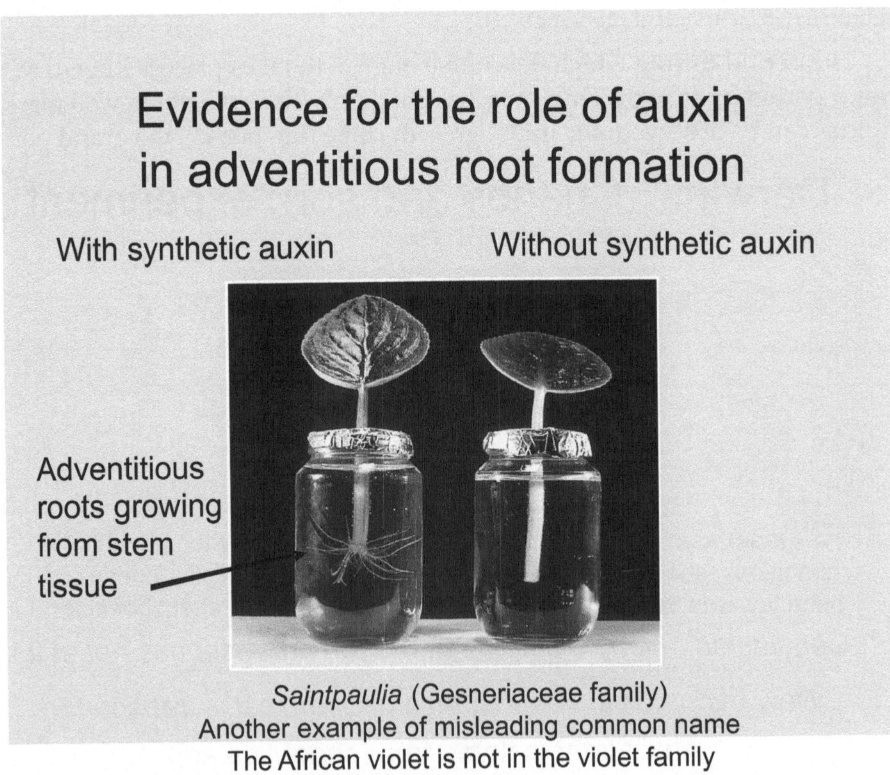

Fig. 3.5: Evidence for the role of auxin in adventitious root formation

(**Source:** Based on Review of Literature)

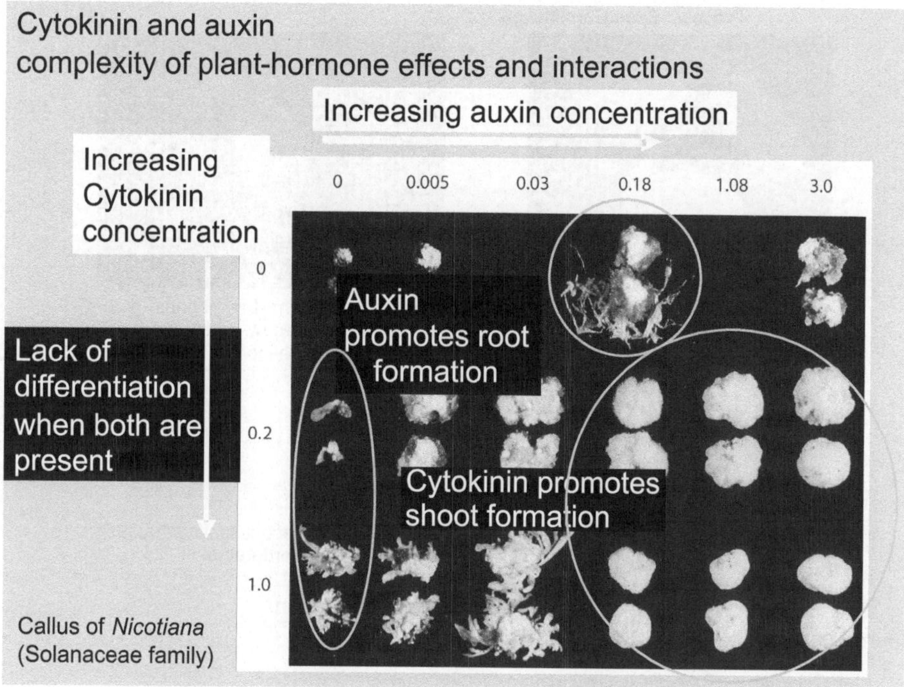

Fig. 3.6: Role of cytokinin and auxin fro growth and development of plant

(**Source:** Based on Review of Literature)

Fig. 3.7: Commercial use of GA

(**Source:** Based on Review of Literature)

Process: Seed Germination

htp://www.buzzle.com/articles/steps-of-seed-germination.html

http://bonnieplants.com/library/bonnie-herb-and-vegetable-plant- food-now-available-for-home-gardens/seed-germinating/

http://www.rollitup.org/cfl-fluorescent-lighting/492395-best-way-germinate-feminized-ordered.html

Fig. 3.8: Process of seed germination

(**Source:** Based on Review of Literature)

Process: Seed Germination

5. Hydrated starch moves to the cotyledon and radicle to initiate growth

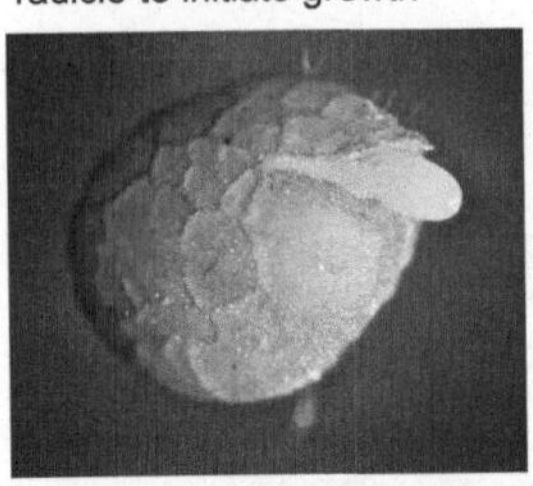

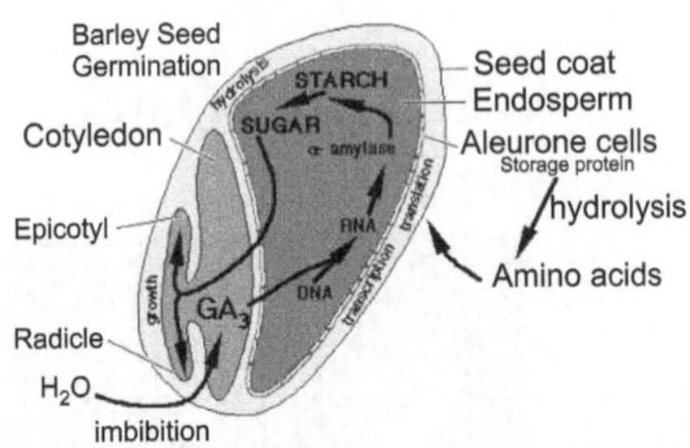

Fig. 3.9: Hydrated starch moved to the cotyledon and radical to initiate growth

(**Source:** Based on Review of Literature)

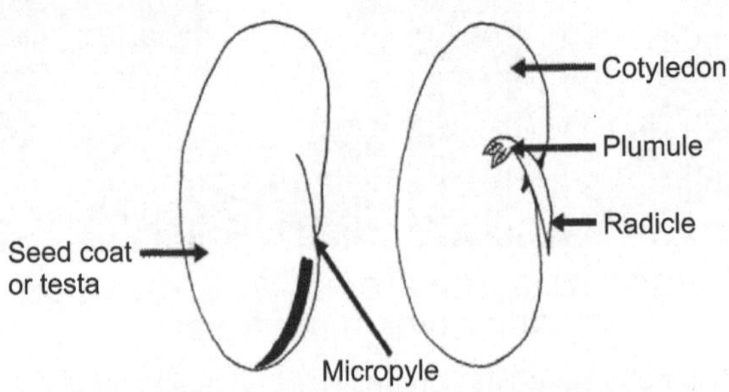

Fig. 3.10. Schematic diagram of Seed structure

(**Source:** Based on Review of Literature)

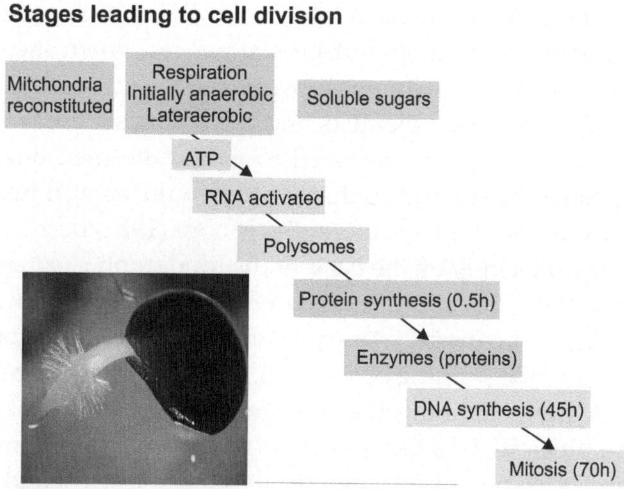

Fig. 3.11. Schematic diagram of stages leading to cell division

(**Source:** Based on Review of Literature)

TETRAZOLIUM TEST FRO SEED VIABILITY

Germination test is the best indication of the potential of a seed lot to emerge under field conditions. However, it takes from days to weeks and in some cases even months to complete. Tetrazolium test, commonly known as the TZ test for seed viability have, therefore,. been developed to furnish quick estimates of seeds' germinability. The test is very useful in processing, handling, storing and marketing. large quantities of seed in a short time, testing dormant seed lots, vigour rating of the seed lots, upplernentinggermination test results and diagnosing the cause of seed deterioration.

Mechanism of the Reaction

Mechanism of the Reaction The TZ test is reliable and widely utilized. The method was pioneered by the German scientist Lakon during the mid nineteens(1939-1958), who recognised that all living tissues, which respire, are capable of reducing a colourless chemical 2,3,5 triphenyl tetrazolium chloride or bromide) into a red coloured compound formazen by H transfer reactions catalysed by the enzyme dehydrogenases (Figure 3.12).

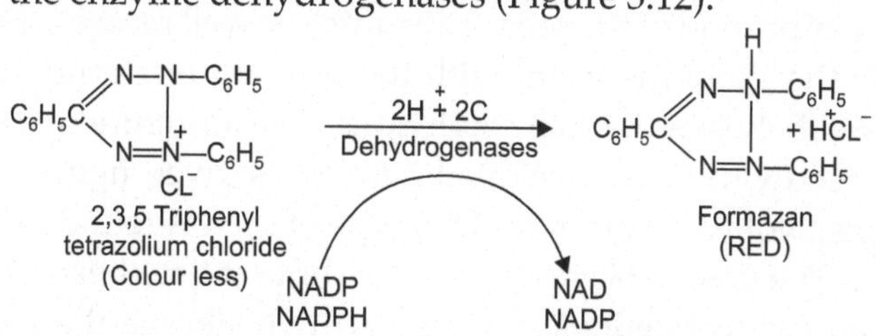

Fig. 3.12: Mechanism of the reactions

(**Source:** Review Literature)

Formazan being non-diffusable, stains the living tissues red. Thus, the living parts of a viable seed should be stained red when incubated in the solution of this chemical. The immense significance and practi~l utility of this test was realised by the See9scientists and technologists the world over and it was suitably modified and improved to assess the seed quality in terms of its viability Since the tissues within a seed could be at different states of viability they would be stained differently. Moore (1973) described the use of TZ staining more efficiently on the basis of the topographic pattern of the seed. The accuracy of the tetrazolium test requires: 1. A sound knowledge of the seed and seedling structures, 2. An understanding of the machanisms of the reactions leading to the staining of the seed. 3. Ability to interpret the staining pattern by critically examining the seed topography and by keeping other visible seed qualities such as tissue turbidity, abnormal or missing structures etc., in view and, 4. Experience gained through keen interest and natural skill. Essential Seed Structures for TZ Test Evaluation Seeds can be grouped into monocots, dicots and polycots on the basis orthe presence of one, two or more than two cotyledons. Embryo structures or structure primordia arc. relatively similar for embryos within each groups, though the ym11Y differ in shape. size and differentiation/development of embryo structures. The critical features of the seeds of these groups me described below. Monocotyledons: Seeds of Gramineae family are a classical example of this class. Tbe most critical features are the growing root and shoot tips and the scutellum. The root region comprise mainly of the radicle which may be theonly root primordia in some cases e.g. small seeded grases or it may have severalseminal root primordia besides the radicle c.g. wheat, maize. barley etc. The radicleties below the mesocotyl region covered under a sheath coleorhiza. The shoot region or the plumule consists of the shoot meristem along with one or more leaf primordia near the base, enclosed within the coleoptilc. Mesocotyl seperates plumule from the point of attachment to tbe scutel1um. The main embryo structures of maize. Dicotyledons: In the dicot seeds with a low degree of differentiation the embryo is embedded in nutritive tissues and consists of a radicle and two cotyledons. In the seeds with a higher degree of differentiation. Embryo occupies a larger portion of the seed. The radicle is well recognizable part of the embryo while the shoot meristem with the primary leaf primordia generally lies compressed between the two cotyledons. The structure of a bean seed - a typical dicot seedwith well developed embryo is given figure 3.13 and 3.14. Polycotyledons: Not very common. This type of seed is found in Pinaceae and other conifers. The embryo is not very well differentiated except for a radicle and more than two cotyledons. Living nutritive storage tissues encircle the embryo while the shoot meristem is encircled by the base of the cotyledons.

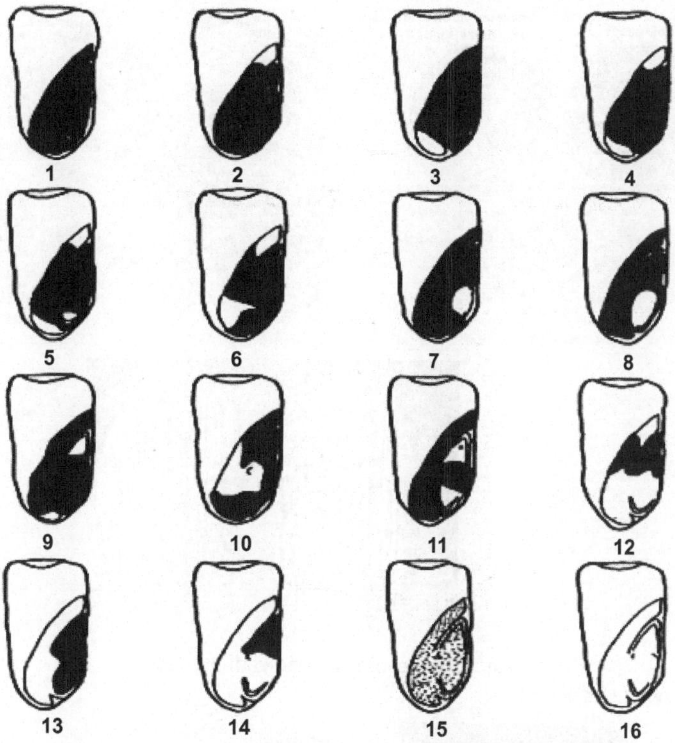

Fig. 3.13. Schematic diagram of embryo of monocot seed

(**Source:** Review Literature)

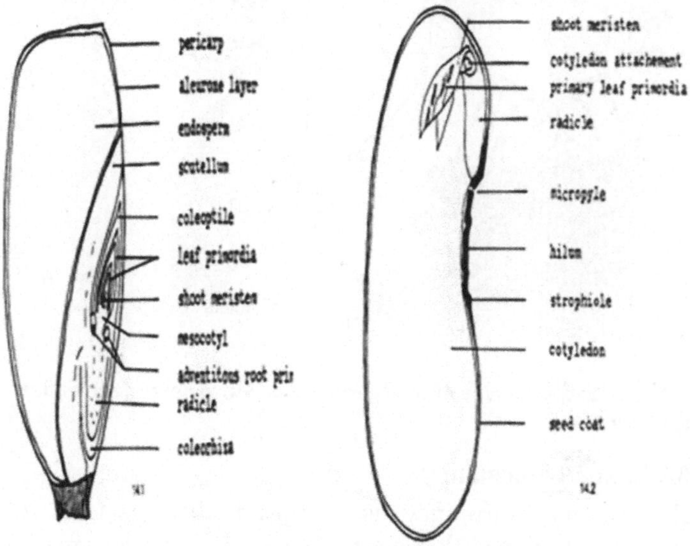

Fig. 3.14. Schematic diagram of Seed Anatomy

(**Source:** Based on Review of Literature)

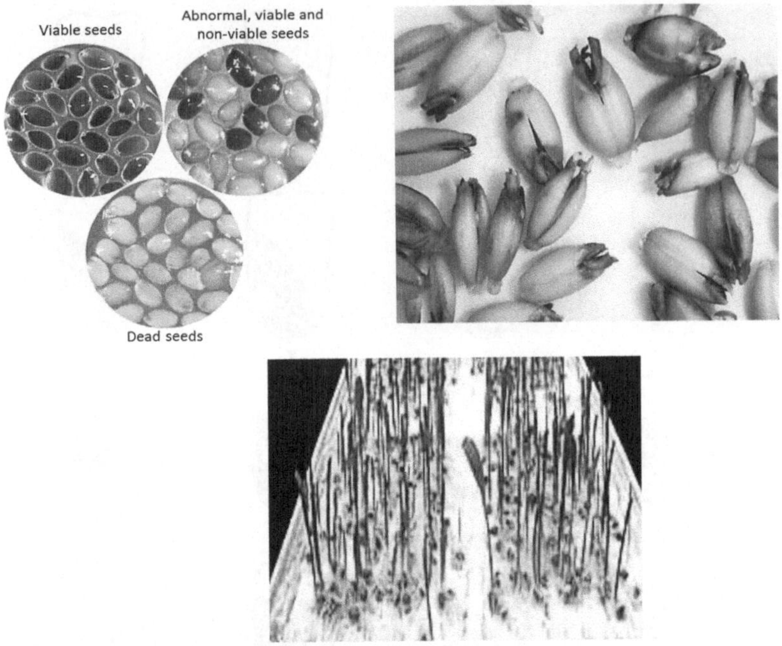

Fig. 3.15: Results of seed viability test

(**Source:** Review of Literature)

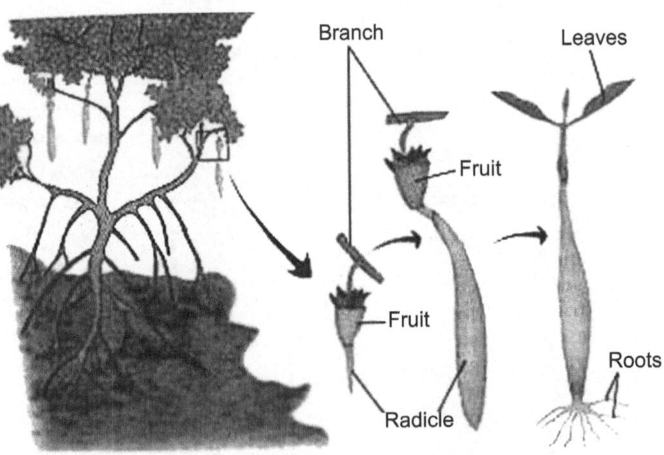

Fig. 3.16: Special type of seed germination viz. vivipery germination

(**Source:** Review Literature)

Role of ABA in Seed Dormancy

In general, primary dormancy is imposed during seed and embryo development so that varying degrees and types of dormancy may be exhibited by the seed during the later stages of development (Kermode 1990; Bewley and Black 1994; Leadem 1990; Hilhorst 1995). Dormancy is generally classed

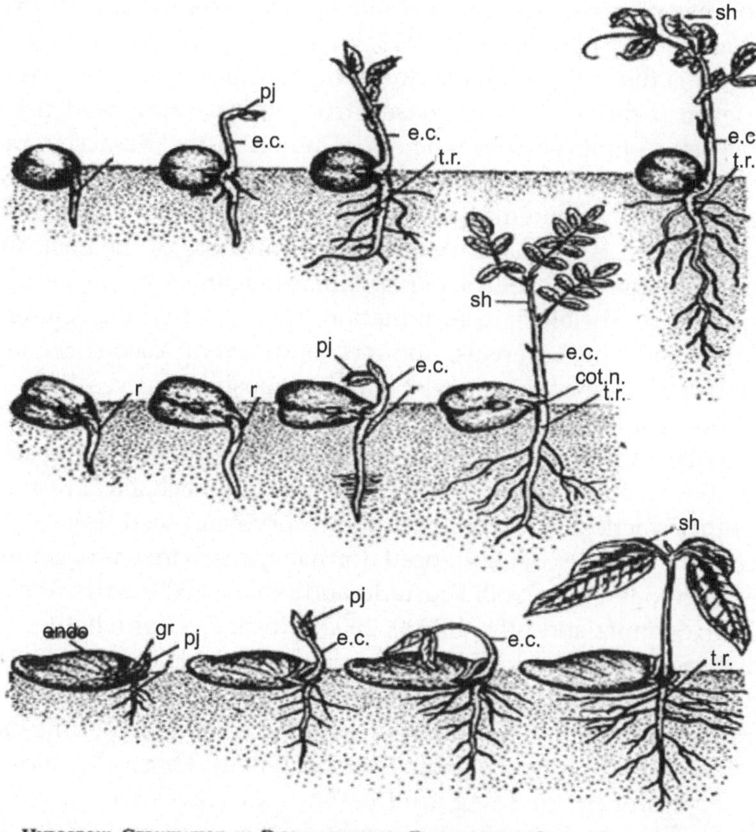

HYPOGEOUS GERMINATION IN DICOTYLEDONOUS EXALBUMINOUS SEEDS. Successive stages in pea (FIG. 56), gram (FIG. 57) and mango (FIG. 58). *r*=radicle; *pl*=plumule; *e.c.*=epicotyl; *t.r.*=taproot; *sh*=shoot; *cot. n.*=cotyledonary node; *endo*=endocarp; *gr*=groove through which radicle and plumule come out.

Fig. 3.17: Common germination of seeds

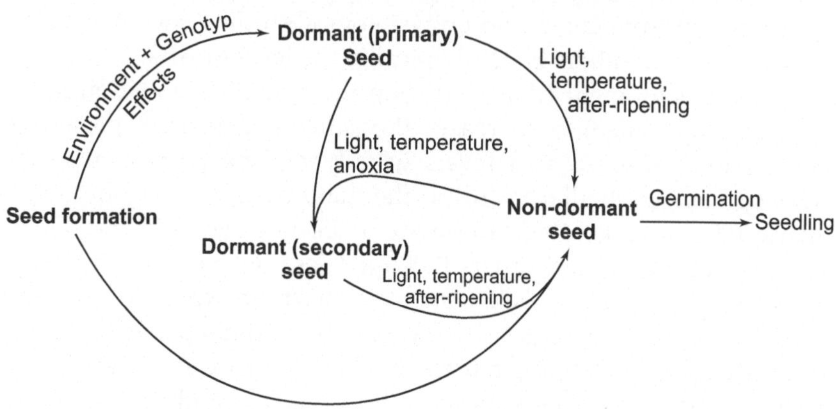

Fig. 3.18: Development of Primary and Secondary Dormancy of Seeds

(**Source:** Based on Review of Literature)

into two major types: embryo dormancy and coat-enhanced dormancy (Bewley and Black 1994) (Figure 3.13, 3.14, 3.15, 3.16, & 3.17). In embryo dormancy, it is the embryo that is dormant, and the embryonic axis will not elongate even if the embryo is excised from its enclosing seed tissues and placed on water. Embryo dormancy is common in the Rosaceae and other woody species, and in some grasses such as wild oat (*Avena fatua*). In coat-enhanced dormancy, the embryo, when isolated is capable of germination, but the intact seed is dormant; thus, it is one or more of the enclosing seed tissues (for example, endosperm, perisperm, megagametophyte, pericarp, and testa) that imposes the block to germination. Species exhibiting coat-enhanced dormancy include most cereals, conifers, and several dicots. Some degree of both types of dormancy can exist simultaneously or successively in some species (Bewley and Black 2004). The inhibitory nature of the enclosing seed tissues may be attributed to one or a combination of the following effects: (1) interference with water uptake or gas exchange, (2) mechanical restraint, and (3) biosynthesis/action of inhibitors in the embryo and seed tissues. All these factors contribute to the coat-enhanced dormancy mechanisms of conifer seeds (Ren and Kermode 1999, 2000; Feurtado and others, 2003, 2004; Terskikh and others 2004; Schmitz and others 2000, 2002). Regardless of whether a seed is dormant or non-dormant at maturity, an important role of ABA during early seed development is to maintain embryos in a developmental mode until they are fully formed and have accumulated sufficient reserves to permit successful germination and subsequent seedling establishment. Thus, ABA biosynthesis in the embryo and surrounding seed tissues encourages the continuation of maturation processes, including the synthesis of storage proteins and storage lipids; it also suppresses precocious germination of embryos (reviewed in Kermode 1990, 1995). Seeds of different species show differences in the timing of dormancy inception during development; the role of ABA in this process is evident from genetic and physiological studies (reviewed in Bewley 1997; Koornneef and others 2002). Typically, the level of ABA in seeds is low during early development (that is, during the histodifferentiation and early pattern formation stage); it increases thereafter and usually peaks around mid-maturation. Abscisic acid levels usually decline precipitously during late development, particularly during the maturation drying phase (Bewley and Black 1994; Meinke 1995; Kermode 1995; Bewley 1997 and references therein; also see Taylor and others [2005]). These developmental changes in endogenous ABA correlate well with the pattern of expression of the gene encoding the ABA biosynthesis enzyme zeaxanthin epoxidase (reviewed in Seo and Koshiba 2002; see references therein). However, several factors add to the complexity of the pattern of ABA increase and decline, including developmental changes in the sensitivities of embryo and seed tissues to ABA and the differential thresholds for the initiation and maintenance of developmental events (for example, the expression of certain developmental genes and the induction and maintenance of dormancy) (Xu and Bewley 1991; Jiang and others 1996; Kermode 1995). Moreover, the environment during seed development (for example, light, temperature, and water availability) can strongly influence the ABA content and sensitivity of the mature seed. In wheat, low temperatures can effect changes in ABA content or sensitivity, which in turn influence the degree of dormancy during development and in the mature grain (Walker-Simmons 1990; Garello and LePage-Degivry 1999). Likewise, water stress imposed during the development of *Sorghum bicolor* seeds decreases both their ABA content and sensitivity, and the seeds have an increased capacity for germination during development (Benech-Arnold and others 1991). In the barley cultivar Triumph and its mutant line TL43, endogenous ABA contents during grain development alone do not adequately account for genetic differences in germination percentages within two environments—one conducive to low dormancy and the other promotive of high dormancy (in Spain and Scotland, respectively) (Romagosa and others 2001). Often there is no clear relationship between the ABA content of the mature dry seed or grain and the degree of dormancy. Thus, although ABA is important for dormancy inception in developing seeds, high levels of ABA need not be present to maintain the state of dormancy (for example, during late maturation and desiccation). However, during the process of imbibition, dormant versus non-dormant seeds can be clearly differentiated. Seeds remaining dormant continue to synthesize ABA during imbibition; those seeds that have been subjected to an effective dormancy-breaking treatment (for example, after-ripened or moist-chilled seeds) still synthesize ABA, but generally, ABA catabolism is favored—that is, there has been a shift in the ratio of the capacity for ABA biosynthesis versus catabolism (see below, under *Dormancy Termination is Accompanied by Changes in ABA Biosynthesis, Turnover, and Sensitivity*). Some mutants characterized by maternally inherited reduced seed dormancy exhibit altered testa characteristics (reviewed in Koornneef and others 2002; Debeaujon and others 2000, 2001). This indicates the importance of the testa structure as a constraint to radicle emergence; seeds weakened in testa structure or having reduced pigmentation exhibit reduced seed dormancy. In the case of reduced testa pigmentation, structural weakening may arise because of reduced anthocyanidins. Thus, it is the polymeric nature of proanthocyanidins and their ability to bind proteins that confers the cell-cementing properties to the testa and allow it to act as an impermeable barrier that contributes to the inhibition of water uptake and germination (Debeaujon and others 2001). In *Arabidopsis*, removal of the testa allows germination of both GA-deficient mutants (Debeaujon and Koornneef 2000) and accessions that have a very strong dormancy (Koornneef and others 2002). The abnormal fragility of the testa of *dag1* mutants of *Arabidopsis* (Papi and others 2000) may allow them to germinate in response to much lower red light fluence rates, and may allow more rapid progression to the phytochrome-independent stage (Papi and others 2002). A regulatory role of ABA in testa development requires further investigation (reviewed in Hilhorst 1995). Abscisic acid–deficient and ABA-insensitive mutants of *Arabidopsis* exhibit reduced thickness of the mucilage layer surrounding the testa (Karssen and others 1983), which in turn is expected to alter the rate of water and oxygen uptake. The ABA-deficient mutant of tomato (*Lycopersicon esculentum*) (*sit* ^{w}) produces seeds that have thinner testas because they are comprised of fewer cell layers (one cell layer, versus the 5-cell layer characteristic of the wild-type); the mutant seeds are less sensitive to highly negative osmotic potentials, perhaps as a consequence of their structure (Hilhorst and Downie 1994; Hilhorst 1995).

ABA Signaling Pathways

Elucidating the role of ABA in controlling seed and embryo maturation processes, including the inception of dormancy, has been facilitated by the generation and analysis of mutants (for example, of tomato, maize, and *Arabidopsis*) that are either deficient in ABA or that exhibit a relative insensitivity to ABA (so-called response mutants). These latter mutants have defects in ABA signaling pathways and are characterized by reduced dormancy, which is generally accompanied by disruption of seed maturation and precocious expression of germinative/postgerminative genes. Screens to identify suppressors of ABA signaling mutants have helped to define some of the components of ABA signaling that interact with other signaling pathways and thus form the basis of hormonal networks that control the dormancy-to-germination transition. Dormancy of developing seeds is dependent on ABA that is synthesized in the embryo and not on maternal sources of ABA (Karssen and others 1983; Frey and others 2004). However, the surrounding seed tissues and parent plant may nonetheless play an important role in maintaining or encouraging ABA biosynthesis in developing embryos. The various ABA mutants have been important in linking ABA to key developmental processes, including the acquisition of desiccation tolerance, prevention of vivipary, and induction of primary dormancy. Vivipary is characterized by germination of the embryo within the fruit on the parent plant. There is an uninterrupted progression from embryogenesis to germination, with little or no cessation of growth (quiescence) and, in most cases, little or no dehydration. Vivipary is a normal occurrence in *Rhizophora mangle* (the mangrove), in which seeds and seedlings exhibit a relative insensitivity to ABA (Sussex 1975). The ABA-deficient *sitiens* mutant of tomato has approximately 10% the ABA content of its wild-type counterpart. This mutant exhibits reduced dormancy, and its seeds germinate viviparously in overripe fruits (Groot 1987; Groot and others 1991). Low endogenous ABA may not directly contribute to vivipary in this case, however, because the embryos also exhibit reduced sensitivity to the highly negative osmotic potential of surrounding seed tissues. Abscisic acid–deficient mutants of maize, *Arabidopsis*, and tobacco (*viviparous* (*vp*)5 or *vp*14, *aba1*, and *aba2*, respectively), exhibit reduced dormancy (*Arabidopsis* and tobacco) or vivipary (maize) (Karssen and others 1983; Tan and others 1997; Frey and others 1999; White and others 2000). Severe mutants of *Arabidopsis*exhibiting relative ABA insensitivity—that is, some of the *abi3* mutants, as well as double mutant *aba/abi* plants—produce seeds that are intolerant of desiccation (reviewed in Kermode 1995; see references therein). Seeds of the *abi3-7* mutant exhibit reduced dormancy and sensitivity to ABA and have undetectable *Em6* mRNA and protein and reduced transcripts for two 2S albumin proteins (Bies-Etheve and others 1999).

Conclusion

Dormancy is a mechanism to prevent germination during unsuitable ecological conditions, when the probability of seedling survival is low. One important function of most seeds is delayed germination, which allows time for dispersal and prevents germination of all the seeds at the same time. The staggering of germination safeguards some seeds and seedlings from suffering damage or death from short periods of bad weather or from transient herbivores; it also allows some seeds to germinate when competition from other plants for light and water might be less intense.

REFERENCES

Achard P, Vriezen WH, Van Der Straeten D, Harberd NP. 2003. Ethylene Regulates Arabidopsis Development via the Modulation of DELLA Protein Growth Repressor Function. Plant Cell 15:2816–2825.

Adkins SW, Loewen M, Symons SJ. 1986. Variation within Pure Lines of Wild Oats (*Avena fatua*) in Relation to Degree of Primary Dormancy. Weed Sci 34:859–864.

Ali-Rachedi S, Bouinot D, Wagner M-H, Bonnet M, Sotta B, *et al.* 2004. Changes in Endogenous Abscisic Acid Levels during Dormancy Release and Maintenance of Mature Seeds: Studies with the Cape Verde Islands Ecotype, the Dormant Model of *Arabidopsis thaliana.* Planta 219:479–488.

Amaral da Silva EA, Toorop PE, van Aeist A, Hilhorst HWM. 2004. Abscisic acid controls embryo growth potential and endosperm cap weakening during coffee (*Coffea arabica* cv. Rubi) seed germination. Planta 220:251–261.

Anderberg RJ, Walker-Simmons MK. 1992. Isolation of a wheat cDNA clone for an abscisic acid-inducible transcript with homology to protein kinases. Proc Natl Acad Sci USA 89:10183–10187Audran C, Borel C, Frey A, Sotta B, Meyer C, others. 1998. Expression studies of the zeaxanthin epoxidase gene from *Nicotiana plumbaginifolia.* Plant Physiol 118:1021–1028

Audran C, Liotenberg S, Gonneau M, North H, Frey A, others. 2001. Localisation and expression of zeaxanthin epoxidase mRNA in *Arabidopsis* in response to drought stress and during seed development. Aust J Plant Physiol 28:1161–1173

Barthe Ph, Garello G, Bianco-Trinchant J, le Page-Degivry MT. 2000. Oxygen availability and ABA metabolism in *Fagus sylvatica* seeds. J Plant Growth Regul 30:185–191

Bäumlein H, Misera S, Luerben H, Kolle K, Horstmann C, others. 1994. The *FUS3* gene of *Arabidopsis thaliana* is a regulator of gene expression during late embryogenesis. Plant J 6:379–387.

Benech-Arnold RL, Fenner M, Edwards PJ. 1991. Changes in the germinability, ABA content and embryonic sensitivity in developing seeds of *Sorghum bicolor* (L.) Moench. induced by water stress during grain filling. New Phytol 118:339–347.

Benech-Arnold RL, Giallorenzi MC, Frank J, Rodriguez V. 1999. Termination of hull-imposed dormancy in barley is correlated with changes in embryonic ABA content and sensitivity. Seed Sci Res 9:39–47.

Bethke PC, Gubler F, Jacobsen JV, Jones RL. 2004. Dormancy of *Arabidopsis* Seeds and Barley Grains can be Broken by Nitric Oxide. Planta 219:847–855.

Bewley JD. 1997. Seed Germination and Dormancy. Plant Cell 9: 1055–1066.

Bewley JD, Black M. 1994. Seeds: Physiology of Development and Germination. 2nd ed. New York, New York, USA, Plenum Publishing Corporation, 445 p.

Bianco J, Garello G, Le Page-Degivry MT. 1997. *De novo* ABA Synthesis and Expression of Seed Dormancy in a Gymnosperm: *Pseudotsuga menziesii*. J Plant Growth Regul 21:115–119.

Bies-Etheve N, da Silva Conceicao A, Giraudat J, Koornneef M, Léon-Kloosterziel K, *et al.* 1999. Importance of the B2 Domain of the *Arabidopsis* ABI3 Protein for Em and 2S Albumin Gene Regulation. Plant Mol Biol 40:1045–1054.

Bove J, Lucas P, Godin B, Ogé L, Jullien M, *et al.* 2005. Gene Expression Analysis by cDNA-AFLP Highlights a Set of New Signaling Networks and Translational Control during Seed Dormancy Breaking in *Nicotiana plumbaginifolia*. Plant Mol Biol 57:593–612.

Brocard-Gifford IM, Lynch TJ, Finkelstein RR. 2003. Regulatory Networks in Seeds Integrating Developmental, Abscisic Acid, Sugar, and Light Signaling. Plant Physiol 131:78–92.

Calvo AP, Nicolás C, Nicolás G, Rodriguez D. 2004. Evidence of a Cross-talk Regulation of a GA 20-oxidase (*FsGA20ox1*) by Gibberillins and Ethylene during the Breaking of Dormancy in *Fagus silvatica* Seeds. Physiol Plant 120:623–630.

Carrari F, Benech-Arnold R, Osuna-Fernandez R, Hopp E, Sanchez R, *et al.* 2003. Genetic Mapping of the *Sorghum bicolor vp1* gene and its relationship with preharvest sprouting. Genome 46:253–258.

Carrari F, Perez-Flores L, Lijavetzky D, Enciso S, Sanchez R, *et al.* 2001. Cloning and Expression of a Sorghum Gene with Homology to Maize *vp1*. Its Potential Involvement in Pre-harvest Sprouting Resistance. Plant Mol Biol 45:631–640.

Carson CB, Hattori T, Rosenkrans L, Vasil V, Vasil IK, *et al.* 1997. The Quiescent/Colorless Alleles Of Viviparous1 Show that the Conserved B3 Domain of VP1 is not Essential for ABA-Regulated Gene Expression in the Seed. Plant J 12:1231–1240.

Cheng W-H, Endo A, Zhou L, Penney J, Chen H-C, *et al.* 2002. A Unique Short-Chain Dehydrogenase/Reductase in *Arabidopsis* Glucose Signaling and Abscisic Acid Biosynthesis and Functions. Plant Cell 14:2723–2743.

Chiwocha SDS, Abrams SR, Ambrose SJ, Cutler AJ, Loewen S, *et al.* 2003. A Method for Profiling Classes of Plant Hormones and their Metabolites using Liquid Chromatography-Electrospray Ionization Tandem Mass Spectrometry: An Analysis of Hormone Regulation of Thermodormancy in Lettuce (*Lactuca sativa* L.) Seeds. Plant J 35:405–417.

Chiwocha SDS, Cutler AJ, Abrams SR, Ambrose SJ, Yang J, *et al.* 2005. The *etr1-2*mutation in *Arabidopsis thaliana* affects the Abscisic Acid, Auxin, Cytokinin and Gibberellin Metabolic Pathways during Maintenance of Seed Dormancy, Moist-Chilling and Germination. Plant J 42:35–48.

Colucci G, Apone F, Alyeshmerni N, Chalmers D, Chrispeels MJ. 2002. *GCR1*, the Putative *Arabidopsis* G Protein–coupled Receptor Gene is Cell Cycle-Regulated, and Its Over Expression Abolishes Seed Dormancy and Shortens Time to Flowering. Proc Natl Acad Sci USA 99:4736–4741.

Corbineau F, Bianco J, Garello G, Côme D. 2002. Breakage of *Pseudotsuga menziesii* Seed Dormancy by Cold Treatment as Related to Changes in Seed ABA Sensitivity and ABA levels. Physiol Plant 114:313–319.

Curaba J, Moritz T, Blervaque R, Parcy F, Raz V, *et al.* 2004. *AtGA3ox2*, a Gene Responsible for Bioactive Gibberellin Biosynthesis, is Regulated During Embryogenesis by *LEAFY COTYLEDON2* and *FUSCA3* in *Arabidopsis*. Plant Physiol 136:3660–3669.

Cutler AJ, Krochko JE. 1999. Formation and Breakdown of ABA. Trends Plant Sci 4:472–478.

Cutler S, Ghassesmian M, Bonetta D, Cooney S, McCourt P. 1996. A Protein Farnesyl Transferase Involved in Abscisic Acid Signal Transduction. Science 273:1239–1241.

Debeaujon I, Koornneef M. 2000. Gibberellin Requirement for *Arabidopsis* Seed Germination is Determined Both by Testa Chacteristics and Embryonic Abscisic acid. Plant Physiol 122:415–424.

Debeaujon I, Léon-Kloosterziel KM, Koornneef M (2000) Influence of the Testa on Seed Dormancy, Germination and Longevity in *Arabidopsis*. Plant Physiol 122:403–414.

Debeaujon I, Peeters AJM, Léon-Kloosterziel KM, Koornneef M. 2001. The *TRANSPARENT TESTA12* gene of *Arabidopsis* Encodes a Multidrug Secondary Transporter-like Protein Required for Flavonoid Sequestration in Vacuoles of the Seed Coat Endothelium. Plant Cell 13:853–871.

Delseny M, Bies-Etheve N, Carles CH, Hull G, Vicient C, *et al.* 2001. Late Embryogenesis Abundant (LEA) Protein Gene Regulation During *Arabidopsis* Seed Maturation. J Plant Physiol 158:419–427.

Derxk MPM, Vermeer E, Karssen C. 1994. Gibberellins in Seeds of *Arabidopsis thaliana*: Biological Activities, Identification and Effects of Light and Chilling on Endogenous Levels. J Plant Growth Regul 15:223–234.

Downie B, Hilhorst HWM, Bewley JD. 1997. Endo-β-mannanase Activity during Dormancy Alleviation and Germination of White Spruce (*Picea glauca*) Seeds. Physiol Plant 101:405–415.

Egerton-Warburton LM. 1998. A Smoke-induced Alteration of the Sub-testa Cuticle in Seeds of the Post-fire Recruiter, Emmenanthe penduliflora Benth. (Hydrophyllaceae). J Exp Bot 49:1317–1327

El-Kassaby YA, Chaisurisri K, Edwards DGW, Taylor DW. 1993. Genetic Control of Germination Parameters of Douglas-fir, Sitka spruce, Western red cedar, and yellow-cedar and its impact on container nursery production. In: Edwards DGW, Editor. Dormancy and Barriers to Germination. Proceedings of an International Symposium of IUFRO Project Group P2.04-00 (Seed Problems). Victoria, B.C., Canada: Forestry Canada, Pacific Forestry Centre. p. 37–42.

Feurtado JA, Xia J-H, Ma Y, Kermode AR. 2003. Increasing the Temperature of the Water Soak Preceding Moist Chilling Promotes Dormancy-Termination in Seeds of Western White Pine (*Pinus monticola* Dougl.). Seed Sci Technol 31:275–288.

Feurtado JA, Ambrose SJ, Cutler AJ, Ross ARS, Abrams SR, *et al.* 2004. Dormancy Termination of Western White Pine (*Pinus monticola* Dougl. Ex D. Don) Seeds is Associated with Changes in Abscisic Acid Metabolism. Planta 218:630–639.

Finkelstein RR, Lynch TJ. 2000. The *Arabidopsis* Abscisic Acid Response Gene *ABI5*encodes a Basic Leucine Zipper Transcription Factor. Plant Cell 12:599–609.

Finkelstein RR, Somerville CR. 1990. Three Classes of Abscisic Acid (ABA)-Insensitive Mutations of *Arabidopsis* Define Genes that Control Overlapping Subsets of ABA Response. Plant Physiol 94:1172–1179.

Finkelstein RR, Gampala SSL, Rock CD. 2002. Abscisic Acid Signaling in Seeds and Seedlings. Plant Cell, Supplement, S15–S45.

Flematti GR, Ghisalberti EL, Dixon KW, Trengove RD. 2004. A Compound from Smoke that Promotes Seed Germination. Science 305:977.

Foley ME. 2001. Seed Dormancy: An Update on Terminology, Physiological Genetics, and Quantitative Trait Loci Regulating Germinability. Weed Sci 49:305–317.

Frey A, Audran C, Marin E, Sotta B, Marion-Poll A. 1999. Engineering Seed Dormancy by Modification of Zeaxanthin Epoxidase Gene Expression. Plant Mol Biol 39:1267–1274.

Frey A, Godin B, Bonnet M, Sotta B, Marion-Poll A. 2004. Maternal Synthesis of Abscisic Acid Control Seed Development and Yield in *Nicotiana plumbaginafolia*. Planta 218:958–964.

Fukuhara T, Kirch H-H, Bohnert HJ. 1999. Expression of Vp1 and Water Channel Proteins during Seed Germination. Plant Cell Environ 22:417–424.

Garello G, LePage-Degivry MT. 1999. Evidence for the Role of Abscisic Acid in the Genetic and Environmental Control of Dormancy in Wheat (*Triticum aestivum* L.). Seed Sci Res 9:219–226.

Giraudat J, Hague BM, Valon C, Smalle J, Parcy F, *et al.* 1992. Isolation of the *ArabidopsisABI3* Gene by Positional Cloning. Plant Cell 4:1251–1261.

http://www.biologydiscussion.com/seed/seed-dormancy/seed-dormancy-meaning-types-and-effects-biology/34493

https://biologyboom.com/definitions-and-key-points-for-seed-dormancy/

https://biologyboom.com/methods-of-breaking-seed-dormancy/

https://biologyboom.com/seed-dormancy/

https://biologyboom.com/tag/seed-dormancy/

http://www.sproutnet.com/Seed-Dormancy

https://en.wikipedia.org/wiki/Seed_dormancy

Plant Physiology : *Stress, Diseases and Management* **Pages 51-75**
Edited by: **Mr. Prasann Kumar; Dr. Pawan Kumar 'Bharti'**
ISBN: 978-93-88854-00-9
Edition: **2019**
Published by: **Discovery Publishing House Pvt. Ltd., New Delhi (India)**

4 Role of Polyamines and Mycorrhiza for the Mitigation of Salinity Stress in Sorghum

[1]Prasann Kumar and [2]Shweta Pathak

ABSTRACT

Sorghum bicolor, commonly called sorghum and also known as great millet,*durra*, jowari, or milo, is a grass species cultivated for its grain, which is used for food for humans, animal feed, and ethanol production. Sorghum originated in northern Africa, and is now cultivated widely in tropical and subtropical regions. Sorghum is the world's fifth-most important cereal crop after rice, wheat, maize, and barley. *S. bicolor* is typically an annual, but some cultivars are perennial. It grows in clumps that may reach over 4 m high. The grain is small, ranging from 2 to 4 mm in diameter. Sweet sorghums are sorghum cultivars that are primarily grown for foliage, syrup production, and ethanol; they are taller than those grown for grain.

Keywords: Agriculture, Biotic, Crop, Density, Energy, Forage, Gap.

Introduction

The leading producers of sorghum bicolor in 2011 were Nigeria (12.6%), India (11.2%), Mexico (11.2%), and the United States (10.0%).Sorghum grows in a wide range of temperature, high altitudes, toxic soils and can recover growth after some drought. It has four features that make it one of the most drought-resistant crops:

- It has a very large root-to-leaf surface area ratio.
- In times of drought, it will roll its leaves to lessen water loss by transpiration.
- If drought continues, it will go into dormancy rather than dying.
- Its leaves are protected by a waxy cuticle.

Richard Pankhurst reports (citing Augustus B. Wylde) that in 19th-century Ethiopia, *durra* was "often the first crop sown on newly cultivated

1 Department of Agronomy, School of Agriculture, Lovely Professional University, Jalandhar, Punjab, 144411, India

2 Department of Plant Physiology, I.Ag.Sci., BHU., Varanasi, 221005, U.P., India

land", explaining that this cereal did not require the thorough ploughing other crops did, and its roots not only decomposed into a good fertilizer, but they also helped to break up the soil while not exhausting the subsoil. Sorghum is cultivated in many parts of the world today. In the past 50 years, the area planted with sorghum worldwide had increased 66%. In many parts of Asia and Africa, its grain is used to make flat breads that form the staple food of many cultures. The grains can also be popped in a similar fashion to popcorn. The species can be used as a source for making ethanol fuel, and in some environments may be better than maize or sugarcane, as it can grow under harsher conditions. It typically has protein levels around 9%, enabling dependent human populations to subsist on it in times of famine, in contrast to regions where maize has become the staple crop. It is also used for making a traditional corn broom. The reclaimed stalks of the sorghum plant are used to make a decorative millwork material marketed as Kirei board. Sweet sorghum syrup is known as molasses in some parts of the U.S., although it is not true molasses.

In China, sorghum is known as *gaoliang* , and is fermented and distilled to produce one form of clear spirits known as *baijiu* of which the most famous is Moutai (or Maotai). Sorghum was ground and the flour was the main alternative to wheat in northern China for a long time.

In India, where it is commonly called *jwaarie, jowar, jola,* or *jondhalaa,* sorghum is one of the staple sources of nutrition. An Indian bread called *bhakri, jowar roti,* or *joladarotti,* is prepared from this grain. In some countries, sweet sorghum stalks are used for producing biofuel by squeezing the juice and then fermenting it into ethanol. Texas A&M University in the United States is currently running trials to find the best varieties for ethanol production from sorghum leaves and stalks in the USA. In Korea, it is cooked with rice, or its flour is used to make cake called *susubukkumi*. In Australia, South America, and the United States, sorghum grain is used primarily for livestock feed and in a growing number of ethanol plants.

In Central America, tortillas are sometimes made using sorghum. Although corn is the preferred grain for making tortillas, sorghum is widely used and is well accepted in Honduras. White sorghum is preferred for making tortillas. In several countries in Africa, including Zimbabwe, Burundi, Mali, Burkina Faso, Ghana, and Nigeria, sorghum of both the red and white varieties is used to make traditional opaque beer. Red sorghum imparts a pinkish-brown colour to the beer. Sorghum is one of a number of grains used as wheat substitutes in gluten-free recipes and products.

Agricultural Uses

It is used in feed and pasturage for livestock. Its use is limited, however, because the starch and protein in sorghum is more difficult for animals to digest than the starches and protein in corn. Research is being done to find a process that will predigest the grain. One study on cattle showed that steam-flaked sorghum was preferable to dry-rolled sorghum because it improved daily weight gain. In hogs, sorghum has been shown to be a more efficient feed choice than corn when both grains were processed in the same way.

The introduction of improved varieties, along with improved management practices, has helped to increase sorghum productivity. In India, productivity increases are thought to have freed up six million hectares of land. The *International Crops Research Institute for the Semi-Arid Tropics* (ICRISAT) in collaboration with partners produces improved varieties of crops including sorghum. Some 194 improved cultivars of sorghum from the institute have been released.

Salinity

Salinity is the saltiness or amount of salt dissolved in a body of water (see also soil salinity). This is usually measured in g*salt*/*kg*sea water{\displaystyle {\frac {g\ {\textrm {salt}}}{kg\ {\textrm {sea}}\ {\textrm {water}}}}} (note that this is technically dimensionless). Salinity is an important factor in determining many aspects of the chemistry of natural waters and of biological processes within it, and is a thermodynamic state variable that, along with temperature and pressure, governs physical characteristics like the density and heat capacity of the water. A contour line of constant salinity is called an *isohaline*, or sometimes *isohale*. Salinity in rivers, lakes, and the ocean is conceptually simple, but technically challenging to define and measure precisely. Conceptually the salinity is the quantity of dissolved salt content of the water. Salts are compounds like sodium chloride, magnesium sulfate, potassium nitrate, and sodium bicarbonate which dissolve into ions. The concentration of dissolved chloride ions is sometimes referred to as chlorinity. Operationally, dissolved matter is defined as that which can pass through a very fine filter (historically a filter with a pore size of 0.45 μm, but nowadays usually 0.2 μm). Salinity can be expressed in the form of a mass fraction, *i.e.*, the mass of the dissolved material in a unit mass of solution.

What is Polyamine?

A *polyamine* is an organic compound having two or more primary amino groups –NH Low-molecular-weight linear polyamines perform essential functions in all living cells. Primary examples are putrescine, cadaverine, spermidine, and spermine. In animals, their levels are maintained from both the diet and de novo synthesis, and their decline with age is associated with various pathologies. Polyamine metabolism is regulated by the activity of the enzyme ornithine decarboxylase (ODC). Polyamines are found in high concentrations in the mammalian brain. The part of polyamine in abiotic push resilience to begin with came beneath seriously investigation after an increment in Put due to K+ lack was detailed decades back. As a result, analysts broadly explored changes in PA, when plants are uncovered to single or combined stresses (Camacho-Cristóbal *et al.*, 2004; Kuthanová *et al.*, 2004; Liu *et al.*, 2006; Moment and Pua, 2002; Shen *et al.*, 2000; Urano *et al.*, 2003). Polyamine biosynthesis pathway and the foremost chemicals of this pathway are beneath complex metabolic and formative control and such control is fundamental for effective control of cell digestion system. In Arabidopsis, differential expression of ADC (ADC1 and ADC2) has been detailed beneath stretch conditions. In reality, ADC2 expression is emphatically initiated by a few abiotic stresses like dry season, tall saltiness, mechanical damage, potassium lack (Alcázar *et al.*, 2006; Armengaud *et al.*, 2004; Hummel *et al.*, 2004; Peréz-Amador*et al.*, 2002; Urano *et al.*, 2003), whereas ADC1 is primarily initiated by cold (Hummel *et al.*, 2004). Essentially, the expression design of SPMS takes after that of ADC2 coming about in polyamine aggregation beneath lack of hydration and tall saltiness (Alcázar *et al.*, 2006; Urano *et al.*, 2003). Be that as it may, SPDS2 has constitutive expression beneath diverse stresses in differentiate to SPDS1 which shows expanded expression beneath lack of hydration. On the other hand, expression of SAMDC1 and SAMDC2 are emphatically initiated by cold and SAMDC2 has slight acceptance in expression beneath salt push (Vergnolle *et al.*, 2005). The expression designs of CPA, AIH and ACL5 are not influenced by any stretch (Alcázar *et al.*, 2006). Dad biosynthesis chemicals (ODC, ADC and SAMDC) are controlled at transcriptional, translational and post-translational levels (Hu *et al.*, 2005); it is curiously to note that these proteins are at first synthesized as an inert forerunner (proenzyme), which are afterward subjected to post-translational preparing coming about in develop chemicals (Xiong *et al.*, 1997). For case, an amassing of Puthas been recognized in reaction to natural changes concomitant with ADC2 and ADC1 up-regulation. In any case, Put collection and acceptance of downstream qualities included in Spdand Spm biosynthesis (SAMDC2, SPDS1, SPMS) did not influence the substance of both polyamines. This might be due to the translational or post-translational direction of SAM decarboxylase, which could be a key chemical in polyamine biosynthesis. Essentially, Hu *et al.* (2005) found that a 52-untranslated grouping plays a central part in both transcriptional and post-transcriptional control of SAMDC quality expression. Beneath push conditions, the level of Dad in plant organs may too be directed by its debasement. Cellular Dad is controlled by catabolic pathway (Bagni and Tassoni, 2001; Cona *et al.*, 2006), which comprises of two amine oxidases, doamine oxidase (DAO) and polyamine oxidase (PAO). The function of DAO is to convert Put into Pyrroline, ammonia and H_2O_2. PAO oxidizes Spd to Pyrroline, 1,3-diamine propane (DAP), H2O2 and Spm to aminopropylpyrroline, DAP and H2O2 (Cona *et al.*, 2003, 2006; Martin-Tanguy, 2001; Sebela *et al.*, 2001). Capell *et al.* (2004) found that rice produces high levels of Spd and Spm until 3 days after drought stress but the level sharply dropped after 6 days, probably because of the action of PAO. It is well-known that ABA contents increase under drought, salinity and other abiotic stresses (Christmann *et al.*, 2005). ABA induces the expression of a plethora of genes involved in defense against these abiotic stresses (Yamaguchi *et al.*, 2007). It is established that genes involved in PA biosynthesis are also inducible by ABA (Alcázar *et al.*, 2006; Kasinathan and Wingler, 2004; Urano *et al.*, 2004). Alcázar *et al.* (2006) also showed that the dehydration inducible expression of ADC2, SPDS1 and SPMS is an ABA-dependent response because up-regulation of these genes is not observed in ABA deficient (aba2) and insensitive (abi1) mutants. Moreover, it is further revealed that stress (DRE and LTR) and ABA responsive elements (ABRE and/or ABRE related motifs) are present in the promoters of these genes. Furthermore, microarray analysis has revealed that most of the genes involved in PA metabolism in Arabidopsis respond to a range of abiotic stresses such as drought (Öztürk *et al.*, 2002); wounding or methyl jasmonate treatment (Peréz-Amador *et al.*, 2002; Sasaki *et al.*, 2001). However, the use of microarray technology for unraveling molecular mechanisms underlying PA effects on abiotic stress tolerance is in its infancy.

Plant Stress Tolerance Modulated by Polyamine Treatment

Stress-derived changes in cellular polyamines give clues on their conceivable suggestion in stretch but don't give prove of their part in checking stretch. Classical approaches utilizing exogenous PA application/mutant/use of inhibitors of proteins included in PA biosynthesis pathway speak to an great demonstrate to test various hypotheses and to reply crucial organic questions inferred from pathway control (Alcázar *et al.*, 2006; Bhatnagar *et al.*, 2002; Liu *et al.*, 2007). Exogenous application of polyamines, which is anticipated to extend levels of an endogenous polyamine, has been endeavored some time recently or amid push (Navakouidis *et al.*, 2003; Wang *et al.*, 2007). There's a huge body of prove to propose that exogenous application of PAs seem, in changing degrees, (1) protect plant cell film keenness, (2) switch development or minimize development restraint caused by stretch, (3) direct expression of osmotically responsive qualities, (4) decrease superoxide radical and H_2O_2 substance, (5) decrease aggregation of NA^+ and Cl^- particles totally different organs, and (6) increment exercises of antioxidant chemicals (Ali, 2000; Iqbal and Ashraf, 2005; Afzal *et al.*, 2009; Ndayiragiji and Lutts, 2006; Tang and Newton, 2005; Yiu *et al.*, 2009; Zhang *et al.*, 2009). Be that as it may, the defensive impacts of person PAs are to some degree distinctive. The reason for such a disparity may be due to contrasts in assimilation, transport and utilization among plant species. These discoveries recommend that exogenous PA application acts as an elicitor of qualities included in abiotic stretch reactions (Gill and Tuteja, 2010). In another approach, treatment with Dad biosynthesis inhibitors, such as x-difluoromethylarginine (DFMA), x-difluoromethylornithine (DFMO), and D-arginine, to decrease endogenous PA brought about in stresssensitive phenotypes. Be that as it may, this impact is switched by the concomitant application of exogenous polyamine (He *et al.*, 2002; Navakouidis *et al.*, 2003). The impacts of these inhibitors are variable, extending from hindrance to incitement or no impact depending on the inhibitor soundness and specificity, formative organize, plant framework tried and presence of productive compensatory components (Kaur- Sawhney *et al.*, 2003). Another hereditary approach utilized for analyzing organic capacities of polyamine digestion system in push reaction is the utilize of mutants lacking in polyamine biosynthesis (Kaur-Sawhney *et al.*, 2003; Urano *et al.*, 2004; Watson and Malmberg, 1998). Watson *et al.* (1998) disconnected EMS mutants of Arabidopsis with decreased ADC action, spe-1 and spe-2. These mutants are lacking in Dad collection and displayed diminished salt resilience compared with the wild sort (Kasinathan and Wingler, 2004). On the other hand, the ADC2 knockout mutant (adc2-1) appeared no self-evident phenotype alter beneath typical development conditions and was more touchy to salt stretch, which can be somewhat switched by exogenous application of Put (Urano *et al.*, 2004). These comes about clearly uncovered that ADC2 could be a key gene and Put inferred from the ADC pathway was imperative in stretch reaction. As of late, a imperfect part for Spm in abiotic stresses such as dry season and saltiness was set up by the Arabidopsis acl5/ spms mutant, imperfect for Spm generation. This mutant displayed a delicate phenotype beneath dry spell and saltiness stresses but recuperated when treated with Spm (Yamaguchi *et al.*, 2006, 2007). Taken together, point by point characterization of mutants, flawed in other PA genes, ought to help in decoding the exact mode of activity of PA genes in reaction to abiotic stresses.

Plant Abiotic Stress Tolerance Modulated by Engineering the Polyamine Synthesis Pathway

Later progresses in molecular science with accentuation on hereditary designing and accessibility of PA biosynthesis genes makes it conceivable to assess and give a effective methodology to recognize the conceivable part of PAs in stretch reaction (Groppa and Benavides, 2008). A common marvel watched is that PAs can change their titres in reaction to different sorts of natural stresses such as water stretch (Capell *et al.*, 2004; Kasukabe *et al.*, 2004; Ma *et al.*, 2005), moo and tall temperatures (Hummel *et al.*, 2004; Imai *et al.*, 2004; Melody *et al.*, 2002) and saltiness (Liu *et al.*, 2006; Maiale *et al.*, 2004; Roy *et al.*, 2005). In arrange to get principal data on the part of Pas amid push, plant PAs have been tweaked by the over-expression/ down-regulation of adc/odc/samdc qualities (Kakkar and Sawhney, 2002; Minocha and Sun, 1997; Thu-Hang *et al.*, 2002). Over-expression of Dad biosynthetic qualities like adc (Capell *et al.*, 1998; 2004; Roy and Wu, 2001), odc (Kumria and Rajam, 2002), samdc (Roy and Wu, 2002; Waie and Rajam, 2003) and spd syn (Franceschetti *et al.*, 2004; Kasukabe *et al.*, 2004, 2006) in plants like O. sativa, N. tabacum, A. thaliana and I. batatas has expanded resilience to different abiotic stresses. There are a few reports on making transgenic plants harboring polyamine biosynthetic qualities in an endeavor to upgrade push resilience. Transgenic work is based on the perceptions that AtADC2 transcripts connects with the amassing of free Put beneath distinctive abiotic stresses in plants (Urano *et al.*, 2004).

For illustration, in a later consider, transgenic rice plants communicating the Datura stramonium adc (arginine decarboxylase) quality created higher levels of Put beneath dry season push than wild sort plants, which driven to higher levels of Spd and Spm and moved forward dry season resilience; transgenic plants shown less chlorophyll misfortune and leaf action, spe-1 and spe-2. These mutants are insufficient in PA aggregation and shown diminished salt resistance compared with the wild sort (Kasinathan and Wingler, 2004). On the other hand, the ADC2 knockout mutant (adc2-1) appeared no self-evident phenotype alter beneath ordinary development conditions and was more delicate to salt push, which can be in part switched by exogenous application of Put (Urano *et al.*, 2004). These comes about clearly uncovered that ADC2 could be a key quality and Put inferred from the ADC pathway was critical in stretch reaction. As of late, a inadequate part for Spm in abiotic stresses such as dry season and saltiness was set up by the Arabidopsis acl5/ spms mutant, flawed for Spm generation. This mutant displayed a delicate phenotype beneath dry spell and saltiness stresses but recouped when treated with Spm (Yamaguchi *et al.*, 2006, 2007). Taken together, point by point characterization of mutants, imperfect in other PA qualities, ought to help in decoding the exact mode of activity of PA qualities in reaction to abiotic stresses. In differentiate, wild-type Datura stramonium display expanded endogenous Put levels on the onset of drought stretch but this Put level isn't sufficient to trigger the transformation of Put into Spd and Spm (Capell *et al.*, 2004). Another case is the presentation of the Tritordeum SAMDC (S-adenosylmethionine decarboxylase) quality into rice, which come about in a three to four-fold increment in Spd and Spm levels in changed plants, which at that point had ordinary development and advancement indeed beneath NaCl stretch (Roy and Wu, 2002). In another illustration, Waie and Rajam, 2003, watched that transgenic tobacco plants over-expressing a human SAMDC quality had higher Spd and Put levels and displayed resilience to dry season and salt push. Franceschetti *et al.* (2004) moreover appeared that over-expression of Arabidopsis SAMDC in tobacco plants come about in expanded SAMDC action, aggregation of dcSAM, irritation of PA levels and transgenic plants displayed numerous stretch resilience. As of late, Peremarti *et al.* (2009) created transgenic rice plants constitutively communicating heterologous SAMDC quality from Datura stramonium to dismember the parts of Put from higher polyamines Spd and Spm. Both transgenic and wild sort plants appeared indistinguishable side effects when uncovered to dry season push but transgenic plants recuperated much more rapidly on re-watering. Additionally, transgenic carrot lines over-expressing mouse odc, which changes over ornithine to diamine putrescine were able to resist salt and osmotic push over brief period (Minocha and Sun, 1997). In another set of tests, ADC communicating transgenic rice plants delivered higher levels of Put, Spd and Spm and displayed dry spell resilience. Advance, it has been proposed that Put may reflect the sub ideal development conditions whereas Spd and Spm may offer assistance detoxifying free radicals (Larher *et al.*, 2003). These comes about affirmed the inclusion of polyamines in dry season stretch and assist credited person parts to Put, Spd and Spm. Interests, presentation of a single polyamine biosynthesis quality has been appeared to bestow resilience to different stresses. Illustrations of these are when Kasukabe *et al.* (2004, 2006) and Wi *et al.* (2006) found wide range resistance to abiotic stresses—drought, chilling, solidifying, saltiness and oxidative stress—by over-expression of SPDS (Spermidine synthase) from Curcurbita ficifolia in Arabidopsis, sweet potato (Ipomoea batatas) or tobacco. A cDNA microarray examination between chilled clears out of a transgenic line and wild sort uncovered that qualities encoding translation variables such as WRKY, B-box zinc finger proteins, NAM proteins, DREB2B and NAC space proteins are up-regulated in transgenic plants. Wen *et al.* (2008) illustrated that overexpression of an apple MdSPDS1 quality in European pear significantly expanded resistance to different stresses by modifying PA levels. Additionally, Prabhavathi and Rajam (2007) illustrated that transgenic eggplant harboring the oat ADC quality shown expanded resistance to dry season, saltiness, moo and tall temperature and overwhelming metals. These information illustrated that a transgenic approach including PA biosynthetic qualities may be a great methodology to progress edit resistance to different abiotic stresses to meet the necessities of a challenging worldwide environment.

Polyamine and Plant Stress Response: Potential Mechanism of Action

Polyamine: A compatible solute in higher plants Metabolic acclimation via the accumulation of compatible solutes is regarded as a basic strategy for the protection and survival of plants under abiotic stresses (Bartels and Hussain, 2008). Compatible solutes are non-toxic molecules, serve in turgor maintenance and stabilize macromolecular structures under unfavorable conditions (Bohnert and Shen, 1999; McNeil *et al.*, 1999). The notion of PA as a compatible solute is controversial in plants and needs further investigation. However, stress-induced PAs are often considered better stabilizers than others for protecting biomolecules and preventing the membrane system from denaturing under stress conditions (Liu *et al.*, 2007). PAs share many properties, for example, hydropholicity, protection of macromolecules, active oxygen scavengers, maintenance of cellular pH etc., which are close to those of proline and other compatible solutes (Liu *et al.*, 2007; Wi *et al.*, 2006). However, the concentration of stress-induced PAs is lower than proline and other solutes, which suggests that PAs are not compatible solutes. On the other hand, Duhazé *et al.* (2002) showed that products of PA catabolism, like β-alanine, can convert into β-alanine betaine which is required for osmoregulation in some halophytes. Proline is one of the most common osmolytes in stressed plants(Bartels and Hussain, 2008; Delauney and Verma, 1993; Sharma and Dietz, 2006; Urano *et al.*, 2009). Polyamine catabolism is closely related to proline accumulation in response to stress conditions (Aziz *et al.*, 1998; Bouchereau *et al.*, 1999). Öztürk and Demir (2003) showed that exogenous PA increases activity of peroxidase (POD) and catalase (Cat), along with proline production. PA metabolism is unique in that Put, proline and GABA share a common substrate, glutamate, and these metabolites often respond similarly to abiotic stresses (Seki *et al.*, 2007; Sharma and Dietz, 2006; Simon-Sarkadi *et al.*, 2005, 2006). There is no evidence yet about the mechanism of their coordinated accumulation (Radukina *et al.*, 2007). However, it is possible that a common signal triggers all three sub-pathways in a coordinated manner. Ornithine is a key intermediate in the biosynthesis of both Put and proline (Coruzzi and Last, 2000; Roosens *et al.*, 2002; Slocum, 2005) and is a possible candidate for a regulatory role in coordinating biosynthesis of these metabolites (Mohapatra *et al.*, 2010). Similarly, a hierarchical accumulation of PAs in different transgenic tissues/ organs has been observed (Lepri *et al.*, 2001) which suggest that PAs might act as compatible solute in specific organs, cells or organelles.

What is Mycorrhiza Mycorrhiza?

A *mycorrhiza* (from Greek µõêüò *mykós*, "fungus", and (íζα *rhiza*, "root"; pl. *mycorrhizae* or *mycorrhizas*) is a symbioticassociation between a fungus and the roots of a vascular host plant. The term mycorrhiza refers to the role of the fungi in the plants' rhizosphere, its root system. Mycorrhizae play important roles in soil biology and soil chemistry. In a mycorrhizal association, the fungus colonizes the host plant's root tissues, either intracellularly as in arbuscularmycorrhizal fungi (AMF or AM), or extracellularly as in ectomycorrhizal fungi. The association is generally mutualistic, but in particular species or in particular circumstances, mycorrhizae may be variously pathogenic in the host plants.

Mechanism of Sorghum Physiology for Salinity

Usually, salinity is measured in units of electrical conductivity (EC_e) of a standard soil paste extract taken from the root zone of the plant. Electrical conductivities are measured on the filtered water extracts from these samples in units of deciSemiens per meter (dS m^{-1}) . The soils with ECe<4 dS m^{-1} are considered as non-saline; those with ECe=4 to 16 dS m^{-1} are considered as in saline-phase and those with ECe>16 dS m^{-1} are considered as saline (www. cahe.nmsu.edu).

Crop Responses to Salinity

Sorghum crop responses to salinity depends on several factors such as soil, environment and genetic and their interrelationships. Plants grown in high saline soils experience low water potential and mineral toxicity due to high Na^+ concentration in external solution of plant cells. Plants challenged by this water potential develop a large soil-to-leaf gradient of potentials and are unable to meet transpiration demand, and ultimately may wilt and desiccate. Water stress is therefore considered a component of salinity injury. Na^+ toxicity results in disturbances in the mineral nutrition of the plant. The cell metabolism is seriously affected when cytoplasm Na^+ concentration reaches 50 to 100 mM. However, under natural conditions, such high salinity level is not experienced by plants at once during the crop growth period. Instead, salinity level increases progressively due to soil drying, which provides ample time for osmotic adjustment of plants to regulate their water uptake. In controlled conditions also, plants adjust osmotically in response to salinity stress, and therefore may overcome the osmotic effect of salt within a few days and symptoms of wilting disappear .The water stress and mineral toxicity induced by soil salinity reduces photosynthesis per unit leaf area indirectly through stomatal closure, and to a smaller extent through direct interference with the photosynthetic apparatus. At whole plant level, soil salinity stress results in delayed flowering, reduced plant height and grain and fodder yields in sorghum, although the degree of these responses varies with the genetic background of the lines . However, grain yield may not decrease until a 'threshold' salinity level is reached. The comprehensive survey of responses of different crop species to salinity stress indicated that 'threshold' level of grain sorghum is 6.8 dS m^{-1} and that grain yield starts declining at 6.8 dS m^{-1} and the reduction are up to 25% at 7 dS m^{-1} and 50% at 10 dS m^{-1} .

Soil Salinity Tolerance

The plant growth and economic product (grain/fodder) producing ability in saline soils relative to that in non-saline soils in comparable environments is termed their salt tolerance. From an agronomic context, salinity tolerance is described as a complex function of yield decline across a range of salt concentrations. Shannon (1997) has empirically described salinity tolerance (S) as a reduction in yield at a given salinity level (Y_s) with respect to a measured yield under non-saline conditions (Y_e): $S = Y_s/Y_e$. This index may change with the severity and duration of the salinity stress that is imposed.

Mechanisms of tolerance: While osmoregulation, which allows maintenance of turgor, is an important mechanism for tolerance to salinity-induced water stress, Na^+ exclusion from the vital parts of the plant such as roots appears to be an important mechanism for tolerance to salinity-induced mineral toxicity. Exclusion of Na^+ from the xylem and compartmentalization in non-vital parts of the plant (apoplast or vacuoles) are other mechanisms to cope with excess salts. The concentration of proline and HCN increases with an increase in salinity levels in tolerant genotypes but not in the sensitive genotypes of sorghum at the seedling stage. Maiti *et al.* (1994) have reported that presence of a specific protein of 22 Kda molecular weight might confer tolerance to salinity in sorghum. More complete characterization of such a specific protein associated with salinity tolerance would aid in mapping and/or cloning of the genes involved, which could then be deployed in elite agronomic background through marker-assisted selection or genetic engineering approaches.

Screening methods: The selection for tolerance under field conditions is usually inaccurate because of the difficulty in assessing the physical and temporal variability in salinity in soil solutions proximal to the root zone, resulting in a large portion of the observed variation in plant growth and yield being due to micro-environmental variation that renders selection ineffective. It may be possible to compensate for these problems to some extent by using very large numbers of populations, and replications, as space is not a major limiting factor and by making a judicious selection of breeding strategy and experimental design, and precisely controlling irrigation in artificially salinized plots. A good alternative combination would be to do an early evaluation in controlled conditions and then extend the evaluation of promising lines to field conditions, in large and replicated plots to account for the within-field variability. Two *in vivo* methods have been suggested by Montemurro *et al.* (1994) for early screening for salinity stress tolerant sweet sorghum genotypes. The methods are: (1) growing the seedlings on sand in polystyrene containers, and (2) growing the seedlings in spectrophotometer cuvettes. Genotypic response to salinity stress was similar in both the methods and classification of sweet sorghum genotypes for salinity tolerance was effectively demonstrated. However, seedling tolerance to salinity may not be translated in adult plant tolerance (Krishnamurthy *et al.*, 2007, Munns *et al.*, 2002). Considering this, a laboratory screening method is standardized at International Crops Research Institute for the Semi-Arid Tropics (ICRISAT), Patancheru, India. The method allows evaluation of sorghum lines for salinity tolerance at all stages from germination to adult plant stage. In this method, plants are grown in large pots containing 9 kg Alfisol. The salt is applied at a rate of 22.22 g NaCl pot^{-1} basis, which would correspond to a NaCl solution of 200 mM concentration, in sufficient amount to saturate that Alfisol at field capacity. However, to avoid a rapid build up of salt, the quantity of salt is applied in three split doses of 7.40 g NaCl pot^{-1} each time, dissolved at first application in 1.8 L, and subsequently in a sufficient amount to avoid water logging. This method is being followed at International Biosaline Agriculture (ICBA) Dubai and is similar to the one reported by Munns *et al.* (2002).

Genetic Variability, Inheritance And Breeding

Genetic variability: Significant genetic variability for salinity tolerance at different stages of crop growth in sorghum have been reported The research at ICRISAT indicated genetic variability for salinity tolerance at all the growth stages, starting from germination to grain formation in sorghum. For instance, taking 80% germination under non-saline control as a minimum acceptable germination standard for good plant stand required for satisfactory crop productivity, a laboratory study at ICRISAT showed that about half of the test sorghum genotypes with >80% germination under control had<80% germination under induced saline condition (23.4 dSm^{-1}).

Inheritance: The genetic control of salinity tolerance in sorghum appears to be complex. Although both additive and dominance gene effects are important in controlling the expression of salinity tolerance at germination and seedling emergence stages, dominance gene effects appear to be predominant. However, relatively high heritability for salinity tolerance suggests the possibility of rapid improvement in salinity tolerance using high selection pressures and replicated progenies in a hydroponics-based screening system combined with field screening.

Breeding: Reports of attempts to breed sorghum for salinity tolerance are rather limited. A practical problem when breeding sorghum for environments prone to abiotic stresses such as salinity is the choice of optimum selection environment(s). The evaluation of large numbers of sorghum genotypes across a broad range of salinity levels showed large and significant genotype × salinity level interactions. When confronted with this situation, the plant breeder must decide whether to work over the whole target environment (breeding for wide adaptation), or subdivide it into more homogeneous sub-environments (breeding for specific adaptation), or work with physiologists to understand some of the reasons for such high genotype × salinity level interactions. In theory, this decision depends mainly on the relative sizes of the genotype × year and genotype × location interactions. Unfortunately, the option of breeding for specific adaptation does not exist when working in areas with saline soils, since salinity levels varies concurrently in the same field, and also in the same spot at different times because of increasing salinity levels due to receding moisture. Thus, breeding for saline areas should follow the approach of breeding for wide adaptation. Calhoun *et al.,* (1994) summarized three strategies that address the issue of choice of selection environment for the situations discussed so far: (1) make selection in a stressful environment, (2) select under optimum production conditions, and (3) use a combination of both the approaches, *i.e.,* select materials that perform well under both stress and non-stress conditions. Igartua (1995) is of the opinion that option (3) is the best. The more environments used, the better will be the results obtained. However, as testing resources are limited, a sensible compromise seems likely to be combination of a non-stress location and at least one stress environment (within the range of target stress environments) between which there is crossover-type genotype × salinity level interaction. Based on the three-component linear equation Maas and Hoffman (1977) and Igartua (1995) conclusively demonstrated the usefulness of the option (3) to select for improved yield in grain sorghum in saline soils. Considering that good germination (80% is considered minimum acceptable for crop cultivation in non-saline soils), and seedling emergence and establishment are crucial for whole-plant productivity and that these stages are more sensitive to soil salinity toxicity than any later stages, enhancing the salinity-tolerance at the germination, emergence, and) concentration in the shoot was significantly but negatively correlated (r = -0.65**) with total dry matter yield at 39 days after sowing (DAS) in sorghum (unpublished data), indicating that this simple non-destructive ionic concentration measurement can be effectively used to discard those genotypes which are likely to have lower dry matter yield in saline soils. Seedling establishment stages should be one of the breeding objectives. Discarding all those genotypes that have <80% germination under saline condition in the laboratory test can routinely be used as the first-stage selection in genetic improvement for salinity tolerance. However, seedling stage tolerance must be combined with adult plant tolerance to achieve reasonable levels of crop productivity under saline conditions. This is because, normally in farmer's fields, seeds germinate under high moisture, whereby seedlings are exposed to relatively lower salinity stress and as soil moisture depletes in later stages plants are exposed to severe stress. Therefore, the genotypes selected from germination test under salinity stress can then be moved to pot-culture evaluation and field evaluation for salinity tolerance for grain and fodder yields. Results of pot-culture studies at ICRISAT have shown highly significant positive correlation (r = 0.75**) between total dry matter yield under salinity and salinity tolerance index (ratio of dry matter yield under salinity stress to that under non-salinity) in sorghum, indicating that selection for high dry matter yield under saline conditions, besides improving the yield potential, will also improve salinity tolerance. However, highly significant correlation (r = 0.97**) between the panicle weight ratio (ratio of panicle weight under salinity to that under non-salinity) and grain yield ratio (ratio of grain yield under salinity to that under non-salinity) in sorghum showed panicle weight ratio as a highly effective selection criterion. Research at ICRISAT has also showed that sodium (Na^+) concentration in the shoot was significantly but negatively correlated (r = –0.65**) with total dry matter yield at 39 days after sowing (DAS) in sorghum (unpublished data), indicating that this simple non-destructive ionic concentration measurement can be effectively used to discard those genotypes which are likely to have lower dry matter yield in saline soils. Igartua and Gracia (1998) assessed the effectiveness of divergent selection for tolerance to salinity at germination-seedling emergence stage in grain sorghum composite population AD11B. A recurrent selection scheme based on the evaluation of S_1 progenies in the laboratory was carried out for two cycles. In each breeding cycle, the subsets of the progenies showing best and least tolerance to salinity were selected and recombined to constitute the next cycle. Evaluation of the original and four subpopulations under saline conditions in the laboratory for germination and emergence ability revealed the effectiveness of selection in separating the subpopulations. Such selections at seedling and maturity stages are likely to be effective in improving whole plant tolerance to salinity in sorghum. Field emergence in induced saline soils confirmed the effectiveness of the selection procedure to shift the populations in the desired direction. Krishnamurthy *et al.* (2003) at ICRISAT have shown that some of the released and popular sorghum varieties that are bred for normal production conditions also exhibited better performance under induced salinity (23.4 dS m^{-1}) relative to non-saline control in a series of pot-culture experiments. Field evaluation of the lines selected from the pot-culture experiments confirmed the superior performance of these released and popular sorghum cultivars under natural salinity (8 dS m^{-1}) in a research station in India and farmers' fields (at 10 dS m^{-1}) in Oman (Ramesh *et al.*, 2005). From the agronomy and plant breeding points of view, cultivars that perform better under both salinity-stress and salinity-free conditions are desirable (Calhoun *et al.*, 1994). Theoretical investigations (Rosielle and Hamblin, 1981) indicating general increase in mean yield in both stress and stress-free environments if selection is practiced for mean productivity (average yield in stress and stress-free environments) lend adequate support to these practical considerations.

Cultivar options: Field studies based on limited numbers of genotypes indicated that hybrids have better salinity tolerance than their parental lines, or pure-line varieties. However, pot-culture experiments at ICRISAT, Patancheru, India indicated that the hybrids are not better than varieties under induced salinity (unpublished data). The differences between soil, weather and their interacting factors that prevail in controlled laboratory situations and those that prevail in field could be the likely causes for the differential results on the performance of hybrids relative to pure-line varieties in saline soils. Therefore, extensive studies involving large numbers of hybrids in varied salinity levels in multi-environments are required to establish superiority/otherwise of the hybrids over pure-line varieties.

Main Thrust Areas of Salinity Research

Salinity is not a new phenomenon as it has been with the mankind since agriculturebegan. Irrigation civilizations in Mesopotamia, Nile Valley, Mohanzoadaro, IndusValley and several other places and their subsequent fall bear testimony to theimminent occurrence of salinity following irrigation. Salinity always affected thesociety but the adverse effects could be better realized only when food and nutritional security of the ever-increasing population was at stake. Now, there is an increased awareness about secondary salinization in irrigated command areas and need of biosaline agriculture. In India, Central Soil Salinity Research Institute (CSSRI) and several State Agriculture Universities (SAUs) have made significant contribution in the field of salinity research in agriculture but many problems remain unanswered. In the scenario of population explosion, globalization, and the climate change the responsibility of research scientists has increased manifold. We would have to rethink over our future strategies and research planning so that a vision document/planning for at least 2-3 decades is formulated at national level. CSSRI has already documented a prospective plan for the Institute (CSSRI 1997) which has been handy in preparing this paper. The salient research achievements, gaps, and future strategies may be discussed under the following broad areas:

- Data bases (inventories) on salt-affected soils and poor quality waters.
- Biodiversity and vegetation ecology of inland and coastal saline areas.
- Marine ecology and aquaculture.
- Utilization, reclamation & management technologies of salt-affected and water-logged areas and poor quality waters.
- Assessment, development, management and conservation of genetic resources (biotechnology) tolerant to salinity, sodicity, water logging and submergence.
- Impact assessment, economic appraisal and dissemination of proven technologies.

Databases (Inventories)

Soils

Indians had long back recognized the infertility of soils inflicted by salinity. In ancient India (2500 B.C. to 600 A.D.), soils were known as urvara (fertile) and anurvara(desert). It is only during the middle of the 19th century that salinity was recognized as a potential threat to agriculture. While tracing out the history of soil salinity, Singh (1992a) mentioned that the first complaint of soil salinity came in 1855 from village Moonak in Haryana under the command of the Western Jamuna Canal, which was constructed by Feroze Shah Tuglak in 1351 along the abandoned channel of the Yamuna River and remodeled in 1839 by the British. In 1863, T.E. Brown, Chemical Examiner from Punjab analyzed salt-affected soils from Punjab. Simultaneously reports about soil salinity started pouring in from Faizabad, Bahraich, Lucknow, Sitapur and Hardoi districts of Uttar Pradesh. There is a long list of chronological sequence of events describing soil salinity problem in the country from the year 1869 till date. Salt lands in India occur over varied geological formations, in all kinds of soils, and under different conditions of climate, relief, and human interventions and accordingly, their extent, characteristics, and response to management are highly variable. A total of 27 sub-groups of salt-affected soils, based on clay mineralogy, presence or absence of calcic horizon, textural variations and ground water conditions have been identified. For practical usage, salt-affected lands have been identified as saline, alkali, sodic, saline-alkali or saline sodic. However, for management point of view CSSRI has placed these soils into the saline or alkali groups. Many workers have given detail accounts of classification, characteristics, extent, management and reclamation aspects of salt-affected soils in India (Agarwal *et al.* 1979; Murthy *et al.* 1980; Tiwari *et al.* 1983; Abrol and Gupta 1990; Singh 1992a; Dubey *et al.* 1995). But, the estimates vary widely. Salt-affected soils have been estimated to be 6 million ha by NCA (1976), 7 million ha by Abrol and Bhumbla (1971), 8.6 million ha by Singh (1992b) and 9.38 million ha by IAB (2000). However, for an effective monitoring programme, ground and air-borne geophysical methods like ground electro-magnetic conductivity meters and air-borne electro-magnetic methods for aerial surveys need to be perfected. Generation and upgradation of sound database requires effective use of remote sensing, global positioning systems (GPS), and geo-graphic information systems (GIS) supported by enough ground truth. Standardization of computer based image analysis for mapping and digitization is needed.

Reclamation and Management Technologies for Salt Affected and Waterlogged Areas

Central Soil Salinity Research Institute and State Agriculture Universities have developed several chemical, biological, and hydrological techniques of reclamation of alkali soils in India. A brief account regarding some of these problems along with future research needs is given here.

Chemical Reclamation of Alkali Soils

The technology package based on chemical amendments consists of the components such as land levelling, bunding, flushing, drainage for removal of excess water, good quality irrigation water, application of amendments, selection of crops, and efficient Dagar: Soil Salinity Research in India nutrient management. Alkali soils require application of an amendment before most crops can be successfully grown. The results of various experiments conducted using different amendments such as gypsum, pyrite, sulphuric acid, nitric acid, pressmud, aluminium sulphate, ferrous sulphate and farmyard manure proved that gypsum followed by pyrites are the most useful because of their easy availability and cost consideration (CSSRI 1979, Tyagi and Minhas 1998). Further, field studies have shown that the pyrite was much less effective than gypsum and single application of gypsum at lower dose before the first crop of rice proved as effective as higher and repeated dose in respect of crop yields in subsequent years (Tyagi 1999). The dose of an amendment required for reclamation of alkali soil is governed by its initial exchangeable sodium percentage (ESP), tolerance of crops be grown, texture and minerology of soil and depth to be reclaimed. Abrol *et al.* (1973) established a good relationship between pH (1:2 soil-water suspension) and the gypsum requirement of surface 15 cm soil. For initiation of the reclamation of alkali soils, cultivation of shallow rooted crops like rice, wheat, berseem and barley and application of 50% of gypsum requirement, which amounts to 10-15 Mg ha^{-1} in 0-15 cm soil is sufficient (Abrol and Bhumbla 1971). The pyrites to be effective for reclamation must contain at least 5-6% soluble S. It showed better efficiency when was placed on the soil surface than mixed in shallow soil depth and further keeping the soil moist for 10-15 days could increase its efficiency by improving its oxidation (Sharma and Swarup 1990). Organic materials together with inorganic amendments quicken the reclamation of alkali soils and also reduce the gypsum requirement.

Biological Reclamation

Use of green manure like species of Sesbania is well known for reclamation of alkali lands. Non-conventional crops of high value is an alternative option for amelioration of alkali soils and producing fuelwood, forage, medicinal and other products of economic use. Afforestation and agroforestry practices, on alkali and saline waterlogged soils are well documented (Singh and Dagar 1998, Singh *et al.*, 1997, Tomar *et al.*, 1998, Dagar *et. al.*, 2001). Many promising grass species have been identified for reclamation (Kumar and Abrol 1986), but adoption of the technology is beset with the problem of high uptake of sodium and other toxic elements in the forage. Therefore, there is a need to search for those grasses which can retain high proportion of sodium in roots, rendering the shoots more palatable. Tomar *et al.* (2003a,b) identified and evaluated suitable tree and grass species irrigated with saline water for wood and forage production. These also improved soil health. Non-conventional crops such as Matricariachamomilla, *Plantago ovata* (isabgol) and aromatic grasses like Vetiveriazizanioides, Cymbopogon martini and C. flexuosus stand chance for such areas. The reclamative effect of growing rice on alkali soils is well known. The search must continue for more tolerant rice (like CSR 10 & CSR 13) and other crop varieties must continue which can be grown without or with very small quantity of amendment. More data are required on crop-based biological reclamation technology and inoculation of mycrorrhiza and other nitrogen-fixing micro-organisms in alkali soils.

Conclusion

Attempts to breed sorghum for enhanced salinity-tolerance have been limited owing to the complexity in screening for and inheritance of salinity tolerance. Considerable variability in soil salinity levels both spatially and temporally, and within the same field, favors breeding sorghum for wide adaptation. Enhancing the salinity-tolerance of sorghum at the germination-emergence/ seedling establishment stages should be combined with adult plant tolerance to achieve reasonable levels of productivity under salinity stress. Considering that *Sorghum halepense*is more tolerant to salinity than *S bicolor, S halepense*may be utilized for genetic enhancement of sorghum for salinity-tolerance. Taking a cue from durum wheat, it might be worth assessing genetic variability and unravel inheritance pattern of Na^+ exclusion, an important component trait of salinity tolerance in sorghum, for its possible use in enhancing the genetic potential of sorghum for salinity tolerance

REFERENCES

Abrol, I.P. and Bhumbla, D.R. 1971. Saline and Alkali Soils in India: Their Occurrence and Management. FAO World Soil Resources Report 41, FAO, Rome.

Abrol, I.P. and Gupta, R.K. 1990. Alkali Soils and their Management. Pages 317-334, In: Abrol, I.P. and Dhruvanarayana, V.V. (Editors) Technologies for Wasteland Development. Indian Council of Agricultural Research, New Delhi.

Afzal I, Munir F, Ayub CM, Basra SMA, Hameed A, Nawaz A. Changes in Antioxidant Enzymes, Germination Capacity and Vigour of Tomato Seeds in Response of Priming with Polyamines. Seed Sci Technol 2009;37:765–70.

Alcázar R, Altabella T, Marco F, Bortolotti C, Reymond M, Knocz C, Carrasco P, Tiburcio AF. Polyamines: Molecules with Regulatory Functions in Plant Abiotic Stress Tolerance. Planta 2010a; 231:1237–49.

Alcázar R, García-Martínez JL, Cuevas JC, Tiburcio AF, Altabella T. Overexpression of ADC2 in Arabidopsis Induces Dwarfism and Late-Flowering through GA Deficiency. Plant J 2005; 43:425–36.

Alcázar R, Marco F, Cuevas JC, Patron M, Ferrando A, Carrasco P, Tiburcio AF, Altabella T. Involvement of Polyamines in Plant Response to Abiotic Stress. Biotechnol Lett 2006; 28:1867–76.

Alcázar R, Planas J, Saxena T, Zarza X, Bortolotti C, Cuevas J, Bitrian M, Tiburcio AF, Altabella T. Putrescine Accumulation Confers Drought Tolerance in Transgenic Arabidopsis Plants Over-expressing the Homologous Arginine Decarboxylase2 Gene. Plant Physiol Biochem 2010b; 48:547–52.

Ali RM. Role of Putrescine in Salt Tolerance of Atropa Belladonna plant. Plant Sci 2000;152:173–9.

Allen GJ, Sanders D. Control of Ionic Currents Guard Cell Vacuoles by Cytosolic and Luminal Calcium. Plant J 1996;10:1055–69.

Allen KD. Assaying Gene Content in Arabidopsis. Proc Nat Acad Sci USA 2002;99: 9568–72.

Altabella T, Tiburcio AF, Ferrando A. Plant with Resistance to Low Temperature and Method of Production Thereof. 2009; Spanish Patent Application WO2010/004070.

An Z, Jing W, Liu Y, Zhang W. Hydrogen Peroxide Generated by Copper Amine Oxidase is Involved in Abscisic Acid-induced Stomatal Closure in Vicia faba. J Exp Bot 2008;59: 815–25.

Apel H, Kirt H. Reactive Oxygen Species: Metabolism, Oxidative Stress and Signal Transduction. Annu Rev Plant Biol 2004;55:373–9.

Armengaud P, Breitling R, Amtmann A. The Potassium-dependent Transcriptome of Arabidopsis Reveals a Prominent Role of Jasmonic Acid in Nutrient Signaling. Plant Physiol 2004;136:2556–76.

Aronova EE, Shevyakova NI, Sretsenko LA, Kuznetsov VIV. Cadaverine-induced Induction of Superoxide Dismutase Gene Expression in Mesembryanthemum Crystallinum L. Dokl Biol Sci 2005;403:257–9.

Asthir B, Spoor W, Duffus CM. Involvement of Polyamines, Diamine Oxidase and Polyamine Oxidase in Resistance of Barley to Blumeria Graminis f. sp. Hordei. Euphytica 2004;136:307–12.

Aziz A, Martin-Tanguy J, Larher F. Stress-induced Changes in Polyamine and Tyramine Levels can Regulate Proline Accumulation in Tomato Leaf Discs Treated with Sodium Chloride. Plant Physiol 1998;104:195–202.

Bagni N, Tassoni A. Biosynthesis, Oxidation and Conjugation of Aliphatic Polyamines in Higher Plants. Amino Acids 2001; 20:301–17.

Baileya A, Strema D, Baea H, Myolob G, Guiltinan J. Gene Expression in Leaves of Theobroma Cacao in Response to Mechanical Wounding, Ethylene, and/or Methyl Jasmonate. Plant Sci 2005;168:1247–58.

Bais HP, Ravishankar GA. Role of Polyamines in the Ontogeny of Plants and their Biotechnological Applications. Plant Cell Tissue Organ Cult 2002;69:1-34.

Bartels D, Hussain SS. Current Status and Implications of Engineering Drought Tolerance in Plants using Transgenic Approaches. CAB Reviews: Perspectives in Agri, Vet Sci, Nutri Natur Sci, 3. ; 2008. p. 020.

Bartels D, Souer E. Molecular Responses of Plants to Dehydration. In: Madhava KV, Editor. Plant Responses to Abiotic Stress. Berlin: Springer; 2003. p. 8-38.

Bartels D, Sunkar R. Drought and Salt Tolerance in Plants. Crit Rev Plant Sci 2005;24: Bhatnagar P, Minocha R, Minocha S. Genetic Manipulation of the Metabolism of Polyamines in Poplar Cells: the Regulation of Putrescine Catabolism. Plant Physiol 2002;128:1455–69.

Bohnert HJ, Shen B. Transformation and Compatible Solutes. Sci Hortic 1999;78:237–60.

Bortolotti C, Cordeiro A, Alcázar R, Borrell A, Culiañez-Macià FA, Tiburcio AF, Altabella T. Localization of Arginine Decarboxylase in Tobacco Plants. Plant Physiol 2004;120:84–92.

Bouchereau A, Aziz A, Larher F, Martin-Tanguy J. Polyamines and Environmental Challenges: Recent Development. Plant Sci 1999;140:103–25.

Bowie D, Lange GD, Mayer ML. Activity-dependent Modulation of Glutamate Receptors by Polyamines. J Neurosci 1998;18:8175–85.

Bright J, Desikan R,Hancock JT,Weir IS, Neill ST. ABA-induced NO Generation and Stomatal Closure in Arabidopsis are Dependent on H_2O_2 Synthesis. Plant J 2006;45:113–22.

Brüggemann L, Pottosin I, Schönknecht G. Cytoplasmic Polyamines Block the Fast Activating Vacuolar Cation Channel. Plant J 1998;16:101–5.

Brüggemann L, Pottosin I, Schönknecht G. Selectivity of the Fast Activating Vacuolar Cation Channel. J Exp Bot 1999;50:873–6.

Calhoun, D.S., Gebeyehu, C., Miranda, A., Rajaram, S., Van Ginkel, M. (1994). Choosing Evaluation Environments to Increase Grain Yield Under Drought Conditions. Crop Science, 34, 673-678.

Calhoun, D.S., Gebeyehu, C., Miranda, A., Rajaram, S., Van Ginkel, M. (1994). Choosing Evaluation Environments to Increase Grain Yield Under Drought Conditions. Crop Science, 34, 673-678.

Camacho-Cristóbal JJ, Lunar L, Lafont F, Baumert A, González-Fontes A. Boron Deficiency Causes Accumulation of Chlorogenic Acid and Caffeoyl Polyamine Conjugates in Tobacco Leaves. J Plant Physiol 2004;161:879–81.

Capell T, Bassie L, Christou P.Modulation of the Polyamine Biosynthetic Pathway Intransgenic Rice Confers Tolerance to Drought Stress. Proc Nat Acad Sci USA 2004;101:9909–14.

Capell T, Escobar C, Liu H, Burtin D, Lepri O, Christou P. Over-expression of Oat Arginine Decarboxylase cDNA in Transgenic Rice (Oryza sativa L.) Affects Normal Development Pattern in Vitro and Results in Putrescine Accumulation in Transgenic Plants. Theor Appl Genet 1998;97:246–54.

Cheng L, Zou Y, Ding S, Zhang Y, Yu X, Cao J, Lu G. Polyamine Accumulation in Transgenic Tomato Enhances the Tolerance to High Temperature Stress. J Integr Plant Biol 2009;51:489–99.

Christmann A, Hoffmann T, Teplova I, Grill E, Müller A. Generation of Active Pools of Abscisic Acid Revealed by in Vivo Imaging of Water Stresses Arabidopsis. Plant Physiol 2005;137:209–19.

Cona A, Cenci F, Cervelli M, Federico R, Mariottini P, Moreno S, Angelini R. Polyamine Oxidase, a Hydrogen Peroxide-Producing Enzyme, is Up-regulated by Light and Down-regulated by Auxin in the Outer Tissues of the Maize Mesocotyle. Plant Physiol 2003;131:803–13.

Cona A, Rea G, Angelini R, Federico R, Tavladoraki P. Functions of Amine Oxidases in Plant Development and Defence. Trends Plant Sci 2006;11:80–8.

Coruzzi G, Last R. Amino Acids. In: Buchanan B, Gruissem W, Jones R, Editors. Biochemistry and Molecular Biology of Plants. American Society of Plant Physiologists MD; 2000. p. 358–410.

Crowley T, Walters DR. Polyamine Metabolism in an Incompatible Interaction Between Barley and the Powdery Mildew Fungus, Blumeria graminis f. sp. Hordei. J Phytopathol 2002;150(11–12):1–7.

CSSRI. 1979. A Decade of Research. Central Soil Salinity Research Institute, Karnal. 186 pages.

Cuevas JC, Lopez-Cobollo R, Alcázar R, Zarza X, Koncz C, Altabella T, Salinas J, Tiburcio AF, Ferrando A. Putrescine is Involved in Arabidopsis Freezing Tolerance and Cold Acclimation by Regulating Abscisic Acid Levels in Response to Low Temperature. Plant Physiol 2008;148:1094–105.

Cuevas JC, Lopez-Cobollo R, Alcázar R, Zarza X, Koncz C, Altabella T, Salinas J, Tiburcio AF, Ferrando A. Putrescine as a Signal to Modulate the Indispensable ABA Increase under Cold Stress. Plant Signal Behav 2009;4:219–20.

Danon A, Botari VI, Gordon A, Mailhac N, Gallois P. Ultraviolet-C Overexposure Induces Programmed Cell Death in Arabidopsis, which is Mediated by Caspase-like Activities and which can be Suppressed by Caspase Inhibitors, p. 35, and Defender against Apoptotic Death. J Biol Chem 2004;279:779–87.

Del Duca S, Betti L, Trebbi G, SeraWni-Fracassini D, Torrigiani P. Transglutaminase Activity Changes during the Hypersensitive Reaction, A Typical Defense Response of Tobacco NN plants to TMV. Plant Physiol 2007;131:241–50.

Del Pozo O, Lam E. Caspases and Programmed Cell Death in the Hypersensitive Response of Plants to Pathogens. Curr Biol 1998;8:1129–32.

Delauney AJ, Verma DPS. Proline Biosynthesis and Osmoregulation in Plants. Plant J 1993;4:215–23.

Della Mea M, Caparros-Ruiz D, Claparols I, SeraWni-Fracassini D, Rigau J. AtPng1p: The First Plant Transglutaminase. Plant Physiol 2004;135:2046–54.

Delledonne M, Xia Y, Dixon RA, Lamb C. Nitric Oxide Functions as a Signal in Plant Disease Resistance. Nature 1998;394:585–8.

Demidchik V, Tester M. Sodium Fluxes Through Non-selective Cation Channels in the Membrane of Protoplasts from Arabidopsis Thaliana Roots. Plant Pgysiol 2002;128: 379–87.

Desiderio MA, Grassilli E, Bellesia EE, Salomoni P, Franceschi C. Involvement of Ornithine Decarboxylase and Polyamines in Glucocorticoid-induced Apoptosis of Rat Thymocytes. Cell Growth Differ 1995;6:505–13.

Dobrovinskaya OR, Muñiz J, Pottosin II. Asymmetric Block of the Plant Vacuolar Ca^{2+} Permeable Channel by Organic Cations. Eur Biophys J 1999a;28:552–63.

Dobrovinskaya OR, Muñiz J, Pottosin II. Inhibition of Vacuolar Ion Channels by Polyamines. J Membr Biol 1999b;167:127–40.

Duan JJ, Li J, Guo SR, Kang YY. Exogenous Spermidine Affects Polyamine Metabolism in Salinity-Stressed Cucumis Sativus Roots and Enhances Short-term Salinity Tolerance. J Plant Physiol 2008;165:1620–35.

Dubey, D.D., Sharma, O.P., Sethi, M. and Gupta, R.K. 1995. Salt Affected Soils of Gujarat : Extent, Nature & Management. Central Soil Salinity Research Institute, Karnal. 95 pages.

Duhazé C, Gouzerh G, Gagneul D, Larher F, Bouchereau A. The Conversion of Spermidine to Putrescine and 1,3-deaminopropane in the Roots of Limonium Tataricum. Plant Sci 2002;163:639–46.

Edreva AM, Velikova VB, Tsonov TD. Phenylamides in plants. Russ J Plant Physiol 2007;54:289–302.

El-Ghachtouli N, Paynot M, matin-Tanguy J, Dorandi D, Gianinazzi S. The effect of Polyamines on Endomycorrhizal Infection ofwild-type Pisumsativum, cv Frisson (nod +myc+) and Two Mutants (nod+myc- and nod-myc+). Mycorrhiza 1995;5:189–92.

El-Ghachtouli N, Paynot M, Matin-Tanguy J, Dorandi D, Gianinazzi S. Effect of Polyamines and Polyamine Biosynthesis Inhibitors on Spore Germination and Hyphal Growth of Glomus Mosseae. Mycol Res 1996;100:597–600.

Evans PT, Malmberg RL. Do Polyamines have Roles in Plant Development? Ann Rev Plant Physiol Plant Mol Biol 1989;40:235–69.

Franceschetti M, Fornale S, Tassoni A, Zuccherelli K, Mayer MJ, Bagni N. Effects of Spermidine Synthase Overexpression on Polyamine Biosynthetic Pathway in Tobacco Plants. J Plant Physiol 2004;161:989-1001.

Franceschetti M, Hanfrey C, Scaramagli S, Torrigiani P, Bagni N, Burtin D, Michael AJ. Characterization of Monocot and Dicot Plant S-adenosyl-L-methionine Decarboxylase Gene Families Including Identification in the mRNA of a Highly Conserved Pair of Upstream Overlapping Open Reading Frames. Biochem J 2001;53:403–9.

Gabrijel Ondrasek, Zed Rengel and Szilvia Veres (September 22nd 2011). Soil Salinisation and Salt Stress in Crop Production, Abiotic Stress in Plants Arun Shanker, IntechOpen, DOI: 10.5772/22248.

Galston AW, Kaur-Sawhney R, Altabella T, Tiburcio AF. Plant Polyamines in Reproductive Activity and Response to Abiotic Stress. Bot Acta 1997;110:197–207.

Galston AW, Weinstein LH. Control of Phytopathogen by Inhibitors of Polyamine Biosynthesis. Adv Exp Med Biol 1988;250:589–99.

Garia-Mata C, Lamattina L. Nitric Oxide and Abscisic Acid Cross Talk in Guard Cells. Plant Physiol 2002;128:790–2.

Garufi A, Visconti S, Camoni L, Aducci P. Polyamines as Physiological Regulators of 14-3-3 Interaction with the Plant Plasmamembrane H^+-ATPase. Plant Cell Physiol 2007;48: 434–40.

Ge C, Cui X, Wang Y, Hu Y, Fu Z, Zhang D, Cheng Z, Li J. BUD2, encoding an Sadenosylmethionine Decarboxylase, is Required for Arabidopsis Growth and Development. Cell Res 2006;16:446–56.

Gill SS, Tuteja N. Polyamines and Abiotic Stress Tolerance in Plants. Plant Signal Behav 2010;51:26–33.

Gomez M, Hellstrand P. Endogenous Polyamines Modulate Ca^{2+} Channel Activity in Guinea-pig Intestinal Smooth Muscle. Pflugers Arch 1999;436:445–51.

Greenberg JT, Guo A, Klessig DF, Ausubel FM. Programmed Cell Death in Plants: A Pathogen-Triggered Response Activated Coordinately with Multiple Defense Functions Cell 1994;77:551–63.

Greenland AJ, Lewis DH. Amines in Barley Leaves Infected with Brown Rust and their Possible Relevance to Formation of 'Green Islands'. New Phytol 1984;96:283–91.

Griffin M, Casadio R, Bergamini CM. Transglutaminases: Nature's Biological Glues. Biochem J 2002;368:377–96.

Groppa MD, Benavides MP, Tomaro ML. Polyamine Metabolism in Sunflower and Wheat Leaf Discs Under Cadmium or Copper Stress. Plant Sci 2003;16:481–8.

Groppa MD, Benavides MP. Polyamines and Abiotic Stress: Recent Advances. Amino Acids 2008;34:35–45.

Grün S, Lindermayr C, Sell S, Durner J. Nitric Oxide and Gene Regulation in Plants. J Exp Bot 2006;57:507–16.

Ha HC, Woster PM, Jager JD, Casero RAJ. The Role of Polyamine Catabolism in Polyamineanalogue-Induced Programmed Cell Death. Proc Natl Acad Sci USA 1997;94: 11557–62.

Hanfrey C, Sommer S, Mayer MJ, Burtin D, Michael AJ. Arabidopsis Polyamine Biosynthesis: Absence of Ornithine Decarboxylase and the Mechanism of Arginine Decarboxylase Activity. Plant J 2001; 27:551–60.

Hanzawa Y, Imai A, Michael AJ, Komeda Y, Takahashi T. Characterization of the Spermidine Synthase-related Gene Family in Arabidopsis Thaliana. FEBS Lett Hashimoto T, Tamaki K, Suzuki K, Yamada Y. Molecular Cloning of Plant Spermidine Synthases. Plant Cell Physiol 1998;39:73–9.

Hanzawa Y, Takahashi T, Komeda Y. ACL5: an Arabidopsis Gene Required for Intermodal Elongation After Flowering. Plant J 1997;12:863–74.

Hanzawa Y, Takahashi T, Michael AJ, Burtin D, Long D, Pineiro M, Coupland G, Komeda Y. ACAULIS5, an Arabidopsis Gene Required for Stem Elongation, Encodes a Spermine Synthase. EMBO J 2000;19:4248–56.

He L, Ban Y, Inoue H, Matsuda N, Liu J, Moriguchi T. Enhancement of Spermidine Content and Antioxidant Capacity in Transgenic Pear Shoots Overexpressing Apple Spermidine Synthase in Response to Salinity and Hyperosmosis. Phytochem 2008;69:2133–41.

He L, Nada K, Kasukabe Y, Tchibana S. Enhanced Susceptibility of Photosynthesis to Low Temperature Photohibition Due to Interruption of Chill-induced Increase of Sadenosylmethionine Decarboxylase Activity in Leaves of Spinach (Spinacia oleracea L.). Plant Cell Physiol 2002;43:196–206.

Hiraga S, Ito H, Yamakawa H, Ohtsubo N, Seo S, Mitsuhara I, Matsui H, Honma M, Ohashi Y. An HR-induced Tobacco Peroxidase Gene is Responsive to Spermine, but not to Salicylate, Methyl Jasmonate, and Ethephon. Mol Plant-Microbe Interact 2000;13: 210–6.

Hirschi KD. Expression of Arabidopsis CAX1 in Tobacco: Altered Calcium Homeostasis and Increased Stress Sensitivity. Plant Cell 1999;11:2113–22.

Hu WW, Gong H, Pua EC. Molecular Cloning and Characterization of S-adenosylmethionine Decarboxylase Genes from Mustard (Brassica juncea). Plant Physiol 2005;124: 25–40.

Huang CJ, Moczydlowski E. Cytoplasmic Polyamines as Permeant Blockers and Modulators of the Voltage-gated Sodium Channel. Biophys J 2001;80:1262–79.

Hummel I, Gouesbet G, El Amrani A, Ainouche A, Couee I. Characterization of the Two Arginine Decarboxylase (polyamine biosynthesis) Paralogues of the Endemic Subantarctic Cruciferous Species Pringlea Antiscorbutica and Analysis of their Differential Expression during Development and Response to Environmental Stress. Gene 2004;342:199–209.

Igarashi K, Kashiwagi K. Polyamines: Mysterious Modulators of Cellular Functions. Biochem Biophys Res Commun 2000;271:559–64.

Igartua, E. (1995). Choice of the Selection Environment for Improving Crop Yields in Saline Areas. Theoretical and Applied Genetics, 91(6/7), 1016-1021.

Igartua, E., Gracia, M.P. (1998). Divergent Selection for Salinity Tolerance at the Germination Emergence Stage in Grain Sorghum. Maydica, 43(3), 161-168.

Illingworth C, Mayer MJ, Elliott K, Hanfrey C, Walton NJ, Michael AJ. The Diverse Bacterial Origins of the Arabidopsis Polyamine Biosynthetic Pathway. FEBS Lett 2003; 549:26–30.

Imai R, Ali A, Pramanik HR, Nakaminami K, Sentoku N, Kato H. A Distinctive Class of Spermidine Synthase is Involved in Chilling Response in Rice. J Plant Physiol 2004;161:883–6.

Iqbal M, Ashraf M. Changes in Growth, Photosynthetic Capacity, and Ionic Relations in Spring Wheat (Triticum aestivum L.) Due to Pre-sowing Seed Treatment with Polyamines. Plant Growth Regul 2005;46:19–30.

Iwata Y, Koizumi N. An Arabidopsis Transcription Factor, AtbZIP60, Regulates the Endoplasmic Reticulum Stress Response in a Manner Unique to Plants. Proc Natl Acad Sci USA 2005;102:5280–5.

Janowitz T, Kneifel H, Piotrowski M. Identification and Characterization of Plant Agmatine Iminohydrolase, the Last Missing link in Polyamine Biosynthesis of Plants. FEBS Lett 2003;544:258–61.

Jones JDG, Dangl JL. The Plant Immune System. Nature 2006;444:323–9. Kakehi J, Kuwashiro Y, Niitsu M, Takahashi T. Thermospermine is Required for Stem Elongation in Arabidopsis Thaliana. Plant Cell Physiol 2008;49:1342–9.

Kakkar RK, Sawhney VK. Polyamine Research in Plants. A Changing Perspective. Physiol Plant 2002;116:281–92.

Kasinathan V, Wingler A. Effect of Reduced Arginine Decarboxylase Activity on Salt Tolerance and on Polyamine Formation during Salt Stress in Arabidopsis thaliana. Plant Physiol 2004;121:101–7.

Kasukabe Y, He L, Nada K, Misawa S, Ihara I, Tachibana S. Overexpression of Spermidine Synthase Enhances Tolerance to Multiple Environmental Stresses and Up-regulates the Expression of Various Stress-regulated Genes in Transgenic Arabidopsis Thaliana. Plant Cell Physiol 2004;45:712–22.

Kasukabe Y, He L, Watakabe Y, Otani M, Shimada T, Tachibana S. Improvement of Environmental Stress Tolerance of Sweet Potato by Introduction of Genes for Spermidine Synthase. Plant Biotechnol 2006;23:75–83.

Kaur-Sawhney R, Tiburcio AF, Altabella T, Galston A. Polyamines in Plants: An Overview. J. Cell Mol Biol 2003;2:1-12.

Khurana N, Saxena RK, Gupta R, Rajam MV. Polyamines as Modulators of Microcycle Conidiation in Aspergillus flavus. Microbiology 1996;142:517–23.

Kim SA, Kwak JM, Jae SK, Wang MH, Nam HG. Overexpression of the AtGluR2 Gene Encoding an Arabidopsis Homolog of Mammalian Glutamate Receptors Impairs Calcium Nutilization and Sensitivity to Ionic Stress in Transgenic Plants. Plant Cell Physiol 2001;42:74–84.

Knott JM, Römer P, Sumper M. Putative Spermine Synthases from Thalassiosira Pseudonana and Arabidopsis thaliana Synthesize Thermospermine Rather than Spermine. FEBS Lett 2007;581:3081–6.

Kumar A, Altabella T, Taylor M, Tiburcio AF. Recent Advances in Polyamine Research. Trends Plant Sci 1997;2:124–30.

Kumar, A. and Abrol, I.P. 1986. Grasses in Alkali Soils. Bulletin No. 11. Central Soil Salinity Research Institute, Karnal.

Kumria R, Rajam MV. Ornithine Decarboxylase Transgene in Tobacco Affects Polyamine Metabolism, in vitro Morphogenesis and Response to Salt Stress. J Plant Physiol 2002;159:983–90.

Kusano T, Yamaguchi K, Berberich T, Takahashi Y. Advances in Polyamine Research in 2007. J Plant Res 2007a;120:345–50.

Maas, E.V., Hoffman, G.J. (1977). Crop Salt Tolerance- Current Assessment. J. Irrigation and Drainage Div, ASCE. 103 (IR2), 115-134.

Minhas, P & P. Sharma, O. (2008). Management of Soil Salinity and Alkalinity Problems in India. Journal of Crop Production. 7. 10.1300/J144v07n01_07.

Munns, R. (2002). Comparative Physiology of Salt and Water Stress. Plant, Cell & Environment, 25(2), 239-250.

Munns, R. (2002). Comparative Physiology of Salt and Water Stress. Plant, Cell & Environment, 25(2), 239-250.

Murthy, R.S., Hirekerur, L.R. and Bhattacharjee, J.C. 1980. The Taxonomy of Salt-affected Soils of the Indian Subcontinent. Pages 67-76, In: International Symposium on Salt Affected Soils. Central Soil Salinity Research Institute, Karnal.

Ramesh, S., Reddy, B.V.S., Reddy, P.S., Hebbar, M., Ibrahim, M. (2005). Response of Selected Sorghum Lines to Soil Salinity-Stress under Field Conditions. International Sorghum and Millets Newsletter, 46, 14-17.

Reddy BVS, Dakheel A, Ramesh S, Vadez V, Ibrahim M, and Hebbar M. 2018. Conventional Breeding Sorghum for Soil Salinity-Stress Tolerance. International Crops Research Institute for the Semi-Arid Tropics (ICRISAT), Patancheru, India.

Rosielle, A.A., Hamblin, J. (1981). Theoretical Aspects of Selection for Yield in Stress and Nonstress Environments. Crop Science, 21, 943-946.

Sharma, P and Swarup, A. 1990. Microbial Oxidation of Pyrites in Relation to Its Efficiency for Reclamation of Alkali Soils. Annual Report, Central Soil Salinity Research Institute, Karnal.

Tiwari, K.N., Kumar, A. and Pathak, A.N. 1983. Characteristics of Salt-affected Soils of Central Alluvial Region of Uttar Pradesh. Journal of Indian Society of Soil Science 31: 272-280.

Tomar, O.S., Gupta, R.K. and Dagar, J.C. 1998. Afforestation Techniques and Evaluation of Different Tree Species for Waterlogged Saline Soils in Semiarid Tropics. Arid Soil Research & Rehabilitation 12: 301- 316.

Tomar, O.S., Minhas, P.S., Sharma, V.K. and Gupta, R.K. 2003. Response of Nine Forage Grasses to Saline Irrigation and Its Schedules in a Semi-arid Climate of Northwest India. Journal of Arid Environments 55: 533-544.

Tomar, O.S., Minhas, P.S., Sharma, V.K., Singg, Y.P. and Gupta, R.K. 2003. Response of 31 Tree Species and Soil Conditions in a Plantation Establisged with Saline Irrigation. Forest Ecology & Management 177: 333-346.

Tyagi, N.K. 1999. Management of Salt-affected Soils. Pages 363-401, In: Singh, G.B. and Sharma, B.R. (Editors) Fifty Years of Natural Resource Management Research. Indian Council of Agricultural Research, New Delhi.

Tyagi, N.K. and Minhas, P.S. (Editors). 1998. Agricultural Salinity Management in India. Central Soil Salinity Research Institute, Karnal, 526 pages.

Plant Physiology : *Stress, Diseases and Management* Pages 76-124
Edited by: Mr. Prasann Kumar; Dr. Pawan Kumar 'Bharti'
ISBN: 978-93-88854-00-9
Edition: 2019
Published by: Discovery Publishing House Pvt. Ltd., New Delhi (India)

5

Phenotypic Stability Analysis and DUS Characterization in French Bean

In Context to IPR and Farmers Rights in Mid World Countries

[1]Basavaraj Makanur, [2]Dhirendra Kumar Singh and [3]Esakkimuthu M

ABSTRACT

The phenotypic expression of a character is not always same under all the environments and different genotypes may respond differently to any specified environment. This response of genotypes to environmental fluctuations is due to genotype x environment fluctuations, which is less defined and non-predictable. Thus, study of G x E interactions is essential for the identification of phenotypically stable genotypes. It includes three parameters, mean performance ($\bar{X}_i$), regression coefficient (b_i) and deviation from regression (S^2d_i). A genotype is said to be stable if it had high mean performance above the average of all the genotypes, regression coefficient (b_i=1) *i.e.,* does not differ from unity and deviation from regression approaching to zero (S^2d_i=0).

Most of countries became a signatory of trade related aspects of intellectual property rights agreement (TRIPS) in 1994. Article 27.3(b) of this agreement requires the member countries to provide for protection of plant varieties either by a patent or by an effective *sui generis* system or by a combination thereof.

Index-terms: Bean, IPR, morphological characterization, plant protection, stability analysis,

Introduction

French bean (*Phaseolus vulgaris* L.; 2n=22) a member of the family Leguminoceae (Fabaceae) and sub-family papilionaceae, is most popular leguminous vegetable crop cultivated in tropics, sub tropics and temperate regions in the world. In India and most of the tropical Asia, it is a major vegetable crop, where indigenous pulses are also preferred (Kay, 1979, Duke, 1981 and Adams, 1985). It is a known fact that the genotypes performing well under a particular environment may or may not perform well over other environments due to genotype-environment interactions (GEI). A genotype with low GEI

[1,2] G. B. Pant University of Agriculture and Technology, Pantnagar, Uttarakhand, India
[3] Kerala Agricultural University, RARS, Pilicode, Kerala, India

will have high stability and vice-versa. Therefore, while developing a high yielding cultivar, if care is not taken to select for both yield and stability of performance one may end up with a high yielding genotype that is suitable only for a particular environment. It, therefore, necessitates the development of variety/hybrid including wide adaptability. Allard and Bradshaw (1964) suggested that the selection of genotypes should be based on least interaction with environments. They further opined that heterozygous and heterogeneous populations offer the least opportunity to produce varieties which show a small GEI. They used the term "individual buffering" for genotypes where the individual members of a population are well buffered such that the population is well adapted to a wide range of environments.

There is a provision under the PPV&FR Act, for the registration of Farmers' variety and Varieties of Common Knowledge under the generic class 'Extant Variety'. Under the PPV&FR Act 2001 of India, it requires registration of varieties based on three principles known as Distinctiveness, Uniformity and Stability (DUS) criteria. Thus, DUS testing principles are used for the protection of varieties and award of plant breeders and farmers rights, a system of intellectual property protection which is available to breeders of all types of crops. On practical level, DUS assessment of agricultural crops generally involves growing field crops under appropriate ambient conditions and recording various morphological characteristics at different stages of growing plants. The candidate varieties are compared with existing varieties that are kept as reference collection. It is thus imperative to characterize varieties especially farmers varieties on the basis of DUS criteria and to register them with PPV&FR Authority on behalf of the farmers. There is an urgency to register the farmers' varieties otherwise valuable germplasm which was being conserved by the farmers will remain unprotected and anybody can utilize for pecuniary gains. Plant morphological DUS descriptors have been the universally undisputed descriptors applied for DUS testing of crop varieties (Anonymous, 2001).

Phenotypic Stability Analysis

Plant breeders are mainly interested in increasing the overall level of production and secondly minimizing the fluctuations in the crop performance. This second aim is of crucial importance in underdeveloped and developing tropical countries where, short falls in management, use of agricultural chemicals and machinery that dictate farmers control over seeds, pests and diseases. Stability is the property of a genotype or a population which permits subsequent alteration of the norm of the adaptation in response to changed selection pressure as reported by Simmonds (1962). According to Mather (1943) an adopted genotype or population is one which survives the selection pressures by a performance better than that of standard. The key facts, that the phenotypic performance of a genotype is not necessarily the same under diverse agro-ecological conditions that all the genotypes may not approach the same level of phenotypic expression under all environmental conditions, and that some genotypes may fare well in some environments but not so well in others, are all indicative of only one phenomenon – G × E interaction. The G × E interaction implies differential behavior of genotypes under different environments. The occurrence of G × E interaction has long posed a major challenge to a fuller understanding of the nature of genetic variation, as also to interpreting the evolutionary pattern in plant species. They have, therefore hampered the rationalization of breeding policies and procedures for crop improvement suggested by Breese (1969) and Kang *et al.* (1987). Thus G × E interactions have assumed greater importance in plant breeding in the sense that they violently interfere with precise estimates of genetic parameters and with stability of genetic values under diverse environments. The crops are generally profitable only when grown in a region where they are well adapted. The adapted cultivars usually produce satisfactory yield even on a poor soil and unfavourable environments. The occurrence of G × E interactions confound the selection of superior cultivars can be minimized in two ways. (*i*) By controlling the environments; (*ii*) By developing the varieties which show a high degree of stability over a wide range of environments. In first approach, control over environmental conditions is rather impossible and the only alternative left for breeders is the choice of suitable genotypes as an effective mean to minimize the impact of G x E interaction that is their homeostatic properties or buffering efficiencies as opined by Sharma (1996). There are many approaches now available to measure stability of genotypes over environments.

Stability and Its Concept

Johannsen (1909) was one of the earlier workers to recognize the importance of environment in the developmental process. His work paved the way to a greater understanding of those processes by which genotype and the environment jointly regulate the development of a particular individual. According to Mather (1943) an adopted genotype or population is one which survives the selection pressures by a performance better than that of standard. Stability is the property of a genotype or a population which permits subsequent alteration of the norm of the adaptation in response to changed selection pressure reported by Simmonds (1962).

Lewis (1954) defined the stability as the ability of an individual to produce certain narrow range of phenotypes in different environments. Allard and Bradshaw (1964) stated that stability does not imply general consistency of phenotype in varying environments. It may depend on holding some aspects of morphology and physiology in steady state. Thus the required varieties will show low genotype-environment interaction for agriculturally important characters, particularly yield. A variety which can adjust its genotypic or phenotypic state in response to transient fluctuations in environment in such a way that it gives high and stable economic return, can be termed 'well-buffering'. There are two buffering systems, individual buffering and population buffering. Individual buffering is a property of genetically homogeneous genotype (pure line varieties or single crosses) and denotes the ability of that genotype to produce an acceptable phenotype over a wide range of environmental conditions, where as population buffering is property of the population and arises due to the presence of the genetically diverse genotypes within the population in such a way that in each environment some genotypes do well and have wider adaptability. Lin *et al.* (1986) amplified that (it concept at stability) it is in many ways depending on how the scientist wishes to look at the problem. In fact, depending on goal and on the characters under consideration, two different concepts of stability exists, *i.e.,* static and dynamic concepts of stability.

Genotype x Environment Interaction and Stability Parameters (b_i and S^2d_i)

According to Finlay and Wilkinson (1963) gave the first model for stability and considered linear regression coefficient of mean yield of a variety on the mean yield of the varieties for each environment designating 'b_i' as an index of phenotypic stability of a variety. An ideal variety with general adaptability was defined as the one maximum yield potential under the most favourable environment and with maximum phenotypic stability (b_i=0). Eberhart and Russell (1966) gave the model of stability of genotype(s) and expressed the phenotypic stability of each variety by two parameters; the slope of the line and the sum of squared deviation from regression. They defined a stable variety as one with unit regression ($b_i = 1$) and least deviation from linearity ($S^2d_i = 0$). The linear regression of a genotype should simply be regarded as a measure of response of a particular genotype, whereas the deviation from linearity should be considered as a measure of stability as reported by Paroda and Hayes (1970). Accordingly a variety with least deviation being the stable one and *vice versa.* Perkins and Jinks (1968) used regression coefficient and the deviation from regression as the parameters of stability, but regression of genotype x environment interaction obtained on environmental index. The competition of separate regression coefficient on the two regions of the G x E response curve could be simple and convenient means of detecting theoretically ideal genotypes with relative insensitivity to poor environmental conditions and high sensitivity to favourable ones reported by Verma *et al.* (1978). Dobhal and Gautam (1994) carried out an experiment on phenotypic stability in adzuki bean (*Vigna angularis*) and they reported that analysis of variance for genotypes and environments was highly significant for number of pods/plant, pod length and seed yield per plant, indicating the presence of genetic variability in the material as well as the environments. The genotype x environment interaction was also significant. The pooled analysis of variance indicated that both linear and non-linear components of genotype x environment interaction were significant for all the traits and 'EC 108080' appeared most promising, as it was stable and showed high mean values for all the three traits. Effect of genotype x environment interaction in 11 rice bean genotypes for seed yield over three years was studied by Mishra (1995). Pooled analysis of variance showed the existence of significant genetic differences among the genotypes for seed yield. Experiment revealed that mean square due to environment was highly significant and non-significant genotype x environment (linear) interaction that indicated none of the genotypes differed in the response to environmental change. He reported that, out of the 12 genotypes, 'SRBS 74' genotype was stable as it had high mean yield (0.9 t/ha), showed regression value equal to 1 (1.01) and less deviation from the regression (–0.30) and the genotypes 'SRBS 43', 'SRBS 50' and 'SRBS 60' with regression coefficient equal to 1(1.07-1.34) were high yielders (0.92-1.16 t/ha) but unstable in performance, as they showed high deviation value from regression.

Accordingly, Panwar *et al.* (1995) studied stability in seed yield of 24 French bean genotypes grown in three distinct environments (Sangla, Kukumseri and Leo) in high-hill, dry temperate region of northwestern Himalayas of India over two years and stability performance analysis in six environments revealed significant differences due to genotypes, environments and genotypes × environment (G × E) interactions. Both linear and non-linear components of G × E interaction were present, with predominance of the former component. The genotypes showing wide adaptability and specific adaptation were identified. 'KRC 5', 'KRC 8' and 'KRC 11' were observed high yielding, out of which 'KRC 8' proved widely adaptable and stable. Pal and Prasad (1996) tested thirty three genotypes of French bean grown in three environments *i.e., rabi* 1992, summer 1993 and nineteen of them in summer 1994 to study the reaction of the genotypes to the changing environments. The degree of inter *per se* variability among the genotypes in three environments had similar trend as indicated by the coefficient of variation for all the characters except green pod yield. The analysis of variance for all the characters indicated high significant difference between the genotypes in all the three environments. Stability analysis revealed that two genotypes, CH-348 and CH-815, were found to be the best suitable in less favourable conditions, whereas, CH-909, CH-1113 and CH-1163 are less stable in yield and are suitable for favourable environments. Based on stability analysis and the yield performance, CH-896 could be regarded as relatively more stable and tolerant to summer heat. Sharma (1998) tested genotype-environment interaction and stability parameters in 10 genotypes of mothbean for days to maturity and seed yield as per Eberhart and Russells' model and results showed that genotypes 'Jadia' and 'Jwala' had high mean, b_i values and non-significant S^2d_i and therefore might show prolonged maturation under poor environments. Significant S^2d_i for 'RMO 173', 'RMO 224', 'RMO 225' and 'RMO 256' with low mean value and high bi value than unity indicated instability for this trait with changed environment. 'RMO 40' and 'RMO 257' had the lowest mean with very low regression coefficient value and non-significant S^2d_i value, showing stability for early maturity under poor environment and thus can be good donor for this trait. This experiment concluded that based on stability parameters genotypes 'RMO 40' and 'RMO 257' were found stable for maturity and seed yield under poor environment.

Research evidenced that, Shridhar and Ram (1999) carried out stability analysis for seed yield and its components in twenty eight french bean genotypes under four fertility regime *viz.*, E_1 (0:0:40), E_2 (60:60:40), E_3 (120:60:40) and E_3 (120:120:40 Kg/ha NPK) using Eberhart and Russell's and Perkins and Jink's model and they observed significant G x E interaction for genotypes and environments for all traits *viz.*, number of pods clusters per plant, number of pods per plant, pod length, number of seeds per pod, 100-seed weight and seed yield per plant. They concluded that environment E_3 was found to be beneficial for realization of full genetic potential of genotypes and according to stability criteria three genotypes *viz.*, PI 310706 (pole type), Pant Anupama and UPF 627 (both bush type) were found to be desirable for seed yield per plant over the fertility environments and also suggested that number of seeds per pod appeared to be an important trait for seed yield stability in all three genotypes. Pan *et al.* (2001) estimated the magnitude of G x E and stability parameters of pole beans over a three seasons period in tribal belt of Chotanagpur, Ranchi and experiment found highly significant genotype-environment (linear) components for pod girth and 10 green pod weight and significant pooled deviations for green pod yield, days to 50% flowering and pod length. Study indicated that genotypes responded both linearly and non-linearly to the change in environment. Twelve genotypes of French bean (*Phaseolus vulgaris* L.) were evaluated for 4 years (1995-98) under rainfed conditions at Research Station, Katrain in Kullu valley for stability of yield and maturity by Thakur *et al.* (2001). Pooled analysis of variance revealed significant differences amongst genotypes and substantial G x E interaction effect on grain yield. Linear and non- linear components of G x E interaction were important for both grain yield and maturity period with preponderance of the former. Genotypes '62-1 P1', 'HPR 207' and 'Hans' were found high-yielding and suitable for high-input conditions of cultivation and 'HPR 207' was high-yielding and most stable amongst the three. The phenotypic stability analysis of eight amaranth genotypes over three years (1997-1999) revealed that highly significant genotype x environment interaction (GEI) for all the traits (Sharma *et al.*, 2001). The linear and non-linear components showed predominant G x E interaction for harvest index, whereas only linear component for days to maturity: and non-linear for plant height, panicle length and grain yield. They concluded that, the genotype Amont exhibited stable high mean performance for grain yield, harvest index and plant height whereas Annapurna for grain yield and panicle length.

Research study support has inline with Nimbalkar *et al.* (2002) carried out an experiment on stability of seed yield and yield contributing characters of 16 genotypes of French bean during rainy season of 1998, 1999 and 2000 at Pune, Maharashtra. The genotype × environment interaction was significant for days to maturity, plant height and seed yield/plant. However, linear component was of larger magnitude than of non-linear components for all the traits except branches/plant and pod length, indicating that the variation in the performance of genotypes when grown over environments could be predicted. Environment + (genotype × environment) sum of squares were significant for all the environments. On examination of individual parameter of stability for different genotypes, 'ACPR 94040' possessed stability, indicating its suitability for general cultivation and also to use as one of parents in breeding programme aimed at development of stable French bean varieties. Raffi *et al.* (2004) were conducted experiment on stability analysis for pod and seed production in dry bean and Genotype-environment interaction was studied for number of pods and seeds plant^{-1} in nine genotypes of dry bean under four cultural environments during *rabi* season of 2001-2002. There were significant variations due to genotypes (G), environments (E) and G × E interaction for both the characters, which were also highly correlated between themselves (r=0.920**). On the basis of stability parameters (P_i, b_i, S^2d_i) genotype PB-58 was found to be most desirable and stable. Smitha (2005) was carried out experiment on stability analysis with four french bean genotypes *viz.*, DWD-FB-1, DWD-FB-53, DWD-FB-57 and IIHR-909 using three induced environments (3 fertilizer levels). The experiment found significant genotype x environment interactions for green pod yield per plant and green pod yield per hectare and 'DWD-FB-53' and 'DWD-FB-57' were exhibited stable under favourable environments, while 'DWD-FB-1' had shown stability in all the environments for green pod yield per hectare. An experiment was conducted to study the stability parameters, *viz.*, regression coefficient (b_i) and mean square deviations (S^2d_i) from linear regression, along with per-se performance of 13 varieties of bush type French bean for nine yield related characters. Highly significant pooled deviation for green pod yield/plant, number of branches/ plant, number of pods/plant and pod weight and highly significant/significant G × E (Linear) Interaction for days to 50% flowering, plant height and pod length indicated the preponderance of non-linear components of G × E interaction. The linear and non-linear components of G × E interactions were high and low, respectively, for pod width. The roundish and stringless podded line EC 350949 was better performing, stable and suitable for favourable environment for green pod yield (23.74 t/ha) and number of pods/plant (20.18) and suitable for unfavourable environment for number of branches/plant (5.14). EC 398564 was also better performing, stable and suitable for farourable environment for green pod yield (16.32 t/ha), pod length (17.63 cm), pod width (1.20 cm), pod girth (0.86 cm) and pod weight (10.68 g). EC 398570 was better performing, stable and suitable for favourable environment for pod girth (0.88 cm) and suitable for unfavourable environment for pod length (19.42 cm) and pod width (1.97 cm). EC 350955 was better performing, stable and suitable for favourable environment for number of branches per plant (5.14) and number of pods per plant (18.10) and suitable for unfavouranle environment for pod girth (0.90 cm) reported by Pan *et al.* (2006).

The stability analysis in 10 dry bean genotypes for seed yield per plant, grown over two years and five cultural environments, was done. Significant variation due to genotype (G), cultural environments (E), year (Y), G×E, G×Y and G×E×Y were observed for seed yield per plant. Combined analysis after Eberhart and Russell's model indicated linear and non-linear component of G×E interaction for seed yield per plant. Perkins & Jinks model showed significant G×E interaction but Freeman and Perkins model showed non-significant G×E interaction. Taking into consideration of all the three stability parameters (b_i, S^2d_i & P_i) of all the models, none of none of genotype could be considered stable. G×E×Y interaction study revealed that all the genotypes appeared to be unstable and sensitive to change environments in respect of years in the three models. They concluded that genotype PB147 and PB 152 might be considered as stable genotypes (Islam *et al.*, 2006). Arumugam *et al.* (2007) carried out an experiment to find out stability of twelve rice genotypes for grain yield and its component characters in six environments of sowing dates. They sowed the crop with 15 days interval between each sowing that represented a separate environment and they used Eberhart and Russell's model for analysis. Genotype x environment interaction was significant for grain yield and its components *viz.*, number of productive tillers, panicle length, spikelet fertility per cent, 1000-grain weight and harvest index. Stability parameters of the genotypes exhibited differential response. None of the genotypes used in the study was stable for all the characters. They found genotypes, IET 8116, KMP 101, IR 30864, CTH 1, CTH 3 and IR 64 were stable for grain yield. The study also indicated that sowing of long duration varieties could be extended upto July 1st fortnight and that of medium duration varieties upto 2nd fortnight of July instead of June 2nd fortnight and July 1st fortnight, respectively without significant reduction in grain yield. Singh *et al.* (2007) carried out stability analysis for yield and its components in french bean under three nitrogen fertility regimes *viz.*, N1 (80 kg/ha), N2 (120 kg/ha) and N3 (160 kg/ha). Heterogeneity among regression coefficients accounted for a significant portion of the genotype-environment interaction. The environment N3 was found to be beneficial for realization of full genetic potential of genotypes. Significant G × E (linear) for all the traits except number of branches per plant, pod length and number of seeds per pod revealed that differences among regression coefficient pertaining to various genotypes on the environmental mean were real. According to stability criteria (high mean performance, b_i=1 and S^2d_i=0), four genotypes *viz.*, HUR 137, CH 812, IIHR 909 and Arka Komal were found to be desirable and stable for pod yield per plot over the different fertility environments.

Researcher opined that, Patel *et al.* (2009) evaluated eleven early maturing pigeonpea genotypes for phenotypic stability of yield and related traits over four years (1997-2000) and they found highly significant genotype-environment interaction indicated differential response of the genotypes to the environmental changes and stability analysis showed significance of linear component of variation for important traits including grain yield. The genotype SKNP-9264 showed highest yield (1874 kg/ha) with high stability (b_i=1.09, S^2d_i=0.27) and genotypes SKNP-9264 and SKNP-9256 were also found stable for pods per plant, primary branches per plant, 100-seed weight, plant height and days to maturity. However, genotypes, SKNP-9203-1, SKNP-9217, SKNP-9226 and SKNP-9260-2 were found unstable over environments for yield (b_i=0.64, S^2d_i=1.45). Twelve varieties of bush type French bean were evaluated during summer season of 2006, 2007 and 2008 for the stability parameters *viz.*, regression coefficient (b_i) and mean square deviations (S^2d_i) from linear regression for nine yield related characters by Pan *et al.* (2009). It was observed that highly significant pooled deviation for days to 50% flowering, plant height, pod length, pod width and pod girth and significant G x E (linear) interaction for number of pods/plant and pod weight indicated the preponderance of non-linear components of G x E interaction. They concluded that stringless and round podded line HAFB-2 was high yielding, stable and showed average response to change in environmental condition for green pod yield (14.42 t/ha) and it was also better performing, stable and suitable for favourable environment for pod weight (6.98 g) and pod girth (0.93 cm) and suitable for unfavourable environment for number of pods/plant (13.85). The line HAFB-4 was also found stable and suitable for favourable environment for green pod yield (13.85 t/ha), number of pods/plant (14.94) and pod girth (0.92 cm). The stringless and flat podded variety Swarna Priya was also better performing, stable and suitable for favourable environments for green pod yield (13.86 t/ha) and plant height (45.46 cm). Further they also found that variety Arka Komal was stable and suitable for favourable environment for pod weight (7.19 g), pod length (14.90 cm) and pod width (1.06 cm) and suitable for unfavourable environment for early flowering (37.88 days).

Accordingly, Akhtar *et al.* (2010) tested fifteen mungbean genotypes at five locations in Pakistan in the *kharif* season 2006 to study their yield stability. Pooled analysis of variance and stability analysis were performed. The genotype (G) x environment (E) interaction and both variance due to genotypes and environments were significant. The partitioning of G x E interaction into linear and non-linear components indicated that both predictable and unpredictable components shared the interaction. Three stability parameters were computed to judge the stable and superior genotype. On the basis of these parameters, the top yielding genotype '2 (check) CGM-504' exhibited the stable performance over all five locations. Results also showed that the genotypes; BRM-288, NCM-257-2 and BRM-286 gave higher yield. But their performance was unstable due to high deviation from regression. Seven genotypes NCM-252-7, 2CMG-504, C1/95-3/45, BRM-286, BRM-288, NCM-257-2 and M-8 produced more grain yield than average yield. On the basis of results, 2CMG-504 was the most suitable and desirable genotype which showed stable yields at different sites. Hosamani *et al.* (2010) evaluated six new French bean varieties *viz.*,'HAFB-3', 'HAFB-4','DWD-FB-1','Arka Anoop','VLFB-2004' and 'VLFB-130' for three years along with checks *viz.*, 'IIHR-909' and 'Contender' during 2005, 2006 and 2007 to study the genotype-environment interaction and stability for growth and yield traits at the University of Agricultural Sciences, Dharwad, Karnataka. Considerable amount of variability was noticed among the genotypes as there was a significant varietal difference. Significant mean squares due to environments for many of the traits indicated that the environments were different. Similarly, G x E (linear) were non-significant for many of the traits except average pod weight indicating that the genotypes responded similarly as the environments changes and the magnitude of regression coefficient and deviation from regression varied from genotype to genotype. Results showed that genotypes 'DWD-FB-1' and 'HAFB-3' were stable for many of the traits and these are suitable to cultivate in *kharif* season. Sharma (2010) evaluated fifteen genotypes of French bean (*Phaseolus vulgaris* L.) for stability of green pod yield under north-western Himalayas of India (Kullu, Himachal Pradesh) and the found significant differences amongst genotypes and substantial genotype x environment interaction effect on green pod yield. The results also revealed that the genotypes *viz.*, IIHR-909, DPFBBS-1, HAFB-1, Contender, HAFB-2 and MFB-3 possessed specific adaptability for better/rich/favourable environments and could be cultivated under rich environments created through better or well management practices. In addition to these, genotypes IVFB-1 and IVFB-2 were highly stable and expected to perform in a stable manner over the fluctuating environmental conditions.

Research in support of Gangopadhyay *et al.* (2012) performed the studies on stability and sustainability index in fifty-five fenugreek genotypes over two environments (2005-2007), showed highly significant differences among the genotypes and environments for all the traits. The pooled deviation and G × E (Linear) interaction were found highly significant for plant height, number of primary branches per plant, pods per plant and seed yield per hectare indicated the preponderance of non-linear components of G × E interaction. They concluded that the genotype IC144260 had shown consistent performance and stability in wider environments for seed yield per hectare and pods per plant, whereas IC144243 has shown consistent performance in poor environment for seed yield per hectare. Thirteen cluster bean genotypes were evaluated for stability at two locations of North Gujarat to identify phenotypic stable genotypes for seed yield and its component traits by Jain and Patel (2012). They calculated pooled analysis of variance and found highly significant differences in the performance of different genotypes for stability *viz*., days to 50% flowering, days to 75% maturity, pods per plant, plant height, and seed yield except pod length and seeds per pod. The G × E interactions for all the characters were significant and the significant mean square due to environment (linear) indicated the existence of the real genotypic differences in the characters for regression over the environmental mean. Suggested the genotypes namely GAUG-0309, GAUG-0416, GAUG-0513 and GAUG-0522 were stable for earliness and they can be directly used for breeding for earliness. For improvement of seed yield, the genotypes *viz*., GAUG-0309 and GAUG-0511 were the most stable under rainfed situation. Nath *et al*. (2013) reviewed that plants generally showed variation in their response to changing environment. Stability analysis has become one of the important tools for plant breeders in predicting the response of various genotypes over changing environments. It is imperative to have stable performing cultivars across environment to realize higher seed yield. The interaction of genotype with the environment has an important bearing in breeding improved varieties. Genotype × environment (G × E) interaction has a masking effect on the performance of a genotype and hence the relative ranking of the genotypes do not remain the same over different environments. Adaptability of genotypes to environmental fluctuation is important for the stable crop production over the environments. Several methods such as regression analysis, multivariate clustering analysis, multiplicate formulations such as additive main effects and multiplicative interaction besides nonparametric method may be used for the G × E interaction. Among all, the model is widely used for stability parameters. The genotypes with high mean, regression coefficient (b_i) close to unity and less/no deviation from regression (S^2d_i) is found to be stable. The overall aim of this review is to emphasize the importance of G × E interaction and stability analysis in mungbean for increasing the global mungbean production.

Perspective of Singh *et al*. (2013) conducted an experiment on stability analysis in mungbean [*Vigna radiata* (L) wilczek] for nutritional quality and seed yield. Pooled analysis of variance indicated highly significant differences for genotypes (G), environment (E) and G x E interaction. The partitioning of G x E interaction into linear and non-linear components indicated that both predictable and unpredictable components shared the interaction. Three stability parameters (Mean, b_i and S^2d_i) were computed to judge the suitable and superior genotype. The deviation from regression for majority of the genotypes was highly significant revealing the unpredictable response of these genotypes and better suitability for sites with better environments. On the basis of these parameters, three genotypes MH 565, SML 668 and ML 776 with higher performance for seed yield, protein, iron and zinc content and highly significant deviation from linearity may be recommended for better environment. The studies on 15 coriander genotypes over the environments (2007-2010) showed non-significant differential G × E interaction to the changing environments while pooled deviation found highly significant for all the characters except days to 50 percent flowering, days to maturity and number of umbels per plant whereas G × E (Linear) interaction showed highly significant for number of secondary branches and days to maturity indicated the preponderance of non-linear components of G × E interaction. The estimates of mean performance, regression coefficient and deviation from regression for different traits showed that the genotypes RKD 18 and RKD 16 were more stable and can be a useful source for varietal development as these are the widely adapted landraces under common cultivation (Verma *et al.*, 2014). Singh *et al.* (2014) carried out an experiment on stability analysis for grain yield and its components in 10 exotic verities of cowpea over four seasons at Breeder Seed Production Centre, Pantnagar, Uttarakhand and they reported that genotypes PGCP-3, PGCP-4, PGCP-11 and Pant Lobia-1 emerged as most desirable genotypes showing their stability over range of environments for grain yield. Further they concluded that genotype Pant Lobia-1 was considered to be stable for yield as it did not showed significant deviation from S^2d_i=0 value and b_i value close to unity.

Correlation Analysis

The efficiency of selection can be improved by estimating the relative degree of association between different pairs of characters on the basis of significant correlation coefficient between yield and other economic traits. This correlation indicate the extent of observed relationship between two character and these include both heredity and the environmental influences, while genotypic correlation coefficient provides a real association between two characters and are highly useful in selection as mentioned by Johnson *et al.* (1955). Commacho *et al.* (1963) conducted an experiment with 49 lines of red kidney beans and reported significant negative correlation between number of pods per plant and number of seeds per pod, number of seed per pod and seed size and also between number of seeds per pod and seed size. Pinchinal and Adams (1966) reported that pod number per plant had predominant influence on seed yield. Pod number per plant was negatively correlated with seeds per pod. However, seeds per pod and seed weight were not strongly correlated. Shetter *et al.* (1975) observed positive and significant correlation between pod yield and number of pods per plant. Natrajan and Arumugam (1981) reported that plant height, number of branches per plant, number of pods per plant, pod length and number and weight of seeds per pod showed highly significant positive correlation with green pod yield. Petrova (1984) studied the correlation between some morphological plant characters and yield in French bean. He reported that stem length was significantly correlated with number of pods per plant.

Accordingly, Singh and Saini (1985) reported that yield was positively and significantly correlated with days to flowering and maturity, plant height, branch number and pod cluster. Joshi and Thomas (1987) reported positive correlation of pod yield with pods per plant, 100 seed weight and days to maturity. Nine elite cultivars of French bean were collected and evaluated by Saha *et al.* (1990). They found that pod yield per plant was positively and significantly correlated with plant height, number of pods per plant and weight of pods per plant, days to flowering were significantly and positively correlated with plant height and pods per plant. Dimova *et al.* (1991) studied correlations between yield-related traits in the F from the crosses Dobrudzhanski 2 × 564 and 186 x 564. Seed weight was closely and significantly correlated with number of fertile nodes and number of pods per plant. Path analysis showed that fertile node number had a marked indirect effect through pod number per plant, which had the most marked direct effect on seed weight. The results suggested that in the breeding work the most important traits for selection were pod number per plant and pod length.

According to Gunjal and Mote (1993) conducted a field trial in Maharashtra, India. They reported that plant height had a significant negative correlation with yield, number of pods per plant, pod weight per plant, grain number per plant and grain number per pod but with single pod weight. Singh (1993) recorded positive and significant correlation of green pod yield per plant with plant height, seed yield and seeds per pod and negative correlation with 100 seed weight. Kalia and Kalia (1994) investigated the inter character association among 35 determinate and indeterminate genotypes of *Phaseolus vulgaris* grown either as sole crop or intercropped with maize. Seed yield was positively correlated with biological yield under both cropping system but negatively correlated with seed yield under monoculture. Associations were generally higher under intercropping than monoculture. Samal *et al.* (1996) reported high positive correlation for seed yield per plant with seeds per pod. Escribano *et al.* (1997) observed high correlation of pod texture with seed length wide and width thickness ratios, per cent seed coat, seed water absorption, crude fat, total sugar, starch content and crude fiber. Mishra *et al.* (1997) reported that pod yield per plant had significant and positive correlation with number of pods per plant and days to first flowering, while significant negative association was observed between number of pods per plant and length in 15 F_4 lines of *Phaseolus vulgaris*. Thakur *et al.* (1997) evaluated 54 *Phaseolus vulgaris* L. genotypes and reported that days to 50 per cent flowering, days to first picking, pods per cluster, pods per plant, pod girth, plant height and harvest index exhibited positive correlation with pod yield. Relative degree of association among different quantitative characters of French bean was measured by Chand and Chand (1998). The correlation study indicated that phenotypically yield was positively and significantly correlated with pods per plant, seeds per pod and 100 seed weight but at genotypic level, the association was highest for pods per plant. Arya *et al.* (1999) studied 25 genotypes of French bean and reported positive and significant correlation of green pod yield with pods per plant, branches per plant, plant height, seed vigour and strong positive association of 100-seed weight, plant height and branches per plant with pod number per plant.

Research evidenced has been in support of Agsakall and Olgun (2001) reported that the coefficient of correlation between days to flowering and yield, pod number and yield, 100 seed weight and yield were found to be highly significant. Shinde and Dumbre (2001) reported fifty genotypes of French bean (*Phaseolus vulgaris* L.) for 11 characters, in Pune, Maharashtra, India, during *kharif* 1998. Seed yield per plant was positively and significantly correlated with days to first flower, days to maturity, plant height, plant spread, number of branches per plant, number of pods per branch and number of seeds per pod. It showed positive but non-significant correlation with pod breadth, while negative non-significant correlation with pod breadth, pod length and 100-seed weight both at genotypic and phenotypic levels. The characters 100-seed weight and number of seeds per pod showed strong positive direct effects, while number of pods per plant and number of branches per plant showed moderate direct effects. The direct negative effects on yield were observed for pod length and days to first flower. Berrocal *et al.* (2002) observed positive correlation for seed yield and seed number per plant and seed number per pod. There was a positive correlation between seed number and pod number per plant.

In support of Makhdoomi *et al.* (2002) evaluated 35 germplasm lines of French bean and reported that seed yield per plant had highly significant and positive association with seed per pod, pods per plant, days to 50 per cent flowering and days to maturity. Nemeskari (2002) reported correlation between plant density and yield average and the volume of yield increase in variety of large and medium sized seed and up to a plant density of 285-400 thousand/ha after which it decline. Nath and Korla (2004) studied twenty-eight dwarf French bean (*Phaseolus vulgaris*) genotypes for correlation and path coefficient analysis during 1998 at Solan, Himachal Pradesh, India. Eight quantitative characters were analysed for their path coefficients in relation to pod yield. Number of pods per plant, pod length and harvest index had significant positive association with pod yield. Number of pods per plant had the highest direct effect, while harvest index and pod length had the highest indirect effects through pod numbers. Rai *et al.* (2004) worked on genotypic and phenotypic correlation twenty-seven germplasms of bush type French bean and investigation revealed that pod yield per plant showed significant positive correlation with pod weight at genotypic and phenotypic level. However, pod yield per plant was positively related to pod length at genotypic level. Significant positive association was also observed in between pod weight and pod length; seed weight and pod width, seed diameter and pod width, seed diameter and seed weight, seed length and pod length, seed length and seed weight and seed length and seed thickness, whereas, significant negative correlation was also observed in between pod width and pod length, number of pods per plant and pod width, seed weight and pod width, seed diameter and pod weight.

It's been evidenced that, Kumar (2005) evaluated 441 lines of French bean germplasm and reported that seed yield per plant was positively and significantly correlated with number of pods per plant, pod length and 100-seed weight but negative and significant association with days to 50 per cent flowering and days to maturity was established. Anju *et al.* (2006) reported the direct and indirect effects of the different yield attributing characters on seed yield of 48 French bean genotypes during the *rabi* season of 1998-99 in Haryana, India. Observations were recorded on five competitive plants for 16 quantitative traits (days to first flowering, days to 50% flowering, days to pod initiation, days to maturity, plant height, primary branches per plant, secondary branches per plant, cluster per plant, pods per cluster, pod length, pods per plant, seeds per pod, biological yield, harvest index, 100-seed weight, and genotypic correlations with seed yield). Five pods per plant were selected to study pod characters. Path coefficient analysis of yield attributes and seed yield in 48 French bean genotypes representing wide agroclimatic regions of the world revealed that in selection programme, maximum weight should be given to biological yield, days to pod initiation, number of clusters per plant, seeds per pod and secondary branches per plant since their direct influence on seed yield was highly significant, while their indirect influence via most of the other component characters was negligible.

In view of Singh (2007) observed that seed yield per plant was positively and significantly correlation with number of pods per plant and pod length, but it had negative and significant correlation with plant height and days to maturity. Kandpal (2008) observed that seed yield per plant was positively correlated with pod length, number of pods per plant, plant height and pod yield per plant, but it had positive and non significant correlation with days to 50 per cent flowering and days to 50 per cent pod setting. Asati and Singh (2008) studied the association character for yield and its contributing in French bean revealed that pod yield per plant, had significant positive with plant height, number of branches per plant, inter-nodal length, weight per pod, seed length, seed width, seed thickness, number of pods per plant and 100 seed weight at genotypic and phenotypic levels. Dubey *et al.* (2009) studied character association in 52 germplasm of French bean and the study revealed that only one character length of pod was positively and significantly correlated with pod yield. Among other positive significantly correlations were between height of plant and width of pod, seed yield per plant and weight of 100 seeds. Weight of 100 seeds in general, had negative correlation with most of the characters and so was the association of number of pods per plant revealing negative correlation with length, width and thickness of pod.

The green pod yield per plant showed positive and significant association with number of pods per plant, pod length, number of seeds per pod and 10 pod weights in all the three environments studied in French bean by Singh *et al.* (2009). The magnitude of the genotypic correlation was higher than the phenotypic correlation but both genotypic and phenotypic correlations followed the same direction, indicating that the selection based on phenotypic correlation could be effective. Karasu *et al.* (2010) found that positively significant correlation in all pairs of the characters except between seed yield per hectare and pod length, pod width and first pod height in dry bean. The highest positive correlations were observed between seed yield per plant with biomass yield, number of pods per plant and number of branches per plant. Sofi *et al.* (2011) evaluated forty two genotypes of rajmash for morphological and yield parameters, revealed that the grain yield was significantly correlated with number of pods/plant followed by 100 seed, leaf area, seeds/pod and plant height but it was negatively correlated with days to flowering, days to maturity and pod length. The pod yield per hectare had positive and highly significant association with pod yield per plant, pod length, weight of pod, plant height, leaf area, leaf area index, ovule number per pod, number of seeds per pod at both phenotypic and genotypic level reported under the study of twelve French bean genotypes (Angadi *et al.*, 2012). Ahmed and Kamaluddin (2013) studied 57 germplasm lines of rajmash beans for yield and yield contributing traits, found that the seed yield was positively correlated with days to 50 per cent flowering, plant height, pod length, number of pods/plant and number of seeds/pod. Pandey *et al.* (2013) evaluated twenty genotypes of French bean for assessment of correlations among yield and economically important traits revealed that significant positive correlation between green pod yield and economic traits like number of pods per plant, pod length, individual pod weight and number of seed per pod indicates that improvement in these traits could lead to increase in pod yield. Walling and Chaturvedi (2014) reported that significant positive correlation between grain yield and 100 seed weight in French bean genotypes.

DUS Characterization

Intellectual Property Rights in Agriculture

Increased interest and debate over the ownership of intellectual property has arisen in agriculture also because the protection of research product is necessary to provide incentive for investment (Jondle, 1989). Intellectual property is an idea, a design, an invention, a manuscript, etc which can ultimately give rise to a useful product/application. This is an integral part of agriculture because seeds reproduce themselves indefinitely. Farmers used to replant, sell and share seeds because plant breeding was natural and considered as common property. Seeds were not seen as a commodity and hence there was little or no private investment. As the profitability of seed companies improved, the potential for losses due to theft or infringement also increased. Consequently economy based issues that needed legal interpretation and regulation emerged. Efforts to resolve these issues led to the enactment of intellectual property rights legislation in the United States and Europe reported by Staub *et al.* (1996). Intellectual property rights (IPRs) can be broadly defined as legal rights established over creative or inventive ideas. Such legal rights generally allow right holders to exclude the unauthorized commercial use of their creations/inventions by third persons. The rationale for the establishment of a legal framework on IPRs is that it is a signal to society that creative and inventive ideas will be rewarded as reported by Watal (1998).

Plant Variety Protection Act (PVPA) was enacted in 1970 (Anonymous, 2001). In 1985, the US Board of Patent Appeals allowed patent protection for asexually, sexually or *in vitro* propagated plants (Sahai, 2001). Currently plants can be protected in the United States by PPA of 1930, the PVPA of 1970 as amended in 1994 and with utility patents. Therefore in the US, there exists today a dual system of protection; plants can be protected by a *sui generis* Plant Variety Protection Act as well as by the Patent Act and in Europe by Plant Breeder's Rights and (PBRs) of 1961. The US Plant Patent Act (PPA), enacted in 1930, allowed patenting of asexually propagated plants and over 6,500 of such plant patents have been granted mostly for ornamentals and fruit trees (Pental, 2003). Kochhar (2004) depicted that IPRs in agriculture were seen congruently with the industrial property rights for the first time only under Uruguay round of the General Agreement on Tariffs and Trade (GATT) negotiations in late 1980s that culminated with the signing of Ministerial Declaration at Marrakesh in 1994. However, the IPR protection for plants and plant varieties was in practice in some countries much earlier than the Uruguay round of GATT negotiations or the establishment of WTO.

In 1930, a legislative instrument (Plant Patent Act) was established in the USA for patenting varieties of asexually propagated plants whereas in 1961, an international convention [Convention of the Union for the Protection of New

Varieties of Plants, original in French 'Union Internationale pour la Protection des Obtentions Vegetales]; (UPOV) was held albeit with few countries to negotiate and provide for the protection of new varieties of plants, and triggered enactment of plant variety protection laws in countries of Europe. Intellectual property includes patents, copyrights, trademarks, geographical indications, industrial designs, integrated circuits and trade secrets (Chawla and Singh, 2005). Stein (2005) observed that more than 80 per cent farmers in developing nations rely on saved seeds for the next harvest. In Japan, plant patents are allowed, but there are some disputes over territorial rights. Life forms of plants and animals except microorganisms are not patentable in India. In pursuance to the TRIPs agreement, India has enacted "Protection of Plant Varieties and Farmers' Rights" (PPV&FR) Act, 2001, a *sui generis* system of plant variety protection and in international context dealt with UPOV (Chawla, 2007). Dewan (2011) reported that private rights in living objects have always been controversial. Agriculture provided the first wave in human civilization. Therefore, agriculture including plant breeding and agriculture methods pre-dated any form of IPR protection unlike industry and commerce. Traditionally, IPR was not applied to agriculture. In recent time, this position has changed and increasingly agriculture is seen as an industry that cannot survive without research and development and astute investment. This has made it necessary that IPR in all its forms be extended to agriculture. IPR were essentially recognized and accepted all over the world due to reasons like to provide incentives to the individuals for new creations, providing due recognition to the creators and inventors, ensuring monetary reward for intellectual property, ensuring the availability of the genuine and original products (Dolli, 2012).

UPOV System of Plant Variety Protection

An International convention of the union for the protection of new varieties of plants, original in French Union International Pour La Protection Des Obtentions Vegetales (UPOV) was signed in Paris in 1961 and it entered into force in 1968. The UPOV aimed to ensure protection of Plant Breeder's Rights (PBRs) by the grant of an exclusive right on the protected new plant variety on the basis of a set of uniform and clearly defined principles. The UPOV Act was revised in 1972, 1978 and 1991. The 1978 Act came into force in 1981 and the 1991 Act in April 1998. These are two main Acts of 1978 and 1991 (Dutfield, 2001). Some countries have ratified the 1991 Act whereas others the 1978 Act. The convention has 70 countries. Under the UPOV a plant variety qualifies for protection when it meets the essential criteria (*i*) distinctness, (*ii*) uniformity, (*iii*) stability, (*iv*) novelty (new in commercial sense) and a unique and unambiguous denomination (name of the new variety). Farmers' rights were available to the farmers in the UPOV Act, 1978 but UPOV Act 1991 deprives farmers of their rights to reuse their produce as a seed. Although farmers are broadly exempted from the monopoly for non-commercial use of their produce from a protected variety including propagating another crop from harvested material on their own farm as mentioned by Kochhar (2004). As per the 1991 Act of UPOV, protection granted for the new variety authorizes the breeder with the exclusive right to commercially exploit the variety by direct sale or by licensing to others for sale. Nevertheless, the UPOV Act, 1991 provides that the breeder of an Essentially Derived Variety (EDV) will have to get authorization of the breeder of the original variety for the commercial exploitation of new-variety (Chawla, 2005).

Changing Nature of UPOV Membership and Developing Countries

Belgium, France, the Federal Republic of Germany (FRG), Italy and the Netherlands were the original signatories for UPOV membership on 2 December 1961. UPOV came into force only in August 1968 after the UK, the FRG and the Netherlands had ratified it. Of the five original signatories, France ratified it and joined the Union in 1971, Belgium in 1976 and Italy in 1977. Switzerland also joined in 1977; Sweden, Israel and South Africa became members during the 1970s. Between 1980 and 1983, six countries joined UPOV, including the USA after an amendment in the 1978 Act. Thus, 17 members of UPOV and Australia, which joined in 1989, effectively negotiated the critical amendments for the 1991 Act reported by Dhar (2002). By January 2002, the membership had expanded to 50. Of these, 14 are from developing countries. All are parties to the 1978 Act except the Republic of Korea, which acceded to the 1991 Act. Since 1991, 11 Eastern European countries and former Soviet Republics have also become UPOV members and eight of these have acceded to the 1991 Act (Dhar, 2002). A striking feature about the membership is the high proportion of countries with relatively low shares of their economically active population in agriculture. At the end of 1999, only seven had more than 25 per cent of their workforce in agriculture and just two, China and Kenya, exceed 50 per cent. Most of the early members of UPOV have less than 5 per cent of their economically active population engaged in agriculture. There seems to be a strong correspondence between adoption of IPR in agriculture and low shares of economically active population in this sector (Dhar, 2002).

In August 2001, *sui generis* legislation for the protection of plant varieties was introduced into the Namibian Parliament. It is based on the "African Model Law for the Protection of the Rights of Local Communities, Farmers and Breeders, and for the Regulation of Access to Biological Resources" developed by the Organization of African Unity. The proposed, "Access to Biological Resources and Associated Traditional Knowledge Act" provides for the grant of farmers rights and Plant Breeders Rights, while recognizing the rights of local communities over their biological resources and associated knowledge, innovations and practices (Dhar, 2002). Asian countries that have ratified UPOV include China (1978 Act, not including Hong Kong special administrative region), Japan (1991 Act), Kyrgyzstan (1991 Act) and Vietnam (1991 Act). Notably the most technologically advanced economies in the region are following 1991 Act High proportion of UPOV signatories have a relatively low share of their economically active population engaged in agriculture, though of Asian UPOV members, China and Vietnam are notable exceptions (Robinson, 2008). The majority of East, Southeast Asian countries that have not signed UPOV has a relatively large share of agriculture in their economies. Countries in Asia, which have not signed or ratified UPOV, but have UPOV-style laws, include Hong Kong, Indonesia, Pakistan, Philippines, Taiwan, Malaysia and Sri Lanka (Robinson, 2008).

A view put forth Singh *et al.* (2011) have reviewed the status of farmers' rights in Asian countries which are members of WTO and further sorted into four groups (Group A) Bahrain, Brunei Darussalam, Hong Kong, Kuwait, Macao, Mongolia, Sri Lanka, Chinese Taipei, (Group B) Armenia, Bangladesh, Cambodia, India, Indonesia, Malaysia, Maldives, Myanmar, Nepal, Pakistan, Philippines, Qatar, Saudi Arabia, Thailand, United Arab Emirates, (Group C) China, Israel, Japan, Singapore, Turkey, Vietnam and (Group D) Jordan, Republic of Korea, Kyrgyzstan and Oman based on whether they are members of UPOV and/or ITPGRFA. Out of the four groups of WTO member Asian countries, only some of the Group B countries, who are members of ITPGRFA but not the UPOV members, have opted for a *sui generis* system, which provided for the farmers' rights (Singh *et al.*, 2011). Of the Group A countries, which have not joined either UPOV or ITPGRFA, only Sri Lanka has drafted a plant breeders right legislation, known as Protection of New Plant Varieties (Breeder's Rights) 2001, which follows the model of UPOV 1991 and does not recognize the farmers' rights. Of the Group B countries, which are members of ITPGRFA but not UPOV, India, Thailand, Indonesia, Malaysia and Philippines have enacted legislations with respect to farmers' right; Bangladesh and Pakistan have prepared draft legislations; and Nepal has prepared a policy document, which discusses the farmers' right. Other countries in the group do not have any legislation relating to farmers' rights or plant variety protection.

Philippines and Malaysian

The Philippines Act, provides for a framework for community registration of locally bred varieties. Farming communities and bonafide farmers' organizations can establish their respective local registry system to register or build an inventory of locally bred varieties. Both Malaysian and Philippine Acts use and identify small farmer, a feature absent in the Indian legislation, in the context of the limitations imposed upon the rights of the breeder. Section 2 A of the Malaysian Plant Variety Act defines small farmer in terms of size of holdings while the Philippines Plant Variety Protection Act of 2002 does not define it. However, Magna Carta of Small Farmers, another Philippine Act, defines small farmer in terms of income (Magna Carta, Sec 4 91).

Pakistan

Pakistan has passed Plant Breeders' Ordinance, 2000. As per this ordinance, the farmer has been recognized as a breeder and is entitled to register new varieties (http://www.grain.org/brl_files/pakistan-pbr-2000.doc, October, 2013). Farmers' right to save, use, exchange, share or sell his farm produce of protected variety has been protected but not seed. Section 30 of the ordinance provides for compulsory lincensing also. The ordinance is silent about benefit sharing. Farmers' right in benefit sharing as such has not been recognized but as a community right farmers are entitled to 10% of the benefit obtained from any commercial use of biological resources.

Bangladesh

Farmers' right in Bangladesh draft provision do not recognize the right to seed but provides the protection to the right to collect, conserve, propagate and use the propagation material of any protected variety if it is for personal and non-commercial use (http://www.grain.org/brlfiles/bangladesh-pvp-1998-en.pdf, October, 2013). Exchange of propagating material for any monetary and financial gains is strictly prohibited. Farmer has been explicitly recognized as a breeder and provision for the protection of farmers' variety is missing. However, it recognizes the farmer's right as innovator and rewards have been proposed in the draft provision. Bangladesh draft aims to provide for protection if the infringing act has been done in the good faith or for non-commercial purpose {Article 21 (4)}. Among the Group C countries, which are members of UPOV as well as WTO, China is governed by the UPOV 1978 Act while the other Asian members of UPOV are governed by the UPOV 1991 Act (http://www.upov.int/en/about/members/pdf/pub423.pdf, October, 2013). The provisions of ITPGRFA guide the status of farmers' rights in Group D countries, which are members of WTO, UPOV as well as ITPGRFA. The farmers in these countries enjoy rights such as benefit sharing, and recognition of their contribution in conservation and preservation of plant genetic resource. These countries do not recognize right to seed but have an option to recognize farmers' privilege to seeds.

Plant Variety Protection System in India

India did not have any legislation on protection of plant varieties before 1995, pre WTO. However India became signatory to the TRIPS in 1994 and legislation was necessitated. Article 27.3(b) of TRIPS agreement requires the member countries to provide protection of plant varieties either by a patent or by an effective sui generis system or any combination thereof (Brahmi *et al.*, 2004). Thus the member countries had the choice to frame legislation suiting their own system and consequently Indian Parliament passed the Protection of Plant Varieties and Farmers' Rights Act on August 9, 2001 after protracted legislative and civil society interactive process stretching to eight years. The Act has 97 sections stacked in 11 chapters (Bala Ravi, 2004). Dewan (2011) opined that India is one of the first countries in the world to have passed a legislation granting rights to both breeders and farmers simultaneously under one Act. It is the only legislation in this area that grants formal rights to farmers in a way that grants formal rights to farmers in a way that prevents their self-reliance from being jeopardized while at the same time recognizing the efforts of the plant breeders in developing new plant varieties. By giving protection to farmers' plant variety, the act recognizes the farmer as both a cultivator and a conserver of the agricultural plant variety.

Objective of PPV & FR Act

The *sui generis* system for protection of plant varieties was developed integrating rights of breeders, farmers and village communities, and taking care of the concerns for equitable sharing of benefits. It offers flexibility with regard to protected genera/species, level and period of protection, when compared to other similar legislation existing or being formulated in different countries (Shankar *et al.*, 2000). The objectives of the act are to: (*i*) provide for the establishment of an effective system for protection of plant varieties, (*ii*) protect rights of farmers and plant breeders, (*iii*) encourage development of new varieties of plants (*iv*) stimulate investment for research and development, (*v*) ensure availability of high quality seeds and planting material to the farmers. Other issues related to public interest include compulsory licensing rights and prevention of the propagation of varieties using genetic use restriction technologies (GURT), which are contrary to the interest of the farmers in general as suggested by Swaminathan (2002).

Eligibility, Scope and Duration for Protection under PPV & FR Act

The main feature of the Act is the provision to claim IPRs over varieties through a system of registration. The Act allows different types of varieties to be registered namely new variety, extant variety, essentially derived variety, farmers' variety and transgenic variety. The subsection 15(3) (a) explains the differences in the definition of novelty in respect of new variety bred in India and introduced from outside. Novelty means commercial novelty, *i.e.*, the propagating or harvested material of the variety should not have been sold or otherwise disposed off earlier than one year in India, from the date of filing of application of registration, or outside India, not earlier than six years in the case of trees and wines and not earlier than four years in any other case. Moreover, trial of a new variety, which has not been sold or otherwise disposed off, shall not affect the right to protection. 'Distinctiveness' means that a variety is clearly distinguishable by at least one essential characteristic from any other variety, whose existence is a matter of common knowledge. 'Uniformity' implies that the variety should be sufficiently uniform in its essential characteristics subject to variation as expected from features of its propagation. 'Stability' requires the essential characteristics remain unchanged after repeated propagation.

The Act is explicit also on other requirements to be satisfied while applying for registration of a plant variety. All applications, except those from farmers, are to be completed with respect to the following requirements (*i*) denomination assigned to such variety by applicant, (*ii*) a sworn affidavit affirming absence of terminator technology (genetic use restriction technology) in the candidate variety, (*iii*) a complete passport data of the parental lines from which the variety has been derived along with geographical location in India from where the genetic material has been taken and all such information relating to the contribution, if any farmer, village community, institution or organization in breeding, evolving or developing the variety, (*iv*) a statement containing a brief description of the variety bringing out its characteristics of novelty, uniformity and stability as required for the registration, (*v*) a declaration that the genetic material or parental material acquired for breeding, evolving or developing the variety has been lawfully acquired, and (*vi*) such other particulars may be prescribed (Brahmi, 2004; Dhillon *et al.*, 2006).

Futuristic View

Scope of protection of a plant variety is delineated under section 28 of the Act. Grant of registration confers exclusive right to the breeder, his /her legal successor, agent or licensee to produce, sell, market, distribute, import or export the variety (*i.e.,* the planting material of the variety). This right, referred to as the PBRs, shall not be exercisable in case of EDV as stipulated under section 23 and 43 without entering into mutually agreed terms on its commercialization between the PBR holder of the EDV and the natural/legal owner of the initial variety from which the EDV was derived (Bala Ravi, 2004). According to the Section 47 of the Act the PPV & FR Authority can grant compulsory licence, in case of any complaints about the availability of the seeds of any registered variety to public at reasonable price. The licence can be granted to any person interested to take up such activities after the expiry of a period of three years from the date of issue of the certificate of registration to undertake production, distribution and sale of the seed or other propagating material of the variety. Compulsory licensing is invoked only after allowing reasonable opportunity to the PBR holder for complying with these requirements. Whenever, a variety is compulsorily licensed, a reasonable compensation is awarded to the PBR holder (Brahmi, 2004). The certificate of registration issued under section 24 valid for nine years in case of trees and vines and six years in case of other crops, and may be reviewed and renewed for the remaining period on payment of such fees as may be fixed by the rules made on this behalf subject to the conditions that the total period of validity is not exceed (i) in case of trees and vines, eighteen years from the date of registration of the variety. (ii) in case of extant varieties, fifteen years from the date of notification of that variety by the Central Government under Section 5 of the Seeds Act, 1996, and (iii) in the other case, fifteen years from the date of registration of the variety (Brahmi, 2004).

Criteria for DUS Testing

The PPV&FR Act, 2001 requires that a variety be examined for compliance with the distinctiveness, uniformity and stability criteria. During the course of the examination, the DUS test centre or the Authority may grow the variety or carry out other necessary tests, cause the growing of the variety or the carrying out of other necessary tests, or take into account the results of growing tests or other trials which have already been carried out (Anonymous, 2007). Sharma (1991) proposed that new cultivars of agricultural crops and vegetables must be registered before they can be entered for certification. The registration process is based upon two tests carried out by independent organizations, in which, one case defines distinctiveness, uniformity and stability (DUS) test and in another, assesses value for cultivation and usage (VCU) test. The registration of a new variety in European Economic Community (EEC) requires information from value for cultivation (VCU) and DUS traits (Tandon, 1992). Mucha *et al.* (1994) proposed the organization and methods of testing of varieties for distinctiveness, uniformity and stability (DUS) for entry in the official register and for protection of Plant Breeder's Right in Poland. The essentiality of a DUS type test for materials released and notified in India was indicated by Singh and Sharma (1996).

Veress and Lazer (1997) reported that the most important topic dealt by the Hungarian Institute for Agricultural Quality Control is the distinctness, uniformity and stability (DUS) testing of maize. A new method, the distinctness percentage method, has been developed with the aid of which (*i*) different character types are investigated, (*ii*) minimal distance involved in DUS testing of maize are studied and (*iii*) minimal distance involved in the DUS distinctness tests are studied between the different character types. Veress and Matok (1999) proposed that the determination of the most similar variety or of groups of similar varieties can be carried out using variety descriptors. DUS assessment of agricultural crops generally involves growing field plots under appropriate and ambient conditions and recording various morphological characteristics of the seed and/or growing plants. Laboratory and greenhouse tests can also be involved (Barendrecht, 1999; Mauria, 2000). According to Law *et al.* (1999) distinctness, uniformity and stability (DUS) testing of varieties is currently carried out using morphological and other phenotypic characters.

Camlin *et al.* (2001) proposed that the testing of new cultivars of plants for registration and granting of plant breeders rights involves the determination of DUS of these new cultivars in comparison with existing reference cultivars. According to section 15 of the Act, Novelty means commercial novelty, moreover, trial of a new variety which has not been sold or otherwise disposed off shall not affect the right to protection. Distinctiveness means that a variety is clearly distinguishable by at least one essential characteristic from any other variety, whose existence is a matter of common knowledge. 'Uniformity' implies that the variety should be sufficiently uniform in its essential characteristics subject to variation as expected from features of its propagation. 'Stability requires the essential characteristics remain unchanged after repeated propagation (Dhillon *et al.*, 2006). The new varieties will be subjected to DUS testing by PPV and FR authority. The PPV and FR authority had developed and published in its journal, guidelines for DUS test for different crops (Anonymous, 2007).

The tests are envisaged to generate comprehensive data on the attributes of a variety, so as to compare these with the variety of common knowledge or similar existing varieties. These tests shall be field and multilocation based for at least two crop seasons, at a minimum two locations, along with special chemical laboratory tests (Section 29, PPV & FR rules). The material should be 'sufficiently uniform' for the reason that uniformity depends on the breeding methodology followed in designing a variety. Lack of uniformity indicates that the material is heterozygous or has admixtures and therefore cannot be stable over generations. Analysis of the visual data scored on distinctiveness and uniformity, and inferring stability forms the basis of registration of the new variety. If the DUS field test is not able to establish that the variety under evaluation is distinct, then if the applicant so desires, special laboratory tests can be conducted (physiological/chemical/molecular tests) to establish that the applied variety is distinct and registrable. The standard laboratory procedures of such special tests are to be made known and the laboratory where it is conducted is to be accredited. On completing the DUS test, if the applied variety meets all the requirements of registration, then a part of the original seed supplied is transferred to National Gene bank. The seed lot is stored under low-temperature conditions at 5°C for the entire registration period, and if necessary, after few years of storage in the National Gene Bank, the seed lot will be rejuvenated and replenished at the cost of the applicant. The seed stored in the National Gene Bank will be used for dispute settlement or when an exigency arises for invoking compulsory licensing provision (Nagarajan *et al.*, 2010). Kochhar (2010) stated that there is no provision for the sale of farm-saved seed as branded seed as well as the presence of genetic use restriction technology (GURT) or 'terminator technology' in the varieties to be registered. Developments related to PVP applications filed and recorded in the initial two-and-a-half to three years since the beginning of registration process on the country suggest that the legislation could not be effective, particularly for the protection and commercial use of extant varieties, including the premium farmers' varieties.

Farmers Rights

PPV & FR Act 2001 is the main law in India dealing with Farmers' Rights. The Act emerged from a process of enormous debate and could be passed after about five revisions were made to the draft. The PPV & FR Act initially emerged as a result of the demands of the seed industry for breeder's rights. Agriculture was generally excluded from IPR protection in India and there was no legal system of Plant Breeders' Rights or Farmers' Rights for decades. 'Common heritage' or the principle of free exchange based on the view that the major food plants of the world are not owned by anyone and are a part of our human heritage governed genetic resources. Farmers were free to use, share and exchange seeds and since breeders could not acquire plant variety protection, there was no system of benefit sharing or compensation (Ramanna, 2006).

The initial demands for IPRs in agriculture arose with the change in policy that allowed private sector entry into the seed sector with the New Seed Policy. The Seed Association of India, formed in 1985, first actively promoted the need for plant breeders' rights in India. With the conclusion of the TRIPs agreement there was also external pressure on India to establish PBRs in India. India's public sector had initially objected to plant variety protection partly because it would enable private companies to take advantage of breeding material developed by the public sector, but this stance underwent a change due to the changing role of the private sector and the relationship between the public and private sectors (Seshia, 2001). Enormous protest against implementing TRIPs, and introducing PBRs, arose from non-governmental organizations and farmers' lobbies in India. Their most effective and forceful argument was that the IPR system as outlined in TRIPs recognizes only agricultural innovations of breeders and corporations, but ignores informal innovations of farmers and communities, especially in developing countries. They asserted that TRIPs and western IPR regimes promote 'bio-piracy' as they only recognize formal innovations and ignore indigenous knowledge systems. Bio-piracy refers to the utilization of traditional knowledge or resources by industrialized nations to create profitable products without compensation. TRIPs allow countries to establish 'effective *sui generis*' systems, but many developing countries are implementing even higher standards than the minimum requirement, such as UPOV 1991. Developing countries are also subject to pressure to implement higher standards from TRIPs plus agreements, including regional trade agreements.

In the background of this debate on plant breeders' right in India, the government formulated a draft of a bill to grant PBRs in 1993/94. The draft led to enormous controversy in spite of the government's attempts to take into account the various demands of the actors while framing the bill. The bill provided for plant breeders' rights through provisions based on UPOV. The first draft of the bill also contained a clause on community rights and farmers' rights. The farmers right under this draft included farmers' right to save, use, exchange propagating material of seed and benefit sharing. There was no concept of farmers' rights as ownership rights or rights to register their varieties in this draft. The bill was opposed both by NGOs and industry and with this impasse the government began the process of revising the draft. The Ministry of Agriculture prepared a second draft in 1996 and a third one in 1997. The third draft added the words 'Farmers' Rights' in the title and was labeled the Plant Variety Protection and Farmers' Rights Act. NGOs, however, criticized both of the bills for not providing adequate protection to farmers. NGOs claimed that benefit sharing was vague under the bill, there were no farmer's representatives in the Authority, and there was no system for registering farmers' varieties. The process of accommodating the interests of various actors began with another draft introduced in Parliament in 1999 (Protection of Plant Varieties and Farmers' Rights Bill) and sent to a Joint Committee of Parliament (JPC). The Joint Committee traveled across the country gathering the views of NGOs, industry, scientists and farmers lobbies on the bill. Incorporating the demands of various actors, the Joint Committee redrafted the bill in 2000 and the new version was introduced in Parliament. The Joint Parliamentary Committee's main revision was the inclusion of a separate chapter on Farmers' Rights. In 2001, the bill was passed and made into a law. The final version of the bill was largely accepted by the major stakeholders. Industry understood that the concept of farmers' rights as seen as an alternative IPR system actually reinforces their position on IPRs and enables them to gain plant breeders' rights in India. NGOs accepted the bill as it provided for a mechanism for granting protection for farmers' varieties on par with breeders' varieties.

India is among the first countries in the world to have passed legislation granting Farmers' Rights in the form of the Protection of Plant Varieties and Farmers' Rights Act, 2001. India's experience is important due to its international contribution to negotiations on Farmers' Rights, its position as a centre of biodiversity, and the complexities of agriculture in India within which the country is attempting to implement these rights. India's law is unique not only because of its far-reaching rights for farmers, but also in that it simultaneously aims to protect both breeders and farmers. This attempt to evolve a multiple rights system could, however, pose several obstacles to the utilization and exchange of plant genetic resources among farmers. India has framed a unique legislation, but still faces the task of implementation. This should serve as a signal internationally that establishing legislation is insufficient to effectively promote Farmers' Rights. Failing to implement Farmers' Rights in India would be a heavy loss for all the farmers who need Farmers' Rights to protect their livelihoods, secure their access to resources, protect their rights to seeds, and, above all, lift them out of poverty (Sahai, 1996).

The Act grants plant variety protection on new varieties (largely modeled on UPOV), extant varieties and essentially derived varieties. Extant varieties include farmers' varieties, varieties in the public domain and varieties about which there is common knowledge. Nine rights can be said to have been given to farmers under the Act including: Rights to Seed, Right to Register Varieties, Right to Reward and Recognition, Right to Benefit Sharing, Right to Information and Compensation for Crop Failure, Right to Compensation for Undisclosed use of Traditional Varieties, Right to Adequate Availability of Registered Material, Right to Free Services, Protection from legal infringement in case of lack of awareness (Sahai, 2001). One can categorize nine rights accorded to farmers under The Protection of Plant Varieties and Farmers' Rights Act, 2001 (Bala Ravi, 2004).

Rights to seed: The farmer's right to save and exchange seed has been one of the major demands of the farmers' right movement. India's Act aims to give farmers the right to save, use, exchange or sell seed in the same manner he/she was entitled to before the Act. However, the right to sell seed is restricted in that the farmer cannot sell seed in a packaged form labelled with the registered name [Section 39 (iv)] (Singh *et al.*, 2011).

Right to register varieties: Farmers like commercial breeders can apply for IPR over their varieties. The criterion for registration of varieties is also similar to breeders (distinctness, uniformity, stability) but novelty is not a requirement. The ability to gain IPR type rights over farmers' varieties is a unique aspect of India's law. Farmers' variety is defined as 'a variety which has been traditionally cultivated and evolved by farmers in their fields; or is a wild relative or landrace of a variety about which the farmers possess common knowledge'. The plant breeder's right granted on farmers' varieties provides the exclusive right to produce and market the seed of registered varieties (Bala Ravi, 2004; Singh *et al.*, 2011).

Right to reward and recognition: The Act provides for establishing a National Gene Fund. Through the National Gene Fund, farmers that have played a role in conservation of varietal development of plants can be recognized and rewarded. The fee collected from breeders who are required to pay for benefit sharing is to be deposited in the National Gene Fund. The money collected under the National Gene Fund can be used for support and reward farmers engaged in conservation. The Act provides this general provision to promote conservation but does not provide further specifications regarding the method. The Authority set up under the Act is left with the task of operationalizing this right.

Right to benefit sharing: The Act proposes the setting up of a centralized National Gene Fund through which benefit sharing would be facilitated. The Authority is required to publish the registered varieties and invite claims for benefit sharing. The Act states that any person or group of persons or firm or governmental or nongovernmental organization can submit its claim of benefit sharing. The rewards from the gene fund can only be given to a farmer/ community who can prove that they have contributed to the selection and preservation of materials used in the registered variety (Mauria, 2004).

Right to information and compensation for crop failure: Section 39 (2) of the Act provides that the breeder must give information about expected performance of the registered variety. If the material fails to perform, the farmers may claim for compensation under the Act. This provision attempts to ensure that seed companies do not make exaggerated claims about the performance (yield, pest resistance) to the farmer. It enables farmers to apply to the Authority for compensation in case they suffer losses due to the failure of the variety to meet the targets claimed by the companies (Singh *et al.*, 2011).

Right to compensation for undisclosed use of traditional varieties: In cases where it is established that the breeder has not disclosed the source of varieties belonging to a particular community, compensation can be granted through the Gene Fund. Any NGO, individual or government institution may file a claim for compensation on behalf of the local community in cases where the breeder has not disclosed traditional knowledge or resources of the community.

Right to adequate availability of registered material: The breeder is required to provide adequate supply of seeds or material of the variety to the public at a reasonable price. If after three years of registration of the variety, the breeder fails to do so, any person can apply to the Authority for a compulsory licence. Compulsory licenses revoke the exclusive right given to the breeder and enable third parties to produce, distribute or sell the registered variety.

Right to free services: The Act exempts farmers from paying fees for registration of a variety, for conducting tests on varieties, for renewal of registration, for opposition and for fees on all legal proceedings under the Act (Bala Ravi, 2004).

Protection from legal infringement in case of lack of awareness: Considering low literacy levels in the country, the Act provides safeguards against innocent infringement by farmers. Farmers who unknowingly violate the rights of a breeder shall not be punished if he/she can prove that they were not aware of the existence of breeder's rights (Anonymous, 2001).

Morphological Markers for DUS Characterization

According Kooistra (1964) the morphological characters of plant *viz.*, shape of leaflets, leaf serration, and number of tendrils, shape of flower, pod size and pod shape could be used for distinguishing pea varieties. Elsaeed (1967) reported characterized two broad bean varieties *viz.*, Beladi and Rebaya-34 based on seed weight which was 192.7g and 317.1g, respectively per 500 seeds. Edgar *et al.* (1970) studied the morphological characters for growth habit, nature of stem hairiness, flower colour and pubescence colour of soybean. Tiwari *et al.* (1978) grouped 21 soybean varieties based on 100 seed weight into three groups *viz.*, small, medium and bold. Villalobos and Fournier (1978) studied 13 important characters *viz.*, colour of the seed coat, hilum and 100 seed weight *etc.*, for identification of soybean. Payne and Koszykowski (1979) grouped 18 soybean cultivars based on seed size for cultivar differentiation. Srikantaradya (1980) classified 60 varieties of soybean based on the seed coat colour. Among them, 13 varieties were found black, three varieties were brown to brick red and rests of the 44 varieties were cream to dull white. Stahi and Pandey (1981) evaluated 21 soybean varieties and grouped them on the basis of nature of maturity and number of days to 50 per cent flowering. Wagner and McDonald (1982) characterized 36 soybean cultivars based on hilum colour of the seed. Koszykowski and Burgoon (1983) grouped 64 soybean cultivars on the basis of hilum colour of the seed.

Paramesh (1983) classified 24 soybean genotypes based on the number of seeds per pod, 100 seed weight and seed size. They were separated into small, medium and large seeded groups based on the test weight. Agrawal (1984) classified soybean varieties based on spreading type, pubescence presence on stem, leaf shape and size, flower colour, pod colour at maturity, days to 50 per cent flowering and maturity. Bahrenfus and Fehr (1984) observed differences in two soybean cultivars *viz.*, Cumberland and Harper. Harper has purple flower, tawny pubescence, brown pods at maturity and higher seed yield compared to Cumberland. But both cultivars were similar in days to maturity and plant height. From the French bean varietal trial, ten cultivars were grouped based on morphological characters *viz.*, plant height, number of branches and leaves per plant, seeds per pod, 100 seed weight and pod length (Anonymous, 1985). Tunwar and Singh (1985) recorded salient features of 31 improved soybean varieties based on seed and plant morphological characteristics. Diazcarrasco *et al.* (1986) grouped 17 soybean varieties based on days to maturity, plant height and seed yield per plant. Lirindae (1986) and Terao (1986) classified the rice genotypes based on seedling characters *viz.*, seedling length, coleoptile and sheath colour and mesocotyl colour. Rasaily *et al.* (1986) tabulated 20 soybean genotype characters based on plant height, number of branches, pods per plant and seed yield per plant. Modesta and Cabral (1987) evaluated

11 soybean lines based on the seed coat colour, hilum colour, seed shape and 100 seed weight.

Chakrabarthy and Agrawal (1989) suggested that morphological characters such as stem pigmentation hairiness, leaflet shape and cotyledonary leaf shape could be used for classifying black gram varieties. Reddy *et al.* (1989) recorded variation in five soybean cultivar for days to maturity, period from flower initiation to maturity, plant height, seeds per plant and yield per plant. Smith and Smith (1989) reported that morphological traits were the earliest markers used in germplasm collection, management and utilization in breeding. Agrawal and Pawar (1990) given seed keys for the identification of 13 soybean cultivars on the basis of seed size, colour and hilum colour. Boerma *et al.* (1990) reported soybean cultivar of Colquitt based on morphological characters of determinate growth habit, purple flower, tawny pubescence on pod walls and matured 3 days later than Gorden and one day earlier than Thomas cultivar. From 150 soybean germplasm accessions were characterized based on useful characters *viz.*, plant height, days to flower, days to maturity, pods per plant, seeds per pod, number of branches per plant and seed yield per plant (Anonymous, 1990).

Sun and Chang (1990) analysed for the characteristics of green soybean in China based on 100 seed weight, seed shape and size. Jarman and Hampson (1991) reported that potential problems regarding the measurement of morphological characters can be partially overcome if repeated measurements are made in multiple environments. Although such type of comparative description requires substantial resource investment, it has been useful for the varietal characterization of several high value crop species. For example, candidate cereal varieties in United Kingdom are evaluated on DUS in the F_8 generation over location and years. Vahab *et al.* (1991) worked on evaluation of selected varieties of vegetable cowpea with the objective of identifying high yielding good quality vegetable types suitable for both rainy and summer seasons. Seven selected varieties of cowpea *viz.*, IIHR 61-B (Bangalore) Sel-263 (Ludhiana), Kanakamani (Kerala), Pusakomal (IARI), VS-389 (Kerala), Sel-2-1 (Faizabad), VS-87 (Kerala) were taken for the study. Varieties differed significantly for plant height and spread in all the three seasons as well as the mean values pooled over the seasons. VS-389 was the tallest in all the seasons, with the mean value of 60 cm and Sel-263 the shortest with a mean value of 44 cm. The maximum spreading varieties were IIHR 61-B in rainy and Sel-2-1 in summer season. Sel-263 had the minimum spread in both the seasons. In all the three seasons, IIHR 61-B had maximum pod weight. Sel-2-1 had the longest pods and more seeds per pod.

Venkatareddy (1991) reported that 100 seed weight differed significantly among the soybean genotypes. Bragg recorded the highest 100 seed weight (20.35 g) followed by Hardee (19.53g) and PK471 (19.75 g) while the least (18.89

g) was recorded by Monetta. Smith and Smith (1992) opined that morphological characterization is a first step in description and classification of crop germplasm. Fourty four chickpea cultivars collected from the different sites of Uttar Pradesh were grouped based on their variation in seed size (small, medium to large), seed shape (round and wrinkled), seed colour (light to dark brown, yellow, pink and white), seeds per pod, foliage colour, plant height and branches per plant (Anonymous, 1992a). Twenty two pea cultivars were grouped based on their variation in seed size (Small, medium and large) seed colour (white, pale green, mottled green and grey) and seed shape (round and flattened) (Anonymous, 1992b). Kumar *et al.* (1993) studied varietal identification of six pearl millet varieties through morphological characters and presented list of key characters on the basis of seed shape, leaf characters and head shape at field level. Bonetti *et al.* (1995) reported that 17 bean cultivars were grouped based on leaf colour (very light green, light green, medium green, dark green, very dark green), pod length (very short, short, medium, long, very long), maturity (early, medium, late) and time of flowering (early, medium and late). Excellent work was done for the 18 soybean genotypes and classified based on morphological diagnostic characteristics such as pigmentation colour, presence of pubescence on seedling, growth habit, plant height, stem pattern, leaf surface, foliage, pigmentation on stem, stem hairiness, colour of the hair, days to flowering, flower co1our, pod shape, pod hairiness, pod colour at maturity, pod hair colour at maturity and days to maturity (Anonymous, 1995). Mudzana *et al.* (1995) reported that the morphological characters such as plant height, foliage colour, number of days to 50 per cent flowering, flower length, pod length, pod breadth and number of seeds could be used for variety discrimination of faba beans. Nagapadma *et al.* (1996) characterized 23 maize inbred lines based on seed colour and 100 seed weight. Qualitative and quantitative inherited morphological traits have been used successfully to describe a large number of varieties in various crop species. Phenotypic character expression is however, influenced by inter and intra locus interactions, as well as genotype and environment interactions. Thus, the use of phenotypic traits for the estimation of genetic distance can be problematic since phenotype may not always be a simple expression of genotype. The potential for unexplained epistatic and environmental interactions with phenotype can present problems not only during PVP or patenting application, but also in case of alleged infringement of property rights (Staub *et al.*, 1996).

Copeland and McDonald (1997) identified soybean cultivars of chippewa-64 can easily distinguished from other varieties that do not have black hilum. Sophisticated techniques must be used for distinguishing the varieties with black hilum. Prakash and Singal (1997) reported that seven grain and six vegetable pea cultivars were grouped based on plant height, leaf length, time of flowering, pod length and leaf colour. Sridhara *et al.* (1997) grouped

10 soybean genotypes based on their seed coat colour and 100 seed weight. Surendra and Singhal (1997) reported that seven grain and six vegetable pea cultivars were grouped based on plant height (short, medium, tall, very tall), leaf length (short, medium, long), time of flowering (early, medium) pod length (short, medium, long) and leaf colour (yellow green, blue green, green). Rabbani *et al.* (1999) characterized 52 accessions of Indian mustard for different morphological traits. Sankarapandian (2002) grouped four cowpea varieties based on pod shape, seed colour and leaf shape. Suryawanshi *et al.* (2002) conducted an experiment and characterized seven soybean cultivars based on morphological characteristics and reported that the pigmentation on seedling, foliage colour, pubescence on leaf and stem. Flower colour, pod hairiness and pod colour at maturity were observed to be the most stable diagnostic characters and these are much helpful for identifying the genotypes at flowering and maturity stage.

Yadav and Shrivasthava (2002) characterized chickpea varieties based on seed colour (brown, light brown, dark brown, reddish brown, light green), seed size (bold, medium, small), stem pigmentation (strong, medium and absent), flower colour (white, deep pink, pink, light pink), foliage colour (dark green, light green), plant height (tall, medium, dwarf), podding habit (single, double), pod number per plant (low, medium, high), number of locules per pod (one, two, three) and duration (early, medium and late). Among all characters at seed level, seed shape, hilum shape, seed coat colour and lusture on seed are most stable, uniform and distinguishing characters in green gram (Jain and Khare, 2002a). Jain and Khare (2002b) characterized 15 green gram varieties based on morphological characteristics and reported that variation in pigmentation on hypocotyls, stem, petiole, leaf, leaf midrib and ventral suture of pod and immature and mature pod colour were most stable and uniform distinguishing characters. Density of hairiness on stem, raceme position, growth habit, pod constriction and pod curvature can be used to identify the mung bean varieties effectively. Days to flowering, days to maturity and plant height were the uniform characters but their expression is varied under different environments. Jones *et al.* (2003) have evaluated the morphological grouping characteristics currently used for DUS testing of wheat for varietal discrimination purpose. Kumar *et al.* (2004) reported that 45 cultivars of pearl millet including 14 hybrids and their parental lines were characterized using qualitative morphological characters of seed (seed colour as green, gray, gray brown and brown), seedling characters and plant morphological characters.

Tarasatyavathi *et al.* (2004) reported that 75 released soybean varieties were characterized based on leaf shape (lanceolate, pointed ovate, rounded ovate, triangular), leaf colour intensity (light, medium, dark), flower colour (white, violet), pod pubescence (absent, present), plant height (short, medium, tall), days to flowering (early, medium and late) and days to maturity (early, medium, late). Duran *et al.* (2005) characterized the common bean landraces and cultivars from the Caribbean using morphological descriptors like leaf width, leaf length, leaf shape (as cordate, ovate, rhombohedric, or hastate), growth habit, length of the fifth internode, bracteole shape, bracteole size, outer base of the standard of the corolla classified as striped or smooth and pod beak position. Nkouannessi (2005) evaluated and grouped 20 cowpea genotypes from different countries *viz.*, Cameroon, South Africa and Kenya based on seed and plant morphological characteristics such as seed shape, seed testa texture, hundred seed weight, growth pattern, plant pigmentation, plant hairiness, raceme position, pod attachment to peduncle, immature pod pigmentation, leaf colour, flower colour, number of main branches, number of pods per peduncle, number of pods per plant, pod length, number of seeds per pod and plant height were employed for characterization.

Gosavi *et al.* (2007) reported that 25 varieties of lentil obtained from IIPR, Kanpur were characterized during consecutive three winter (rabi) season (2003-2004, 2004-2005 and 2005-2006) and concluded that Seed coat colour and testa mottling were most stable, uniform and distinguishable traits to distinguish the lentil varieties at seed level; anthocyanin pigmentation on epicotyls at seedling stage; whereas foliage colour, leaflet tendril type, size of leaflet, leaf pubescence, colour of flower, length of calyx teeth, pod pigmentation and pod size at plant level. These traits can be considered for grouping of varieties to perform DUS testing. Expression for seed size, branching pattern, plant height, days to flowering and days to maturity were uniform but their expression may alter with the fluctuations of environment hence should be used only as an indicator to test the genetic purity. No variation was observed for cotyledon colour, pod pubescence and shape of pod surface among the varieties under active seed multiplication chain. These traits may be considered for verification of lentil varieties in future.

Joshi *et al.* (2007) characterized 19 rice varieties taking into account 52 traits from National DUS testing guidelines. Stem length, 1000 grain weight, grain length and width were found to be stable in both the seasons. High difference between PCV and GCV values for panicle number per plant shows high environmental effect. Following the eight grouping characters of National DUS testing guidelines the varieties were grouped. Reddy *et al.* (2007) carried out varietal characterization of cotton hybrids and their respective parents based on quantitative or measurable descriptors like days to 50 per cent flowering, growth habit and plant height. Sarutayophat *et al.* (2007) characterized 13 cowpea accession based growth habit, days to 50 per cent flowering, pod colour, pod length, number of pods per plant, seed yield per plant. Ashok *et al.* (2008) characterized seven french bean varieties based on seed, seedling and plant characters *viz.*, seed coat colour, hilum colour and seed shape, hypocotyl colour, seedling cotyledon colour and pubescence on hypocotyls, flower colour and constriction on pod. Joshi (2008) characterized 26 forage sorghum varieties according to DUS guidelines issued by PPV & FR authority. Smykal *et al.* (2008) characterized twenty one varieties of field pea and four varieties of fodder pea from the list of recommended varieties for cultivation in Czech Republic and made a standard classification by 12 qualitative morphological descriptors.

Cupic *et al.* (2009) analysed European pea (*Pisum sativum* L.) germplasm, to determine differences between *P. sativum* var. *arvense* and *P. sativum* ssp. *sativum* groups, and to estimate genetic variability among and within 18 *P. sativum* accessions. Sixteen morphological traits (shape of seed, colour of hilum, shape of grain starch, unwrinkled seed and simple starch grain, colour of testa, colour of cotyledons, plant height, colour of foliage, anthocyanin, type of node, stipule length, colour of flower, maximum number of flowers per node, days to flowering, pod-shape of distal part, parchment of pod) were used to estimate genetic distances. Joshi *et al.* (2009) studied in twenty six varieties of forage sorghum using 40 morphological descriptors for DUS descriptors. Distinctive unique morphological profiles could be obtained for 11 varieties. However, the rest of 15 varieties remained in groups of two or three varieties. Naima *et al.* (2009) studied 20 landraces of cowpea and characterized based on seed morphological characters such as seed colour, eye colour, shape, texture, weight of hundred seeds and plant morphological characters such as flower colour, seed number per pod, pod purple pigmentation, pod length, number of seeds per pod and days to 50 per cent flowering. An experiment was conducted at VPKAS experimental farm, Hawalbagh, Uttarakhand using genetically pure seeds of 89 soybean varieties released in India to establish distinctness among varieties as per the national test guidelines for the conduct of test for distinctness, uniformity and stability on soybean by Gupta *et al.* (2010) and they reported that, of the 89 soybean varieties studied, 60 varieties were found to be distinct on the basis of 12 essential characters and they classified remaining 29 varieties into 10 groups. These groups were distinct from each other but the varieties within group exhibited similar characters. Further they concluded that characters, *viz.*, flower colour, presence and absence of pod hair, colour of hair, and colour of testa were found reliable and reproducible across the zones.

Patra *et al.* (2010) assessed 60 morphological DUS descriptors of 18 basmati rice varieties. Among the 46 visual characters 26 were monomorphic, 11 were dimorphic and 7 were polymorphic indicating their potential for varietal characterization and distinctiveness. COYD analysis was made on 14 measurable DUS descriptors which revealed distinctiveness for all varieties. COYU analysis for five of the measurable characterization revealed than 15 out of 18 were almost uniform. On the basis of grouping characteristics unique morphological profiles could be established for seven varieties. Joshi *et al.* (2011) studied twenty indigenous aromatic rice varieties using morphological DUS descriptors. Out of 60 morphological characters 46 were visually assessed and 14 measurable. 24 monomorphic, 17 dimorphic and 5 polymorphic characters indicating their potential for varietal characterization and distinctiveness. COYD analysis was made on 14 measurable DUS descriptors which revealed distinctiveness for all except Tilakchandan varieties 3047 and 3048 with respect to each other only. COYD analysis was performed with MJRA analysis revealed that 9 varieties were completely uniform. On the basis of grouping characteristics seven varieties showed unique profile.

Mall (2011) carried out an experiment on DUS characterization of 11 French bean varieties based on morphological markers. Out of 22 morphological characters 19 were visually assessed among them 13 were dimorphic and six were polymorphic and three measurable all were polymorphic indicating their potential for varietal characterization and distinctiveness. Combined over years distinctiveness (COY-D) analysis was made on three measurable DUS descriptors which revealed distinctiveness for all characters. Combined over years uniformity (COY-U) analysis also carried out to find uniformity it revealed that all the varieties were more or less uniform for measurable characters. Modified joint regression analysis (MJRA) also used to supplement COY-D and COY-U. Sood *et al.* (2011) characterized 25 bell pepper genotypes according the national test guidelines for the conduct of test for distinctness, uniformity and stability on soybean. Thirty two jute (*Corchorus olitorius* and *C. capsularis*) varieties, including 25 released/notified and seven of common knowledge, were characterized through distinctness, uniformity and stability (DUS) testing trials for two consecutive years using 17 heritable morphological traits prescribed in the Revised Official DUS Test Guidelines of Jute to enable identification of these varieties and for unambiguous ascertainment of distinctness. Out of 17 traits, 8 were found to be monomorphic, 7 dimorphic and only 2 polymorphic in *C. capsularis,* while 8 traits were dimorphic and 9 polymorphic among *C. olitorius* varieties, indicating their potential for varietal characterization. On the basis of this study no single character could identify all the varieties individually; however, when used in combination, identity and distinctness of almost all the *C. olitorius* varieties and 10 varieties of *C. capsularis* (Padma, JRC-212, Bidhan Pat-2, D-154, KTC-1, KC-1, JRC-80, Bidhan Pat-3, JRC-7447 and JRC-698) could be established individually. The remaining varieties of *C. capsularis* could be classified into two groups: early flowering group (JRC-321, UPC-94) and fine fibre group (JRC-4444, Bidhan Pat-1) (Begum and Kumar, 2011).

Chakrabarty *et al.* (2012) made an attempt to validate the distinctiveness of rice (*Oryza sativa* L.) varieties by taking 106 example varieties. They obtained example varieties from Nodal Officer, DUS Testing, Directorate of Rice Research, Hyderabad. They reported that twenty varieties did not conform to the distinct characteristics for which these were identified as examples. The non-conformity of the example varieties for the particular state of expression of characteristics was further examined with fresh seed lots obtained in the second year from the Directorate of Rice Research, Hyderabad. Six varieties still could not be validated for the identified example characteristics. A strict maintenance breeding of the reference varieties, including the example varieties, and use of alternate example varieties for conduct of DUS testing in rice, if needed, are suggested. For the establishment of distinctiveness as per DUS guidelines among Indian soybean [*Glycine max* (L.) Merrill] varieties, Ramteke and Murlidharan (2012) used 20 characters *viz*., flower colour, hypocotyl anthocyanin pigmentation, seed colour, absence or presence of pod pubescence, pod pubescence colour, plant growth type, pod colour, days to maturity, seed cotyledon colour, days to 50 per cent flowering, seed size, seed shape, leaf colour, plant height (cm), seed hilum colour, seed lusture, plant growth habit, pod shattering, leaf shape and peroxidase activity. They concluded that out of 92 soybean varieties, 42 varieties were found to be distinctive on the basis of 11 essential characters. Remaining 50 varieties can be classified into 19 groups. However, 13 of these groups were distinct from each other on the basis of other remaining nine characters. But one group (four varieties, *viz*. MAUS 1, PK 308, PUSA 20, and PUSA 37) belonging white flowered and five groups (10 varieties, viz. RKS 18 and RAUS 5, MAUS 47 and Monetta, ADT 1 and Co 1, MACS 57 and PUSA 16, Gujarat Soybean 1 and Punjab 1) belonging purple flowered could not be differentiated being similar characters.

Liu *et al*. (2012) evaluated 50 lettuce (*Lactuca sativa*) varieties and used 40 morphological traits for DUS testing. Cluster analysis was done using UPGMA based on morphological traits which divided the varieties into three groups. Yadav *et al*. (2013) characterized 78 Indian mustard genotypes by using morphological descriptors as per DUS guidelines for mustard crop notified by the Protection of Plant Varieties and Farmers' Rights (PPV & FR) Authority. Kumar *et al*. (2014) carried out an experiment in 29 diverse French bean genotypes especially vegetable types, collected from different agro-climatic zones of India and they used 12 agronomic traits for the characterization of genotypes namely, days to first picking, number of pods per plant, per cent pod set per cluster, pod length (cm), pod width (cm), pod thickness (cm), seeds per pod, seed length (cm), seed width (cm), seed thickness (cm), 100 seeds weight (g) and pod yield per plant (g).

Conclusion

It may be concluded that studies may be done with different genotypes to find out those having greater stability for majority of characters. Such genotypes maybe used in breeding programme to evolve stable varieties in French bean and also the morphological DUS descriptors can be effectively used for identification and grouping of the French bean varieties.

REFERENCES

Adams, M. W. (1985): Common Bean (*Phaseolus vulgaris* L.). *In*: Summerfield RJ, Roberts EH, eds. *Gr. Leg. Cr.*, London, K : Collins, 433-476.

Agarwal, V.D. and Singh, T.P. (1973): Genetic variability and interaction in agronomic traits in Kidney bean (*Phaseolus vulgaris* L.), *Indian Journal of Agricultural Sciences* (43): 845-848.

Agrawal, R. L. (1984): Identification of Crop Varieties, *Oxford and IBH Publishing Co.*, New Delhi, pp: 228.

Agrawal, R.L. and Pawar, A. (1990): Identification of Soybean Varieties Based on Seed and Seedling Characteristics, *Seed Res.*, 18 (1): 77-81.

Agsakall, A. and Olgun, M. (2001): Use of Weighted Scaling Method in Dry Beans Breeding Programmes, *Anadolu*. 11 (2): 33- 42.

Ahmad, M.A. Munir, I. Ali, W. Swati, Z.A. Khattaki, M.S. Sohail, Q. and Khan, I. (2013): Assessment of Genetic Diversity of Local and Exotic Brassica Napus Germplasm, *Pak. J. Biol. Sci.* 10 (15): 2490-2494.

Ahmed, S. and Kamaluddin, (2013): Correlation and Path Analysis for Agro-morphological Traits in Rajmash Beans under Baramulla- Kashmir Region, *African Journal of Agricultural Research*, 8 (18): 2027-2032.

Akhtar, L. H., Kashif, M., Ali, M. and Aziz, T. (2010): Stability Analysis for Grain Yield in Mung Bean (*Vigna radiata* L. wilczek) Grown in Different Agro-climatic Regions, *Emir. J. Food Agric.*, 22 (6): 490-497.

Ali, N. Javidfar, F. Elmira, J. Y. and Mirza, M. Y. (2013): Relationship Among Yield Components and Selection Criteria for Yield Improvement in Winter Rapeseed (*Brassica napus* L.), *Pak. J. Bot.*, 35: 167-174.

Allard R.W. (1960): Principles of Plant Breeding, *John Wiley and Sons Inc.*, New York, p:185.

Allard, R.W. and Bradshaw, A.D. (1964): Implication of Genotype Environmental Interactions in Applied Plant Breeding, *Crop Sci.*, 4: 503-598.

Angadi, P., Patil, M.G. and Angadi, A. (2012): Correlation Studies in French bean (*Phaseolus vulgaris* L.), *The Asian Journal of Horticulture*, 7 (1): 55-59.

Anju, D., Sharma, S.K., Singh, K.P. and Luthra, O.P. (2006): Path Analysis of Seed Yield Components in French Bean (*Phaseolus vulgaris* L.), *CCS. Research on Crops*, 7 (1): 255-257.

Anonymous, (1985): NBPGR, *Ann. Rep.*, New Delhi, pp: 133.

Anonymous, (1990): NBPGR, *Ann. Rep.*, New Dehi, pp: 197.

Anonymous, (1992a): NBPGR, *Ann. Rep.*, New Delhi, pp: 197.

Anonymous, 1992b. NBPGR, *Ann. Rep.*, New Delhi, p:125.

Anonymous, (1995): ICAR, *National Seed Projects (Crops)*, New Delhi, pp: 26.

Anonymous, (2008): ICAER, *News letter. Tech. Bull.*, 10, pp: 13.

Anonymous. (2001): Manual of Patent Examining Procedures, 8th Edn., pp: 21-50.

Anonymous. (2007): General Guidelines to the Examination of DUS and the Development of Harmonized Descriptors of Plant Varieties, *Plant Variety Journal India*, 1 (1): 192-201.

Arumugam, M., Rajanna, M.P. and Vidyachandra, B. (2007): Stability of Rice Genotypes for Yield and Yield Components Over Extended Dates of Sowing under Cauvery Command Area in Karnataka, *Oryza*, 44 (2): 104-107.

Arya, P. S., Ram, A. and Rana, A. (1999): Study of Direct and Indirect Influence of Some Yield Traits on Green Pod Yield in French Bean (Phaseolus vulgaris L.), *Adv. In Horti. and Forest*, 6: 99 – 106.

Asati, B. S. and Singh, A. K. (2008): Genetic Components Studies in French Bean (*Phaseolus vulgaris* L.), *New Agriculturist,* 19 (1/2):117-123.

Ashok S.S., Prashanth, N. D. and Hosmani, R. M. (2008): RAPD Markers and Morphological Characteristics for Identification of French Bean (*Phaseoous vulgaris* L.) Cultivars, *Seed Res.,* 36 (1): 81-83.

Bahrenfus, J.F. and Fehr, W.R. (1984): Registration of 'Harper' and 'Lakota' Soybean, *Crop Sci.,* 21: 385.

Bala Ravi. (2004): DUS Test in Rice. In: Proceedings of Training Programmes in Rice, DRR, Hyderabad, pp. 119.

Barendrecht, C.J. (1999): The Concept of Grouping in UPOV Guidelines Focused on Ornamental, *Plant Var. & Seeds,* 5: 175-182.

Begum, T. and Kumar, D. (2011): Usefulness of Morphological Characteristics for DUS Testing of Jute (*Corchorus olitorius* L. and *C. capsularis* L.), *Spanish Journal of Agricultural Research,* 9 (2): 473-483.

Berrocal, I.S., Cereceres, O.J. and Pena, V.C.B. (2002): Yield Components, Harvest Index and Leaf Area Efficiency of a Sample of a Wild Population and a Domesticated Variant of the Common Bean (*Phaseolus vulgaris* L.), *South African Journal of Botany,* 68: 205-211.

Bhushan, K.B., Singh, B.P., Dubey, R.K. and Ram, H.H. (2007): Correlation Analysis for Seed Yield in French Bean (*Phaseolus vulgaris* L.), *Pantnagar Journal of Research,* 5 (1): 104-106.

Boerma, H. R., Hussey, R.S., Phillips, D.V. and Wood, E.D. (1990): Registration of 'Colquitt' Soybean, *Crop Seed.,* 30 (3): 748.

Bonetti, A., Miggiano, A., Dinelli, G. and Lovato, A. (1995): Identification of bean (*Phaseolus vulgaris* L.) Cultivars Grown in Italy by Field and Electrophoresis Tests: A Comparative Study, *Seed Sci. Tech.,* 23: 69 – 84.

Brahmi, P. Saxena, S. and Dhillon, B.S. (2004): The Protection of Plant Varieties Rights Act of India, *Curr. Sci.,* 86: 392-398.

Breese, E.L. (1969): The Measurement and Significance of Genotype Environment Interaction in Grasses, *Heredity,* 24: 27-44.

Burton, G.N. and Devane, E.M. (1953): Estimating Heritability in Tall Fescue (*Fesluca arundinacea* L.) from Replicated Clonal Material, *Agronomy Journal,* 45: 478-481.

Camlin, M. S.; Watson, S.; Waters, B. G. and Weatherup, S. T. C. (2001): The Potential for Management of Reference Collections in Herbage Variety, *Pl. Var. Seeds,* 14(1): 1-14.

Chakrabarthy, S. K. and Agrawal, R. L. (1989): Identification of Blackgram Varieties-I Utilization of Seed Characteristics, *Seed Res.,* 17 (1): 23-28.

Chakrabarty, S.K., Joshi, M.A., Singh, Y. and Dadlani, M. (2012): Example Varieties for DUS Testing in Rice (*Oryza sativa*), *Indian Journal of Agricultural Sciences,* 82 (12): 1011-1015.

Chand, P. and Chand, P. (1998): Character Association and Path Analysis in Rajmah, *Madras Agric. J.,* 85: 188-190.

Chawla, H.S. (2005): Patenting of Biological Material and Biotechnology, *J. Intellec. Prop. Rights,* 10: 44-51.

Chawla, H.S. (2007): Managing IPRs for Better Transfer and Commercialization of Agricultural Technologies, *J. Inellec. Prop. Rights,* 12: 330-340.

Chawla, H.S. and Singh, A.K. (2005): Intellectual Property Rights. Vol. II: Copyrights, Trade Marks, Trade Secrets and Geographical Indications, *Pantnagar University Press,* pp: 75.

Commacho, L.H., Durate, N.A. and Orozeo, S.H. (1963): Relationship Between Growth Habit and Yield Components in French bean, *Revista Instituto Colombiano Agropecuaro.,* 1: 718-722.

Comstock, R.E. and Moll, R.R. (1963): Genotype-environmental Interactions, Symposium on Statistical Genetics and Plant Breeding, *NAS-NRC Publication*, 982: 164-196.

Cook, S.A. and Johnson, M.P. (1968): Adaptation to Heterogeneous Environments, Variation in Heterophylly in *Ranunculus flammula* L. *Evolution*, 22: 495-516.

Copeland, L. O. and McDonald, M. B. (1997): Principles of Seed Science and Technology, III Edition, *Pub., New York*, pp: 393.

Cupic, T., Tucak , M., Popovic, S., Bolaric, S., Grijusic, S. and Kozumplik, V. (2009): Genetic Diversity of Pea (*Pisum sativum* L.) Genotypes Assessed by Pedigree, Morphological and Molecular Data, *J. Food Agric. Environ.*, 7 (3&4): 343-348.

Desmae, H. (2007): Genetic Diversity and Variability in Grain Quality of Sorghum (*Sorghum bicolor* (L.) Moench) landraces from Northeastern Ethiopia, PhD Thesis, *School of Land, Crop and Food Sciences, University of Queensland*, pp. 239.

Dewan, R. K. (2011): IPR Protection in Agriculture: An Overview. *Journal of Intellectual Property Rights*. 16: 131-138.

Dhar, B. (2002): Sui Generis Systems for Plant Variety Protection: Options under TRIPS, A Discussion Paper, *Quaker House*, United Nations Office, Geneva, Switzerland, pp: 62.

Dhillon, B.S., Brahmi, P. and Saxena, S. (2006): Crop Improvement Programmes in India, *Emerg. Scenar.*, 90: 780-783.

Diazcarrasco, H., Abreuferrer, S., Velazquez. O. and Garcia, O. (1986): Similarities between Some Agronomic Characters in Soybean, *Ciencias de la Agricultura*, 27: 108-113.

Digby, P. G. N. (1979): Modified Joint Regression Analysis for Incomplete Variety ÷ Environment Data, *J. Agric. Sci.*, 93: 81–86.

Dimova, D., Svetleva, D. and Lozanov, I. (1991): Correlation and Path Coefficient Analysis of Some Quantitative Characters in French Bean, *Genetika I Selektsiya*, 24 (4): 221-225.

Dobhal, V.K. and Gautam, N.K. (1994): Phenotypic Stability in Adzuki Bean (*Vigna angularis*), *Indian Journal of Agricultural Sciences*, 64 (3): 179-181.

Dolli, M. (2012): Intellectual Property Rights: Regulations and Trends in India, *Int. J. Eco. Res.*, 3(2): 16-27.

Dubey, A.K., Singh, N.P. and Srivastava, J.P.(2009): Character Association and Coefficient Analysis in French Bean (*Phaseolus vulgaris* L.), *Veg. Sci.*, 36 (3 Suppl.): 378-379.

Duke, J. A. (1981): Handbook of Legumes of World Economic Importance, *Plenum Press*, UK: 195-200.

Duran, L. A., Blair, M.W., Giraldo, M.C., Macchiavelli, R., Prophete, E., Nin, J.C. and. Beaver, J.S. (2005): Morphological and Molecular Characterization of Common Bean Landraces and Cultivars from the Caribbean, *Crop Sci.*, 45: 1320–1328.

Dutfield, G. (2001): Intellectual Property Right, Trade and Biodiversity: The Case of Seed and Plant Varieties, In: Background Study Material, Vol. I. For Training on IPR and WTO to NARS Scientists, ICAR, New Delhi.

Eberhart, S.A. and Russell, W. L. (1966): Stability Parameters for Comparing Varieties, *Crop Sci.*, 6: 36-40.

Edgar, E., Hartwig, Calton, J. and Edwards, J. R. (1970): Effects of Morphological Characteristics Upon Seed Yield in Soybean, *Agron. J.*, 62: 64-65.

Elangovan, M., Prabhakar and Reddy, D.C.S. (2007): Characterization and Evaluation of Sorghum [*Sorghum bicolor* (L.) Moench] Germplasm from Karnataka, India. *Karnataka J. Agric. Sci.*, 20 (4): 840-842.

Elsaeed, E. A. K. (1967): Seed Size as a Varietal Differences in Broad Beans (*Vicia faba* L.). *J. Agric. Sci., Camb.*, 68 : 69-73.

Escribano, M.R., Santalla, M. and De Ron, A.M. (1997): Genetic Diversity in Pod and Seed Quality Traits of Common Bean Populations from North Western Spain, *Euphytica*, 93: 71-81.

FAO, (2012): Food and Agriculture Organization, Bean World Statistics, pp. 236. (http://faostat.fao.org.site/339/default.aspx; Accessed on: 1st September 2014).

Finlay, K.W. and Wilkinson, G.N. (1963): The Analysis of Adaptation in a Plant Breeding Programme, *Aust. J. Agri. Res.*, 14: 742-754.

Gangopadhyay, K.K., Tehlan, S.K., Saxena, R.P., Mishra, A.K., Raiger, H.L., Yadav, S.K., Kumar, G., Arivalagan, M. and Dutta, M. (2012): Stability Analysis of Yield and Its Component Traits in Fenugreek Germplasm, *Indian Journal of Horticulture*, 69 (1): 79-85.

Gosavi, S., Singh, K. and Khare, D. (2007): Characterization of Lentil (*Lens culinaris*) Varieties for DUS Testing, *Indian Journal of Agricultural Sciences*, 77 (8): 529-532.

Gunjal, S.B. and Mote, U.N. (1993): Determination of Economic Injury Level of Stemfly, Ophiomyis Phaseoli (Tryon) on French Bean, *Plant Protection Bulletin*, Faridabad, 45 (1): 37-41.

Gupta, A., Mahajan, V., Khati, P. and Srivastva, A. K. (2010): Distinctness in Indian Soybean (*Glycine max*) Varieties Using DUS Characters, *Indian Journal of Agricultural Sciences*, 80 (12):1081-1084.

Hosamani, R.M., Patil, B.C., Ajjappalavara, P.S., Naik, B.H., Smitha, R.P., Ukkund K.C. and Mohammadali, A. (2010): Comparing Stability of Snap Bean Genotypes, *Indian Journal of Horticulture*, 67(Special Issue): 174-178.

Islam, A.K.M.A., Newaz, M.A., Jahan, M.M.A. and Islam, M.A. (2006): Stability Analysis of Seed Yield in Dry Bean (*Phaseolus vulgaris* L.) Genotypes Following Different Models, *Bangladesh J. Pl. Breed. Genet.*, 19 (1): 7-14.

Jain, K.C. (1978): Studies on Genetic Diversity and Phenotypic Stability in Chickpea (*Cecer arietinum* L.), Ph.D. Thesis, G.B. Pant University of Agriculture and Technology, Pantnagar, pp: 265.

Jain, S. and Khare, D. (2002a): Characterization of Mung Bean Varieties for Verification of Genetic Purity at Seed Level, *JNKVV Res. J.*, 36 (1&2): 35-37.

Jain, S. and Khare, D. (2002b): Characterization of Mung Bean Varieties for Verification of Genetic Purity at Plant Level, *JNKVV Res. J.*, 36 (1&2): 38-43.

Jain, S. K. and Patel, P. R. (2012): Stability Analysis for Seed Yield and their Component Traits in Breeding Lines of Guar (*Cyamopsis tetragonoloba* L.), *Legume Res.*, 35 (4): 327-331.

Jarman, R.J. and Hampson, A.G. (1991): The Use of Computer Management System for Testing Candidate Cereal Varieties for Distinctness, Uniformanity and Stability and the Award of Plant Breeder's Rights, *Plant Var. Seeds*, 4: 161-168.

Jayanthamma, B.P.N. (1984): Character Association and Stability Analysis in French Bean (*Phaseolus vulgaris* L.), M.Sc. (Agri.) Thesis, University of Agricultural Sciences, Bangalore, pp. 456.

Johanson, W.L. (1909): Elements Dev Extateten Exblichkeitslahre, Jena, Gustar Gishy, pp: 236.

Johnson, H.W., Robinson, H.F. and Comstock, R.E. (1955): Estimates of Genetic and Environmental Variability in Soybean, *Agron. J.*, 47: 314 -318.

Jondle, R.J. (1989): Overview and Status of Plant Proprietary Rights, In: Intellectual Property Rights Associated with Plants (Caldwell, B.E., Barton, J.H., Schillinger, J.A., Qualset, C.O., Duvick, N.N. and Barnes, R.F., eds.), *Amer. Soc. Agron. Madison*, pp: 1-15.

Jones, H. U. W; Jarman, R. and Austin, J. (2003): The Management of Variety Reference Collections in Distinctness, Uniformity and Stability Testing of Wheat, *Euphytica,* 32(2): 175-184.

Joshi, A. Agrawal R. C. and Chawla H. S. (2011): Assessment of Distinctiveness, Uniformity and Stability of Indigenous Aromatic Rice (*Oryza sativa*) Varieties Based on Morphological Descriptors, *Indian J. Agri. Sci.,* 81 (7): 595-601.

Joshi, B.D. and Thomas, T.A. (1987): Genetic Resources in Temperate Grain Legumes, *In*: Plant Genetic Resources in Indian Prospective, *In*: Paroda, R.S., Arora, R.K. and Chandel, K. P. S. ed Proc. Natl, *Plant Genet. Resources,* NBPGR, New Delhi, pp: 255-167.

Joshi, D. C. (2008): DUS Characterization of Forage Sorghum (*Sorghum bicolor* (L.) Moench) Cultivars by Morphological, Biochemical and Molecular Markers, Ph.D. Thesis, G.B. Pant University of Agriculture and Technology, Pantnagar, pp. 65.

Joshi, D.C. Shrotria P.K. Singh, R. and Chawla, H. S. (2009): Assessment of Distintiveness, Uniformity and Stability of Sorghum (*Sorghum bicolor* (L.) Moench) Varieties Based on Morphological Descriptors, *Indian J. Genet.,* 69 (4): 1-11.

Joshi, M. A. Sarao, N. K. Sharma, R. C. Singh, P. and Bharaj T. S. (2007): Varietal Characterization of Rice (Oryza sativa L.) based on Morphological Descriptors, *Seed Research,* 35 (2): 188-193.

Kakaei, M. Mostafaie, A. and Zebarjadi, A. (2011): Genetic Variability of Some Traits in Rapeseed (*Brassica napus* L.) Under Drought Stress and Non-stress Conditions, *Biharean Biologist,* 5 (2): 127-131.

Kalia, N.R. and Kalia, R.K. (1994): Character Association and Path Coefficient Analysis in French Bean, *Indian J. Pulse Res.,* 7: 165-167.

Kandpal, L.M. (2008): Evaluation of French Bean (*Phaseolus vulgaris* L.) germplasm, M.Sc. (Ag.) Thesis, G.B. Pant University of Agriculture and Technology, Pantnagar, pp: 63.

Kang, M.S., Miller, J.D., Tai, P.Y.P., Dean, J.L. and Glaz, B. (1987): Implications Confounding Genotypes x Year and Genotypes x Crop Effects in Sugarcane, *Crop Sci.,* 15: 349-355.

Karasu, A. and Oz, M. (2010): A Study on Coefficient Analysis and Association between Agronomical Characters in Dry Bean (*Phaseolus vulgaris* L.), *Bulgarian Journal of Agricultural Science,* 16 (2): 203-211.

Kay, D. E. (1979): Food legumes. Tropical Products Institute, London, *Crop and Product Dig.,* 3: 124-176.

Khulbe, R.K. Pant, D.P. and Saxena, N. (2000): Variability, Heritability and Genetic Advance in Indian Mustard (*Brasisca juncea* (L.) Czern and Coss), *Crop Res. Hisar.* 20 (3): 551-552.

Kochhar, S. (2004): Systems Perspective for IPR Protection in the Plant Kingdom, *Journal of Intellectual Property Rights,* 342: 342-355.

Kochhar, S. (2010): How Effective is *Sui Generis* Plant Variety Protection in India: Some Initial Feedback, *J. Intellec. Prop. Rights,* 15: 273-284.

Kooistra, E. (1964): Identificaion Research On Pulses, *Proceedings of Intl. Seed Testing Assoc.,* 29 (4): 937 – 947.

Koszykowski, W. J. and Burgoon, A. C. (1983): Soybean Cultivar Testing Update, *Newslett. AOSA,* 57 (2): 32-39.

Kumar, A. Chowdhury, R.K. and Kapoor, R. (1993): Varietal Identification in Pearlmillet Through Morphological Characters, *Seed Research,* 25(1): 53-58.

Kumar, A., Singh, P.K., Rai, N., Bhaskar, G.P. and Datta, D. (2014): Genetic Diversity of French Bean (*Phaseolus vulgaris* L.) Genotypes on the Basis of Morphological Traits and Molecular Markers, *Indian Journal of Biotechnology,* 13: 207-213.

Kumar, B.B. (2005): Evaluation of Exotic French Bean (*Phaseolus vulgaris* L.) Germplasm and Estimation of Character Association under *Tarai* Region of Uttaranchal, M.Sc. (Ag.). Thesis, G.B. Pant University of Agriculture and Technology, Pantnagar, pp: 153.

Kumar, M.B., Sherry, R.J., Varier, A. and Sharma, S.P. (2004): Seed Esterase-A Descriptor for Characterization of Pearl Millet Genotypes, *Indian J. Genet*, 64(4): 267-270.

Law, J.R., Cooke, R.J., Reeves, J.C., Donini, P. and Smith, J.S.C. (1999): Most Similar Variety Comparisons as a Grouping Tool, Special Issue: Cultivar Group Classification, *Plant Varieties & Seeds*, 12(3): 181-190.

Lewis, D. (1954): Genotype-environment Interactions, The Relationship Between Dominance Heterosis, Phenotypic Stability and Variability, *Heredity*, 14: 333-356.

Lin, C.S., Binns, M.R. and Lafkovitch, L.P. (1986): Stability Analysis: Where do We Stand? *Crop Sci.*, 26: 894-900.

Lirindae, M. A. (1986): Laboratory Methodology for Cultivar Purity Testing in US Rices, *Dissertation Abstracts Int.*, B (Sciences and Engg.), 47 (4): 1336B – 1337B.

Liu, L., Liu, Z., Chen, H., Zhou, L., Liu, Y. and Luo, L. (2012): SRAP Markers and Morphological Traits could be Used in Test of Distinctiveness, Uniformity, and Stability (DUS) of Lettuce (*Lactuca sativa*) Varieties, *Journal of Agricultural Science*, 4 (3): 227-236.

Lush, J.L. (1949): Animal Breeding Plans, *Collegiate Press*, Iowa States, pp. 593.

Magalingam, V., Yassin, M. and Kumar, S.R. (2013): Genetic variability and Character Association in Dolichos Bean, *SAARC J. Agri.*, 11 (2): 161-171.

Makhdoomi, M.I., Wani, M.A., Ahangar, H.V. and Rangraz, M.A. (2002): Correlation and Path Coefficient Analysis for Different Morphological and Sink Parameters of Rajmah bean (*Phaseolus vulgaris* L.) under Different Cropping Systems, *Applied Biological Research*, 4: 71-74.

Mall, N. (2011): DUS Characterization of Maize and French Bean Varieties by Using Morphological, Biochemical and Molecular Markers, Ph.D. Thesis, G.B. Pant University of Agriculture and Technology, Pantnagar, pp. 96.

Mather, K. (1943): Polygenic Inheritance and Natural Selection, *Biol. Rev.*, 98: 32-64.

Mauria, S. (2000): DUS Testing in Crop Varieties-A Synthesis on the Subject for New PVP Opting Countries, *Plant Varieties & Seeds*, 13(2): 69-90.

Mauria, S. (2004): National Conference on 'Seed- A Global Perspective'-'Protection of Plant Varieties and Farmers' Rights Act-Implementation and Likely Impact on Indian Seed Sector', Indian Society of Seed Technology (Division of Seed Science and Technology, IARI,) New Delhi, India, pp: 432.

Mishra, D. (1995): Phenotypic Stability for Seed Yield in Rice Bean (*Vigna umbellata*), *Indian Journal of Agricultural Sciences*, 65 (12): 604-906.

Mishra, H. N., Killadi, B. and Mishra, R. C. (1997): Character Association and Path Coefficient Analysis in Pole Type French Bean, *Environment and Ecol.*, 14 (1): 103-106.

Modesta, R. C. D. and Cabral, L. C. (1987): Characteristics of Seeds of Some Soybean Lines with Coloured Testas, EMBRAPA, *News lett., Brazil*: (17), p: 17.

Mohan, Y. (2000): Stability Analysis for Seed Quality Components in Soybean (*Glycine max* L. Merril), Ph.D. Thesis, G.B. Pant University of Agriculture and Technology, Pantnagar, pp: 23.

Mucha, I., Pospieszna, M.Z. and Walkowiak, A. (1994): Testing and Assessment of the Distinctness. Uniformity and Stability of Grass Varieties, *Genet. Polonica.*, 31: 300-304.

Mudzana, G., Pickett, A. A., Jarman, R. J. and Cooke, R. J. (1995): Variety Discrimination in Faba Beans: An Integrated Approach, *Plant Verities and Seed*, 8: 135-145.

Nagapadma, K., Muralimohanreddy, B., Ankaiah, R. and Sarada, P. (1996): Characterization of Twenty Three Maize Inbred Lines through Seed Morphology, Leaf Stomatal Studies and Response of Seedling to Added Chemicals, *Seed Research*, 24 (1): 15-19.

Nagarajan, S., Trevedi, R.K., Raj Ganesh D. S. and Singh, A. K. (2010): India Registers Plant Varieties under PPV&FR Act 2001, *Curr. Sci.*, 99 (6): 723-725.

Nagarajan, S., Yadav, S. P. and Singh, A. K. (2008): Farmers' Variety in the Context of Protection of Plant Varieties and Farmers' Rights Act 2001, *Curr. Sci.*, 94 (6): 709-713.

Naima G., Marie M., Jacquemin, J.M., Ounane, S.M., Mekliche, L. and Baudoin, J.P. (2009): Morphological and Molecular Diversity within Algerian Cowpea (*Vigna unguiculata* (L.) Walp.) Landraces, *Genet. Resource Crop Evol., springerlink.com.*

Nath, A., Harer, P. N. and Dey, U. (2013): Stability Analysis and G × E Interaction in Mungbean (*Vigna radiate* L. Wilczek): A Review, *African J. Agril. Res.*, 8 (26): 3340-3347.

Nath, S. and Korla, B.N., (2004): Path Analysis of Some Quantitative Characters in Dwarf French Bean (*Phaseolus vulgaris* L.) in Relation to Pod Yield, *Legume Res.*, 27 (3): 228-230.

Natrajan, S. and Arumugan, R. (1981): Inter Relationship of Quantitative Traits with Pod Yield in French Bean *(Phaseolus vulgaris* L.), *Prog. Hort.*, 13: 43-47.

Nemeskari, E. (2002): Investigation of Some Production Factors on Yield and Quality of Dry Beans, *International J. Horti. Sci.*, pp. 83–88.

NHB, (2013): www.nhb.gov.in .Indian Horticulture Database 2013 (Accessed on 1st September 2014).

Nimbalkar, C.A., Baviskar, A.P., Desai, V.T. and Navale, P.A. (2002): Stability of Seed Yield and Yield Contributing Characters in French bean (*Phaseolus vulgaris*), *Indian Journal of Agricultural Sciences*, 72 (7): 433-435.

Nkouannessi M. (2005): The Genetic, Morphologicl and Physiological Evaluation of African Cowpea Genotypes, M.Sc. (Agri) Thesis, *Univ. of Free State, Bioemrontein*, South Africa, pp. 639.

Pal, A.B. and Prasad, K.V.S.R. (1996): Genotype x Environment Interactions and Stability Performance Under Changing Climatic Conditions in French Bean (*Phaseolus vulgaris* L.), *Indian Journal of Horticulture*, 53 (2): 145-149.

Pan, R. S., Singh, A. K., Rai, M. and Kumar, S. (2006): Stability Analysis of Yield and Its Components in Bush Type French Bean, *Veg. Sci.*, 33(2): 145-148.

Pan, R.S., Prasad, K.V.S.R. and Rai, M. (2001): Yield Stability in Pole Bean (*Phaseolus vulgaris* L.). *Veg. Sci.*, 28 (1): 65-66.

Pan, R.S., Singh, A.K. Kumar, S. and Rai, M. (2009): Stability of Yield and Its Components in Bush Type French Bean Under Off-season (summer) Cultivation, *Veg. Sci.*, 36 (1): 35-38.

Pandey, V., Singh, V. K. and Upadhyay, D. K. (2013): Determination of Green Pod Yield Components in French Bean (*Phaseolus vulgaris* L.) Through Correlation and Path Coefficient Analyses, *Vegetos*, 26 (2): 438- 443.

Pandey, V.P., Prashad, G. and Pandey, S. (2004): Stability Analysis in French bean (*Phaseolus vulgaris* L.), *Annals of Agricultural Research New Series*, 25 (2): 200-205.

Panse, V.G. and Kharagonkar, H., (1957): Genetics of Quantitative Characters in Relation to Plant Breeding, *Indian J. Genet.*, 17: 318-327.

Panse, V.G. and Sukatme, P.V. (1969): Statistical Methods for Agricultural Workers, ICAR, New Delhi, pp. 381.

Pant, S.C. and Singh, (2001): Genetic Variability in Indian Mustard, *Agric. Sci. Digest*, 21(1): 28-30.

Panwar, K.S., Chaudhary, H.K. and Thakur, S.R. (1995): Stability in Seed Yield of French Bean *(Phaseolus vulgaris)* genotypes in High~Hill, Dry Temperate Region of North-Western Himalayas, *Indian Journal of Agricultural Sciences*, 65 (5): 341-344.

Paramesh, R. (1983): Screening of Soybean Cultivars for Seed Size, Seed Vigour and Establishment of the Relationship with Yield and Yield Components, M. Sc. (Agri) Thesis, University of Agricultural Sciences, Bangalore, Karnataka, India, pp: 169.

Paroda, R.S. and Hayes, J.D. (1970): An Investigation of Genotype Environment Interaction for Rate of Ear Emergence in Spring Wheat, *Heredity*, 26: 157-175.

Patel, P.T., Chauhan, R.M., Parmar, L.D. and Tikka, S.B.S. (2009): Phenotypic Stability of Yield and Related Traits in Pigeonpea, *Legume Res.*, 32 (4): 235-239.

Patra, N. Agrawal, R. C. and Chawla, H. S. (2010): Assessment of Distinctiveness, Uniformity and Stability of Basmati Rice (*Oryza sativa* L.) Varieties Based on Morphological Descriptors, *Indian J. Genet.*, 70 (1): 48-57.

Patra, N. and Chawla, H.S. (2010): Biochemical and RAPD Molecular Markers for Establishing Distintiveness of Basmati Rice (*Oryza sativa* L.) Varieties as Additional Descriptors for Plant Variety Protection, *Indian J. Biotechnology*, 9: 371-377.

Payne, R.C. and Koszykowski, T.J. (1979): The Effect of Seed Size on Hypocotyl Length of Soybean Cultivars, *Seed Sci. Technol.*, 7: 109-115.

Pental, D. (2003): Transgenics for Productivity and Sustainable Agriculture: Some Considerations for the Development of a Policy Framework, *Curr. Sci.*, 84: 413-424.

Perkins, J.E. and Jinks, J.L. (1968): Environmental and Genotype Environmental Components of Variability III Multiple Lines and Crosses, *Heredity*, 23: 339-356.

Petrova, T. (1984): Correlations Between Some Morphological Plant Characters and Yield in French Bean, *Rastenier dni Naukii.* 21: 38-42.

Pinchinal, A. and Adams, N.W. (1966): Induction of Variation in Dry Bean Population by Combinations of Recurrent Intercrossing and Neutron Irradiation, *Cycles one and the USDA ARS.*, 74: 30-31.

PPV & FR, (2007): Guidelines for the Conduct of Test for Distinctiveness, Uniformity and Stability on Kidney bean (*Phaseolus vulgaris* L.), *Plant Variety Journal of India.*, 1 (1): 192-201.

Prakash, S. and Singhal, N.C., (1997): Characterization of Some Indian Pea (*Pisum sativum* L.) Cultivars, *Seed Research*, 25 (1): 53-58.

Rabbani, M. A. Iwabuchi, A. Murakami, Y. Suzuki, T. and Takayanagi, K. (1999): Collection, Evaluation and Utilization of Oilseed Mustard *(Brassica juncea* L.) in Pakistan, *Pak. J. Biol. Sci.*, 2: 88-94.

Raffi, S.A. Newaz, M.A. and Khan, N. (2004): Stability Analysis for Pod and Seed Production in Dry Bean *(Phaseolus vulgaris* L.), *Asian J. Plant Sci.*, 3 (2): 239-242.

Rai, N., Asati, B.S., Yadav, D.S. and Singh, A.K. (2004): Genetic Analysis in French Bean *(Phaseolus vulgaris* L.), *Veg. Sci.*, 31 (2): 138-141.

Ramanna, A. (2006): 'India's Policy on Genetically Modified Crops' Asia Research Centre, London School of Economics and Political Science, Working Paper 15, pp. 45.

Ramteke, R and Murlidharan, P. (2012): Characterization of Soybean (*Glycine max*) Varieties as Per DUS Guidelines, *Indian Journal of Agricultural Sciences*, 82 (7): 572–577.

Rasaily, S.K., Desai, N.D. and Kukadia, M.U. (1986): Genetic Variability in Soybean (*Glycine max* (L.) Merrill), *Gujarat Agril. Uni. Res. J.*, 11 (2): 57-60.

Reddy, M. Hunje, R. Biradar, D. P. and Vyakarnahal, B. S. (2007): Characterization of Cotton Hybrids and Parental Lines using Morphological Characters, *Karnataka J. Agric. Sci.*, 20 (3): 511-513.

Reddy, P.N., Reddy, K.N. and Singh, S.P. (1989): Effect of Seed Size on Qualitative and Quantitative Traits in Soybean, *Seed Sci. and Technol.*, 17: 289-295.

Robinson, D. (2008): Sui Generis Plant Variety Protection Systems: Liability Rules and Non-UPOV Systems of Protection, *Journal of Intellectual Property Law & Practice*, 3 (10): 659-665.

Ruiz, R. Calsyn, *I.e.*, Gilliland, T.J. Dubreuil, P. Dillmann, C. Lallemand, J. Loose, M. and Baril, C.P. (2001): Estimating Genetic Conformity Between Related Ryegrass (Lolium) Varieties. 2. AFLP Characterization, *Mol. Breed*, 6: 593-602.

Saha, P., Hazra, P. and Maity, T. K. (1990): Genetic Variability and Correlation Studies in French Bean (*Phaseolus vulgaris* L.), *Veg. Sci.*, 17: 213-216.

Sahai, S, (2001): Plant Variety Protection and Farmers Rights Law, *Econo. Politic. Weekly*, (Issue: September, 2001), pp. 45.

Sahai, S. (1996): Protecting Plant Varieties: UPOV Should not be Our Model, *Econo. Politic. Weekly*, (Issue: October 1996), pp. 26.

Salisbury, E.J. (1940): Ecological Aspects of Plant Taxonomy, *In*: The New Systematics (Ed. J. Huxley),: 329-342.

Samal, K.M., Senapati, N. and Nandi, A. (1996): Performance, Variability, Correlation and Coheritability Estimates in Rajmash, *Indian J. Genet. and Plant Breeding*, 56 (4): 505-509.

Sankrapandian, R. (2002): Identifying Some Pulse Cultivars Based on Key Characters Alone Among Popular Varieties of Tamil Nadu, *Seed Tech News*, 32 (1): 146.

Sarutayophat, T., Nualsri, C., Santipracha, Q. and Saereeprasert, V. (2007): Characterization and Genetic Relatedness Among 37 Yard Long Bean and Cowpea Accessions Based on Morphological Characters and RAPD Analysis, *Songklanakarin J. Sci. Technol.*, 29 (3): 591-600.

Searle, S.R. (1961): Phenotypic, genotypic and environmental correlations. *Biometrics*, 17: 474-480.

Seshia, S. (2001): Plant Variety Protection and Farmers' Rights in India: Law-making and the Cultivation of Varietal Control, M.Phil Dissertation, Institute of Development Studies, University of Sussex, U.K.

Shankar R., Kochhar, A.S., Archak, S. and Gautam, P.L. (2000): Plant Variety Protection : Lessons from cross-coutry perspective, Policy Brief No. 11, National Centre for Agricultural Economics and Policy Research, ICAR, New Delhi.

Sharma, J.K., Lata, S. and Sharma, R.P. (2001): Stability for Grain Yield in Amaranth (*Amaranthus hypochondriacus*), *Indian Journal of Agricultural Sciences*, 71 (6): 364-394.

Sharma, J.R. (1996): Principles and Practices of Plant Breeding (1st edition), Tata *Mc Graw – Hill Publishing Co. Ltd.*, New Delhi, pp: 426.

Sharma, K.C. (2010): Stability for Green Pod Yield in Bush Type French Bean (*Phaseolus vulgaris* L.) Under North-Western Himalayas, *Journal of Hill Agriculture*, 1 (2): 197-199.

Sharma, R.C. (1998): Stability in Mothbean (*Vigna aconitifolia*), *Indian Journal of Agricultural Sciences*, 68 (2): 130-131.

Sharma, S.P. (1991): Plant Variety Testing System in U.K. *Seed Res.*, 19(2): 101-105.

Shettar, B.I., Kumar, V.S. and Shethey, M.V.N. (1975): Path Analysis of Yield Components in Snap Bean, *Mysore J. Agric. Sci.*, 9: 649-651.

Shinde, S.S. and Dumbre, A.D. (2001): Correlation and Path Coefficient Analysis in French Bean, Mahatma Phule Krishi Vidyapeeth, Rahuri, India, *J. Maharashtra Agri. Universities*, 26 (1): 48-49.

Shridhar and Ram, H.H. (1999): Stability Analysis for Yield and Its Components under Different Fertility Regimes in French Bean (*Phaseolus vulgaris*), *Veg. Sci.*, 26 (1): 6-11.

Simmonds, N. W. (1962): Variability in Crop Plants, Its Use and Conservation, *Biol. Rev.*, 37: 422-465.

Singh, A. K., Tomer, A. K., Tyagi, K. and Singh, P. P. (2007): Stability Analysis for Yield and Its Components in French Bean (*Phaseolus Vulgaris* Lam.), *Legume Res.*, 30 (3): 166-172.

Singh, A.K. (1993): Genetic Variability and Correlation Studies in French bean, *Haryana J. Hort. Sci.*, 22 (3): 235-339.

Singh, A.K. and Saini, S.S. (1985): Genetic Analysis of Protein Content of French Bean, *Indian J. Hort. Sci.*, 45: 110-114.

Singh, A.K., Singh, A.P., Singh, S.P. and Singh, V. (2009): Relationship and Path Analysis for Green Pod Yield and Its Contributing Characters Over Environments in French Bean (*Phaseolus vulgaris* L.), *Legume Res.*, 32 (4): 270.

Singh, A.P., Padmavati, M. and Chawla. (2011a): Sui Generis IPR Laws vis-à-vis Farmers' Rights in Some Asian Countries: Implications under the WTO, *Journal of Intellectual Property Rights*, 16: 107-116.

Singh, J.P. (1991): Stability Analysis in Rice (*Oryza sativa* L.): I. Yield Characters, *Narendra Deva J. Agric. Res.*, 6 (1): 150-154.

Singh, J.P. and Sinha, P.K. (1993): Stability Analysis for Yield and Quality Characters in Ground Nut (*Arachis hypogea* L.), *Indian J. Genet.*, 53 (1): 97-98.

Singh, J.V., Paroda, R.S., Arora, R.N. and Saini, M.L. (1991): Stability Analysis for Green and Dry Fodder in Cluster bean, *Indian J. Genet. Pl. Br.*, 51: 345-348.

Singh, P. (2007): Diversity Analysis in Indigenous French Bean (*Phaseolus vulgaris* L.), M. Sc. Thesis, G.B. Pant University of Agriculture and Technology, Pantnagar, pp 263.

Singh, R. B. and Sharma, S. P. (1996): Plant Variety Protection and the Indian Agriculture, *Indian Farming*, 46(8): 73-75.

Singh, V. (1983): Genetic Divergence and Stability Analysis in Forage Sorghum (*Sorghum bicolar* (L.) Moench), Ph.D. Thesis, G.B. Pant University of Agriculture and Technology, Pantnagar, pp: 263.

Singh, V., Yadav, R.K., Yadav, R., Malik, R. S., Yadav, N.R. and Singh, J. (2013): Stability Analysis in Mung Bean [*Vigna radiata* (L.) Wilczek] for Nutritional Quality and Seed Yield, *Legume Res.*, 36 (1): 56 – 61.

Singh, Y.V., Nautiyal, M.K., Sharma, C.L., Agrawal, J. and Singh, A. (2014): Stability Analysis for Grain Yield and Yield Components in Exotic Varieties of Cowpea (*Vigna unguiculata* (L.) Walp.), *In*: All India Seminar on "Emerging Technology for Sustainable Resource Management" March 13-14, 2014, Proceedings Organized by Pantnagar Local Centre, The Institution of Engineers, Pantnagar, pp: 143-146.

Singhania, D.L. (1972): Heterosis, Line *per se* Performance, Combining Ability and Stability of Performance in Grain Sorghum (*Sorghum bicolar* (L.) Moench), Ph.D. Thesis, IARI, New Delhi, India, pp: 263.

Smith, J.S.C. and Smith, O.S. (1989): The Description and Assessment of Distances Between Inbred Lines of Maize: II. The Utility of Morphological, Biochemical and Genetic Descriptors and a Scheme for Testing of Distinctiveness Between Inbred Lines, *Maydica*, 34: 151-161.

Smith, J.S.C. and Smith, O.S. (1992): Fingerprinting Crop Varieties, *Advances in Agronomy,* 47: 85-127.

Smitha, D.D.P. (2005): Divergence and Stability Studies in French Bean (*Phaseolus vulgaris* L.), M.Sc. Thesis, University of Agricultural Sciences, Dharwad, Karnataka, India, pp: 263.

Smýkal, P., Horáèek, J., Dostálová, R. and Hýbl, M. (2008): Variety Discrimination in Pea (*Pisum sativum* L.) by Molecular, Biochemical and Morphological Markers, *J. Appl. Genet.,* 49 (2): 155–166.

Snedecor, G.W. and Cochran, W.G. (1967): Statistical Methods, *Oxford and IBH Publishing Co.,* New Delhi, pp: 593.

Sofi, P.A., Zargar, M.Y., Debouck, D. and Graner, A. (2011): Evaluation of Common Bean (*Phaseolus vulgaris* L) germplasm under Temperate Conditions of Kashmir Valley, *Journal of Phytology,* 3 (8): 47-52.

Sood, S., Sood, R. and Vidyasagar, (2011): Morphological Characterization of Bell Pepper (*Capsicum annuum* var. *grossum*) Genotypes and their Application for Distinctness, Uniformity and Stability Testing, *Indian Journal of Agricultural Sciences,* 80 (3):240-246.

Sridhara, S., Thimmegowda, S. and Chalapathi, M. V. (1997): Nutritional Values, Physical and Phsico-chemical Characteristics and Cooking Quality of Soybean Genotypes, *Crop Res.,* 13 (2): 259-266.

Srikantaradya, M.G. (1980): Genetic Variability with Respect to Different Seed Characters in Relation to Viability and Vigour in soybean (*Glycinc max* (L.) Merrill), M. Sc. (Agri) Thesis, University of Agricultural Sciences, Bangalore, Karnataka, India, pp. 263.

Stahi, J. P. and Pandey, M. P. (1981): Association of Seed Impermeability with Flowering and Maturity Duration in Soybean, *Tropical Grain Legume Bull.,* 22: 119-121.

Staub, J.E., Gabert, A. and Wehner, T.C. (1996): Plant Variety Protection: A Consideration of Genetic Relationships, *Hort. Sci.,* 31 (7): 1086-1091.

Stein, H. (2005): Intellectual Property and Genetically Modified Seeds, The United States, Trade and the Developing Worth, *North Western J. Technol. & Intellc. Prop.,* 3(2): 161-173.

Sun, J. and Chang, R. (1990): Analysis of the Characteristics of Green Soybean in China, *Crop Genetic Resources,* 3: 4-6.

Surendra, P. and Singhal, N. C. (1997): Characterization of Some Indian pea (*Pisum sativum* L.) Cultivars, *Seed Res.,* 25 (1): 53-58.

Suryawanshi, V. B., Patil, R. B., Mata, S. N., Gagare, K. C. and Manjare, M. R. (2002): Morphological Characterization of Soybean Cultivars, *Seed Tech. News,* 32(1): p: 211.

Swaminathan, M.S. (2002): The Protection of Plant Varieties and Farmer's Rights Act from Legislation to Implementation, *Curr. Sci.,* 82: 778-780.

Talukdar P. and Konwar, B.K. (1984): Phenotypic Stability of Soybean Genotypes for Field Germination, *Soybean Genet. Newsl.,* 11: 214-216.

Tandon, J.P. (1992): An Appraisal of Variety Testing and Released System in India, pp: 45-52.

Tarasatyavathi, C., Bharadwaj, C. H., Husain, S. M., Karmakar, P. G. and Yogendra Mohan, (2004): Identification Key for Soybean (*Glycine max*) Varieties Released or Notified in India, *Indian J. Agric. Sci.,* 74 (4): 215-218.

Terao, H. (1986): Studies on the Mesocotyl Elongation of Seedling in Japanese Paddy Rice Cultivars, *Oryza sativa* L. *Bull. Institutional Tropical Agril.,* 9: 77 – 87.

Thakur, B.S., Korla, B.N. and Joshi, A.K. (1997): Path Coefficient Analysis in French Bean (*Phaseolus vulgaris* L.), *Annals of Agri. Res.,* 18: 437-440.

Thakur, H.L., Gupta, J.C., Kalin, N.R., Verma, S. and Sharma, K.C. (2001): Phenotypic Stability for Grain Yield and Maturity in French Bean (*Phaseolus vulgaris*), *Indian Journal of Agricultural Sciences,* 71 (11): 721-722.

Tiwari, D. K., Tiwari, J. P. and Agarwal, V. K. (1978): Evaluation of Soybeans for High Germinability and Field Emergence, *Seed Res.*, 6 (2): 125-128.

Tobin, G. and Carpenter, K.J. (1978): The Nutritional Value of Dry Bean (*Phaseolus vulgaris*). A Literature Review, *Nutr. Abst. Review-Series A. 48.*, 11: 919-935.

Tunwar, N.S. and Singh, S.V. (1985): Handbook of Cultivars, *Oxford and IBH Publishing Co.*, New Delhi, India, p. 302.

Tyagi, P.C. and Agarwal, M.C. (1995): Phenotypic Stability for Seed Yield in Pigeonpea, *Indian Journal of Genetics and Plant Breeding*, 55: 148-150.

Ullah, M.Z., Hasan, M.J., Rahman, A.H.M.A. and Saki, A.I. (2011): Genetic Variability, Character Association and Path Analysis in Yard Long Bean, *SAARC J. Agri.*, 9 (2): 9-16.

Vahab, M. A., Joseph, S., Mathe, S.K., Devadas, V. S. and Peter, K. V. (1991): Evaluation of Selected Varieties of Vegetable Cowpea, *Veg. Sci.*, 18 (2): 222-224.

Venkatareddy, D. M. (1991): Investigations on Seed Technology of Soybean, Ph.D Thesis, University of Agricultural Sciences, Bangalore, Karnataka, India, pp: 369.

Venkateswarlu, O. (1998): Phenotypic Stability for Grain Yield in Pigeonpea, *International Journal of Chickpea and Pigeonpea Newsletter*, 5: 41-42.

Veress, Z. and Lazer, L. (1997): Survey on Character Types Involved in DUS Testing Using Distinctness Percentage Method and DUS Data on Maize, *Novenytermeles*, 46: 401-412.

Veress, Z. and Matok, G.Y. (1999): Similarity Groups Based on DUS Variety Description, *Novenytermeles*, 48: 43-54.

Verma, M.M., Chahal, G.S. and Murty, B.R. (1978): Limitations of Conventional Regression Analysis- A Proposed Modification, *Theoretical and Applied Genetics*, 53 (2): 89-91.

Verma, P., Ali, M., Doshi, V. and Solanki, R.K. (2014): Stability Analysis in Coriander (*Coriandrum sativum* L.), *Indian Journal of Horticulture*, 71 (1): 126-129.

Villalobos, E. and Fournier, L. A. (1978): Morphological Identification of Some Soybean Selections Introduced into Costa Rica, *Agronomia Costarricense*, 2 (10): 23-27.

Wagner, C.K. and McDonald, M.B. (1982): Rapid Laboratory Tests Useful for Differentiation of Soybean (*Glycine max* L.) Cultivars, *Seed Sci. Technol.*, 10: 431-449.

Walling, B. and Chaturvedi, H.P. (2014): Genetic Variability, Character Association and Path Coefficient Analysis in French Bean (*Phaseolus vulgaris* L.) Genotypes of Nagaland, *Indian Res. J. Genet. & Biotech.*, 6 (2): 397-401.

Watal, J. (1998): Intellectual Property Rights in Agriculture, *World J.Intellect. Prop.*, 1(2): 1-25.

Watson S. (2004): Using the DUS Software. WORKSHOP ON DATA HANDLING Organized by the International Union for the Protection of New Varieties of Plants (UPOV) in cooperation with the State Forestry Administration of China, the Ministry of Agriculture of China and the State Intellectual Property Office of China with the Financial Assistance of the Ministry of Agriculture, Forestry and Fisheries of Japan, Beijing, June 9 to 11, 2004, UPOV/DATA/BEI/04/ 12: 2-19.

Weiss, E.A. (1971): Caster, Sesame and Sunflower, *Leonard Hill Books*, London, pp: 311-355.

Widdington, C.H. (1942) Canalisation of Development and the Inheritance of Acquired Characters, *Nature*, 150: 563-565.

Yadav, A.K., Singh, D. and Arya, R.K. (2013): Morphological Characterization of Indian Mustard (*Brassica juncea*) Genotypes and their Application for DUS testing, *Indian Journal of Agricultural Sciences*, 83 (12): 1305-1316.

Yadav, R.D.S. and Srivastava, J.P. (2002): DUS Characteristics of Chickpea Varieties. *Seed Tech News*, 32 (32): 29-30.

Plant Physiology : *Stress, Diseases and Management* **Pages 125-142**
Edited by: **Mr. Prasann Kumar; Dr. Pawan Kumar 'Bharti'**
ISBN: 978-93-88854-00-9
Edition: **2019**
Published by: **Discovery Publishing House Pvt. Ltd., New Delhi (India)**

6

CRISPR/Cas9 Technology and Its Potential Role in Plant Disease Resistance

[1]Joginder Pal and [2]Sunita Chandel

ABSTRACT

The targeted genome editing that targets genomic sequences in a site specific manner has recently emerged as a most effective biotechnological weapon for boosting resistance in plants against widespread phytopathogens. Among various gene editing techniques, gene targeting notably by CRISPR-Cas9 (Clustered Regularly Interspaced Short Palindromic Repeats) has abundantly aroused consequential excitement among agricultural scientists since its discovery in 2013. It is an inexpensive, easy, efficent and rapidly flourshing technique that occurs in nature as a prokaryotic immune system and confers resistance to foreign invading genetic elements such as plasmids and bacterial viruses by intruppting compatible host pathogen interaction.The most important advantage of this technique over other gene editing methods is that it enables precise genomic modifications with ease and more effective manner, reducing off targest effects and can also be capable of editing multiple genome site simultaneously. The CRISPR/Cas9 technique offers the opportunities to rewrite the effector-target sequence for avoiding effector-target molecular communication and also to modify effector-target promoters for increasing the expression of target genes and thereby engaged in the resistance process. Besides its widespread role in virus and bacterial disease resistance, recently its potentiality in fungal disease management has also been reported. The technique displayed plant resistance tremendously by acting upon the immunity components and proved as an excellent and indispensable approach for sustainable agriculture. The CRISPR/Cas9 is rapidly evolving technique and its application is constantly expanding year by year. In this review, we have summarized the CRISPR/Cas9 system and its role in developing plant resistance.

Keywords: CRISPR-Cas9, genome modifications, disease resistance, sustainable agriculture.

[1] Department of Plant Pathology, Dr. Y.S. Parmar University of Horticulture and Forestry Nauni, Solan-173230 (Himachal Pradesh), INDIA

Introduction

During the last few decades, the CRISPR-Cas based systems have opened the new era of molecular biology and become the most promising tool among agricultural scientists for editing and modifying genome in widespread organisms especially plants. In general, the CRISPR/Cas9 technology is evolved from prokaryotic organisms (a type II bacterial immune system) that acts on an adaptive immune system and thereby protect these organisms from invading DNA viruses and/or plasmids. Moreover, it represents a new array of targeted genome editing technology globally which can be applied extensively to nearly all organisms in a sustainable manner, including the potential for reduced pesticide usage. In CRISPR/Cas9 technique, site-specific modification is achieved by a single guide RNA (usually about 20 nucleotides) that is complementary to a target gene or locus and is anchored by a protospacer adjacent motif. Cas9 nuclease then cleaves the targeted DNA to generate double-strand breaks (DSBs), which are subsequently repaired by non-homologous end joining (NHEJ) or homology-directed repair (HDR) mechanisms. When combined with double or multiplex guide RNA design, NHEJ may also introduce targeted chromosome deletions, whereas HDR can be engineered for target gene correction, gene replacement, and gene knock-in.

Remarkably, CRISPR/Cas DNA editing system is able to achieve efficient gene editing in plants through either transient experiment or transgenic plants. In many cases, Cas9 and gRNAs are introduced inside plant cells by *Agrobacterium*-mediated T-DNA transformation or physical means, such as PEG-mediated transformation of protoplast or biolistic transformation of callus. In CRISPR technology, the Cas proteins, such as Cas9, are RNA-directed endonucleases which are able to recognize and cleaving nucleic acids on the basis of sequence complementarities and to resite the targeted sequences. Cas9 can be targeted to specific DNA genomic sequences by engineering separately an encoded small guide RNA (sgRNA) with which it forms a complex. Thus, only a short RNA sequence must therefore be synthesized to confer recognition of a new target. Recently, an alternative to the Cas9 enzyme, Cpf1, has also been reported, which is much smaller in size and makes genome editing easier and more precise technique.

Historical Background

S.No.	Year	Contribution
1	1987	First record of CRISPR cluster repeats was reported in *Escherichia coli*
2	2000	Recognition and approval that CRISPR families are present throughout prokaryotic organisms
3	2002	Description of term CRISPR along with defined signature cas genes was coined

4	2005	Identification and description of PAM with foreign origin of spacers and their adaptive immunity function was taken into consideration
5	2007	The CRISPR-cas complex was successfully demonstrated and it was the first experimental evidence for CRISPR adaptive immunity
6	2008	CRISPR system can act upon specified DNA targets; Spacers are converted into mature crRNAs which acts as a small guide RNAs
7	2009	Type III-BCmr CRISPR complexes can cleave RNA of specific region in chromosome with more success than Other Gene Editing Methods
8	2010	Cas9 is Directed by Spacer Sequences and Cleaves Target DNA via Double Strands Breaks
9	2011	Tracer RNA Designs a Twofold Structure with cr RNA in Association with cas9:Type II CRISPR Systems are Transposable and can be Heterologously Expressed in Different Organisms
10	2012	*In vitro* characterization of DNA targeting by cas9
11	2013	First Demonstration of cas9 Genome Engineering in Prokaryotic Cells
12	2014	Description of Genome -Wide Functional Screening with cas9: Crystal Structure of cas9 in Complex with Guide RNA can Rewrite DNA Efficiently
13	2015	CRISPR/Cas Systems were Successfully Refined Against Numerous geminiviruses]
14	2015	The Cas9 Endonuclease from the Bacterium *Francisella novicida* is Demonstrated to Cleave RNA Viruses
15	2016	Development of resistance to a ssRNA plant virus through CRISPR/Cas 9 deal mutagenesis of host gene elF(iso)4E that codes a protein which is necessary for virus replication and Multiplication of Same Virus
16	2016	Evolution of Resistance Against Three ssRNA Plant Viruses Through CRISPR/Cas 9 mediated mutagenesis of Host Gene elF4F that Codes for a Protein Required for Virus Replication

Mechanism of CRISPR/Cas9 Based Genome Editing

CRISPR-Cas9 is a new gene editing technology that offers the potential for substantial improvement over other gene editing technologies which offers the most reliable and versatile platform to engineer plant genome in a sequence specific manner. Irrespective of its large applications in animal sciences, it has now become the method of choice for genome engineering in plants for multipurpose. The CRISPR/Cas technology is initially regulated by the bacterial type-II CRISPR/Cas adaptive immune system that is displayed by the hosts to cleave invading phage or plasmid DNA. In general, CRISPR- Cas9 system just requires three components, *i.e.,* a protospacer-containing CRISPR RNA (crRNA), a trans-activating crRNA (tracrRNA) and a Cas9 endonuclease for function. The Cas9 nuclease is supervised by the crRNA tracrRNA duplex to cleave any trespassing DNA carrying the same protospacer sequence which is escorted by a protospacer adjacent motif (PAM). The PAM is absolutely crucial for target recognition as it carries the platform of the crRNA tracrRNA-Cas9 complex and consequitive and successive base pairing between the crRNA and the protospace.

In CRISPR/Cas9 technology, the Cas9 and sgRNA are expressed and design or construct a complex that fuses on targeted DNA near the NGG (PAM) site. A double stranded break (DSB) is induced at a targeted site that can be repaired either by non-homologous end joining (NHEJ) or homology directed repair (HDR). The repair by NHEJ usually results in the insertion or deletion (indel) or frame shift mutation resulting gene knockout by disruption. If a donor DNA is provided with end homology, then this can be inserted at the targeted site to modify a gene by adding changes in nucleotides or by gene insertion. In type II of CRISPR, attacking viral DNA or plasmids is divided into smaller pieces and integrated in CRISPR locus.The particular loci are reproduced or transcribed and these processed transcripts produce crRNA. These crRNAs regulate effect or endonuclease to target alien DNA depending upon complementarity or matching of sequence. Cas9 produce DSBs (double-stranded breaks) at target site, which on the other hand assists endogenous DNA repair mechanisms leading to rewrite DNA.

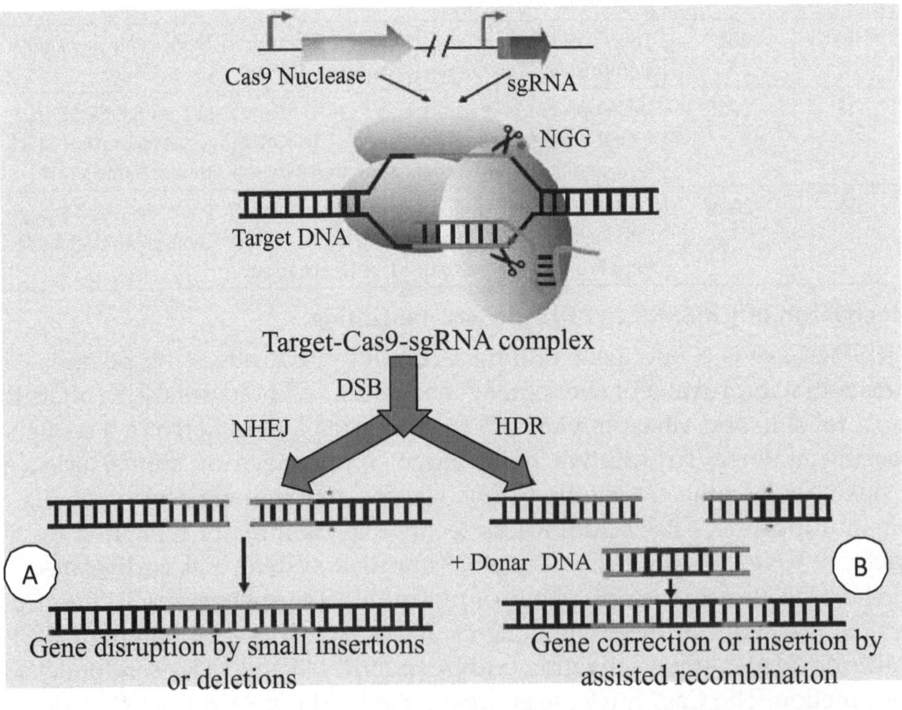

Fig. 6.1: Schematic representation of Targeted genome editing via CRISPR-Cas9 system

Spectacularly, the sgRNA programmed Cas9 appeared more effective in targeted gene modifications rather than individual trRNA and crRNA.Till date, genome-editing protocols have ratify three different types of Cas9 nuclease. The first Cas9 type can cut DNA site-specifically and results in the stimulation of DSB repair event to occur.Cellular NHEJ (Non-Homologous End Joining) mechanism is used to repair DSBs. As a culmination, insertions/deletions (indels) takes place that obstruct the targeted loci immediately. Apart from this, if any similarity between donor template and target locus is witnessed, the DSB may be repaired by HDR pathway (homology directed repair) allowing exact substitute mutations to be prepared. Cong *et al.* introduced advanced Cas9-D10A, as an alternative, in which DNA repairs happens via the HDR pathway only which cuts single strand of DNA without activation of NHEJ. Hence, it produces less indel mutations.

CRISPR/Cas9 Technology Mediated Resistance in Plants

The CRISPR/Cas9 system is a newly developed tool that can furnish important role in developing resistance in different agricultural crops. The CRISPR mediated genome editing has been used as a tool for imparting resistance to viruses in plants composed of Cas9 endonuclease of *Streptococcus pyogenes* and a synthetic guide RNA (gRNA), which combines functions of CRISPR RNA (cRNA) and trans-activating cRNA (tracrRNA) to direct the Cas9 protein to the DNA target sequence leading the protospacer-associated motif (PAM) (NGG in the case of *S. pyogenes*). Because the specificity of the system is determined by the 20-nucleotide sequence of the gRNA, it allows for peculiar and adequate genome. Once again, the CRISPR/Cas9 system can be used to simultaneously editing of multiple genomic targets. The type II bacterial CRISPR/Cas9 system has been used to fluent disruption of target genes in the fungal maize pathogen *Ustilago maydis*.

The Role of CRISPR/Cas9 System for Developing Resistance in Plants can be Described As

1. Antiviral Resistance in Plants Based on CRISPR-Cas Technology: The CRISPR/Cas system of genome editing has now been used efficiently as a tool for imparting resistance to viruses in several crop plants. Very recently, three reports have been documented which described the CRISPR/Cas approach and its wide utility for protection to plants against geminiviruses. This technology admitted enhanced resistance to the plants against the geminiviruses species including BCTV (Beet curly top virus), TYLCV (Tomato yellow leaf curl virus), and MeMV (Merremia mosaic virus) at the same time with single gRNA; BeYDV (Bean yellow dwarf virus), and BSCTV (Beet severe curly top virus).

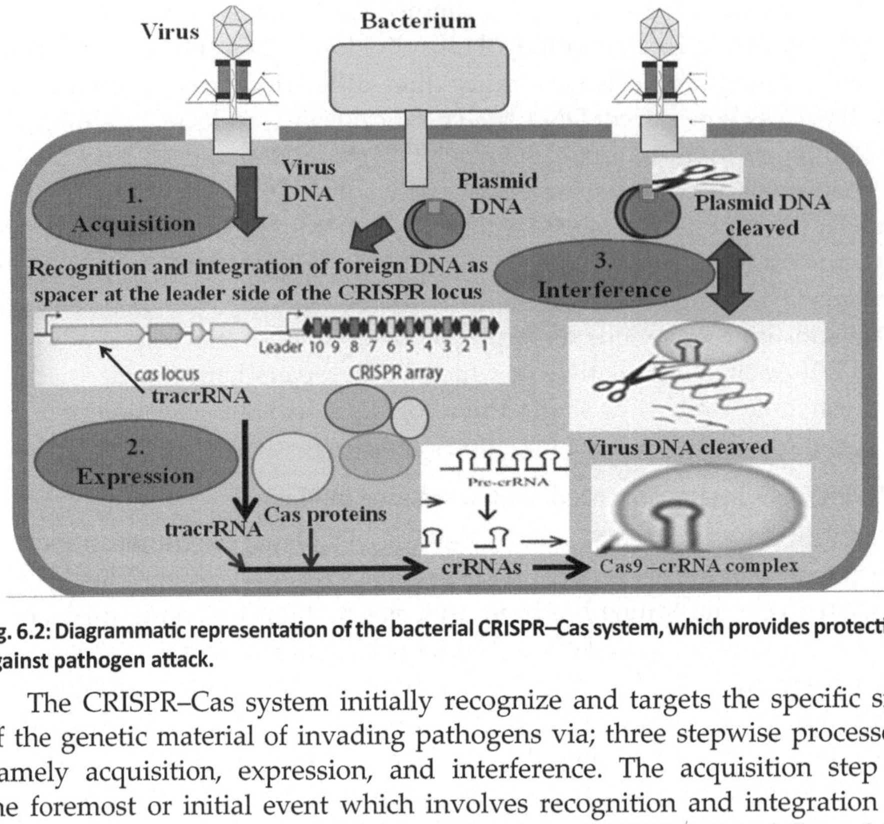

Fig. 6.2: Diagrammatic representation of the bacterial CRISPR–Cas system, which provides protection against pathogen attack.

The CRISPR–Cas system initially recognize and targets the specific site of the genetic material of invading pathogens via; three stepwise processes, namely acquisition, expression, and interference. The acquisition step is the foremost or initial event which involves recognition and integration of foreign DNA as spacer at the leader side of the CRISPR locus, followed by duplication of the repeat. In general, in first step, short fragment of exogenous DNA are incorporated via CRISPR array in the bacterial genome, and acts as a new spacer sequence. In the expression step of the CRISPR–Cas system, the long pre-CRISPR RNA (pre-crRNA) first transcribed and is then actively processed into crRNAs with the help of specific Cas proteins as well as trans-activating crRNA (tracrRNA). During the third or final event as interference, a specific sequence of foreign genomic element is targeted and then cleaved into small fragments. The crRNA directs the Cas9 protein for cleavage to the complementary target region of the DNA of viruses and plasmids and therby leading induction of resistance in plants.

CRISPR/Cas9 based antiviral resistance in plants can be grouped into:

(*a*) Developing Plants Resistant to RNA Viruses: Earlier no single evidence of directly targeting and cleaving RNA viruses were found. But currantly CRISPR-Cas9 sgRNA system has now been used extensively to efficiently inactivate certain target genes and later these target regions of genome were mutated with the CRISPR/Cas9 system, in order to produce virus-resistant plants. The only limitation of directly targeting RNA viral genomes is that the guide RNA-Cas9 system can only be used to target DNA viruses. But this could be change in the future, because Cas9 nuclease can be programmed and modify to cleave RNA and the type III-B CRISPR-Cas system mediates programmable cleavage of RNA sequences that are complementary to a guide RNA. *A. thaliana* mutant plants of these translation initiation factors exhibited *Turnip mosaicvirus* (TuMV) with great success. Currently, the usefulness of CRISPR/Cas9technology for generating novel genetic resistance to the potyvirus TuMV was demonstrated greatly in *A. thaliana*, by deletion of a host factor, *eIF(iso)4E*, which is strictly required for virus growth and multiplication. Development of virus resistance in cucumber (*Cucumis sativus* L.) was also explained by disrupting *eIF4E*, and developing non-transgenic heterozygous *eIF4E* mutant plants. These non-transgenic plants resulted partial resistance to an ipomovirus (*Cucumber vein yellowing virus*) and two important potyviruses (*Zucchini yellow mosaic virus* and *Papaya ring spot mosaic virus*-W) causing severe losses to cucrbits and papaya. Other examples of resistant to RNA viruses includes the targeting of two sites of eIF4 E gene in cucumber allowed developing plants resistant to infection by five positive strand RNA viruses. The targeted genome sites were present with in the first and third exon sequences. Small indel and small nucleotide polymorphisms (SNPs) were also observed in the T1 generation. Homozygous T3 progeny with 20 and four deletions in the eIF4E gene were found immune to infection by cucumber vein yellowing virus (family *Potyviridae*, genus *Ipomovirus*), and resistant to papaya ring spot virus-W and zucchini yellow mosaic virus(family *Potyviridae*, genus *Potyvirus*). As expected, the plants remained susceptible to viruses that donot appear to highjack the host eIF4E to complete their cycle, such as cucumber mosaic virus (members of family *Bromoviridae*, genus *Cucumovirus*) or cucumber green mottle mosaic virus (family, *Virgaviridae*, genus *Tobamovirus*). Pyott *et al.* were also found successful in targeted genome engineering imparting complete resistance in *Arabidopsis* to turnip mosaic virus, a potyvirus, using the CRISPR/Cas9 technology targeting the plante IF (iso) 4E gene.

(*b*) Developing Plants Resistant to DNA Geminiviruses: The geminiviruses are major group of single stranded DNA viruses and most of the previous research regarding CRISPR-mediated viral interference has been done on these ssDNA geminiviruses. But very recently, the application of the CRISPR-Cas systems targeting geminiviruses has been reported to enhance resistance to tomato yellow leaf curlvirus (TYLCV, genus *Begomovirus*) and bean yellow dwarf virus (BeYDV, genus *Mastrevirus*) in *Nicotiana benthamiana* and to beet severe curly topvirus (BSCTV, genus *Curtovirus*) in *N. benthamiana* and in *Arabidopsis*. Ali *et al.* has done excellent work in CRISPR/cas technology and engineered sgRNAs targeting coding and non-coding TYLCV sequences, including the conserved non-coding intergenic region (IR) of about 300 nt that can exhibit a stem- loop structure containing the origin of replication and promoter sequences for RNA polymerase II SgRNAs targeting the IR were demonstrated the most efficient inreducing TYLCV DNA titer that wholly or partially vanish the disease symptoms.The sgRNAs-Cas9 system was also found successful in simultaneously targeting of three geminiviruses TYLCV, beet curly top virus (genus *Curtovirus*) and merremia mosaic virus (genus *Begomovirus*) when sgRNAs specific for the IR sequence of each virus were used. Similarly, Ji *et al.* targeted coding and non-coding sequences of BSCTV genome and recorded enhanced resistance to the virus.

SgRNA-Cas9 constructs intrrupted the virus DNA replication at different levels. Over-expressing sgRNA-Cas9 specifically targeting the viral DNA genome sequences resulted in virus-resistant plants. Disease symptoms were also attenuated to different levels, which ranged from severe to mild leaf curly symptoms. It has been reported that two sgRNAs targeting the same BeYDV genome site in infected *N. benthamiana* plants and can significantly increase resistance response as compared to using only one single sgRNA. Ali *et al.* demonstrateded that *N. benthamiana* plants expressing the CRISPR/ Cas9 machinery mediated widespread resistance against TYLCV, *Beet curly top virus* (BCTV), and *Merremia mosaic virus* (MeMV). Baltes *et al.* and Ji *et al.* showed increased virus interference activities in *N. benthamiana* against *Bean yellow dwarfvirus* (BeYDV) and BSCTV, respectively. Ji *et al.* correlated Cas9 expression patterns with the levels of virus suppression, indicating the necessity to use one background transgenic line with optimum expression of Cas9 and the sgRNA for successful practical applications.

Ali *et al.* engineered sgRNAs targeting open reading frames encoding viral genes such as Rep, coat proteins and conserved noncoding intergenic region (IR) were targeted and it was reported that conserved intergenic region of gene was most effective target for minimizing the virus titre of tomato yellow leaf curl virus (TYLCV). Further, simultaneous resistance to tomato yellow leaf curl virus (TYLCV), beet curly top virus (BCTV) and merremia mosaic virus (MeMV) could be achieved with the use of sgRNA targeting conserved sequence from IR region. Cotton leaf curl disease caused by begomoviruses is one of the major and destructive diseases of cotton. For combating this, a multiplex CRISPR editing technique was developed as a broad spectrum method for control of leaf curl diseases of cotton. Baltes *et al.* showed that one sgRNA targeting the BeYDV genome could confer plant resistance without cleavage activity,which suggests that catalytically inactive Cas9 (dCas9) can be used to mediate virus interference, thereby eliminating concerns of off-target activities in the plant genome. Ali *et al.* analysed that CRISPR/Cas system can be used to target and cleave *Cotton leaf curl Kokhran virus* (CLCuKoV) and they also recorded that this technology not targeting only the conserved nucleotide sequence but can can target multiple begomoviruses simultaneously and therefore conferring broad-spectrum gemini virus resistance activity. All of these studies showed that *N. benthamiana* plants expressing the CRISPR/Cas9 system displayed considerably reduced viral titers, which abolished or significantly reduced disease symptoms.

Ali *et al.* systematically determined the ability of multiple geminiviruses geminiviruses to evade the CRISPR/Cas9 machinery by targeting coding and non-coding sequences.This study reveals that targeting coding sequences led to the generation of viral variants capable of evading the CRISPR/Cas9 machinery. Interestingly, targeting the non-coding intergenic sequences resulted high levels of virus interference, no detectable viral movements from the CRISPR/Cas9 machinery, and there by providing an effective strategy to confer potential durable resistance in plants against numerous DNA viruses.

Table 6.1: Examples of CRISPR/Cas Technology Developed to Confers Virus Resistance in Plants

CRISPR / Cas technology	Virus	Genus	Family	DNA targeted	References
	Bean yellow dwarf virus	Mastrevirus		Viral	Baltes et al.
	Merremia mosaicvirus, Cotton leaf curl Kokhran virus, Tomato yellow leaf curl virus (TYLCV)	Begomovirus	Geminiviridae	Viral	Ali et al.
	Beet curly top virus (BCTV); Beet severe curly topvirus (BSCTV)	Curtovirus		Viral	Ali et al.
	Cucumber vein yellowing virus	Ipomovirus	Potyviridie	Host	Chandra-sekaran et al. [24]
	Zucchini yellow mosaic virus, Papaya ring spot virus, Turnip mosaic virus	Potyvirus		Host	Chandra-sekaran et al.

2. CRISPR/Cas confers resistance in plants against fungal and bacterial pathogens: Despite of large applications of CRISPR/Cas9 in managing plant virus disease, recently it has also proven to be extremely versatile tool for combating fungal and bacterial pathogens. Rice-pathogenic bacteria *Burkholderia glumae, Burkholderia gladioli,* and *Burkholderia plantarii,* which primarily cause grain rot, sheath rot, and seedling blight, respectively, can severely affects and reduce rice yield potential in all the major rice growing countries. For successful managaemnt of these diseases yet requires comprehensive studies and new tool to control these diseases only in the early stages. Although the genome of *B. plantarii* ATCC 43733T has many related features with those of *B. glumae* and *B. gladioli,* but this *B. plantarii* strain also has some distinctive features, including quorum sensing and CRISPR/CRISPR-associated protein (Cas) systems, signifying that *B. glumae* has evolved rapidly or has undergone rapid genome rearrangements or deletions in response to the host plants. Thus, this rice pathogenic Burkholderia species has unique features relative to other Burkholderia species of plants, animals and humans. The type II bacterial CRISPR/Cas9 system has been used to efficiently disrupt target genes in the smut causing maize pathogen *Ustilago maydis*. The utility of this system was explained successfully by disrupting function of two genes bW2 and bE1 responsible for virulence of *U. maydis* causing smut of maize.

Two years ago TALEN and CRISPR/Cas9 technologies were used successfully to target the mildew-resistance locus O (*MLO*) in wheat, generating plants resistant to powdery mildew disease. GETs were used to generate plants resistant to bacterial leaf blight, caused by *Xanthomonas oryzae* pv. *oryzae*, impairing down the transcriptional regulation of S-genes by the effector and thereby leads to resistance process. Indeed, the plants firmly edited in the *OsSWEET14* promoter were resistant to bacterial strains since the effector was found incapable to activate the transcription of its target. The metabolic pathways that regulate hormonal balance can be customized to enhance the IMC component of plant immunity. This goal was achieved by using GETs to cause the down-regulation of ethylene-responsive factors (*ERF*). In particular, the ethylene pathway in rice was successfully modified by targeting a mutation in OsERF922 using CRISPR/Cas9 technology to increase resistance to rice blast pathogen caused by *Magnaporthe oryzae*.

The CRISPR/Cas9 system has been used to commence targeted mutations in the three homoeoalleles that encode MILDEW-RESISTANCE LOCUS (MLO) proteins in hexaploid bread wheat. The CRISPR/Cas9 also holds potential for generating mlo-type resistance in tomato against powdery mildew and other pathogens. *Pectobacterium atrosepticum*, a plant pathogen that causes soft-rot and blackleg disease in potato, has been used to explore protein-protein interactions and complex formation in the subtype I-F CRISPR/ Cas system including Cas1, Cas3, and the four subtype specific proteins Csy1, Csy2, Csy3 and Cas6f. The CRISPR/Cas9 system and a synthetic sgRNA targeting the CsPDS gene were delivered into sweet orange leaves via agroinfiltration facilitated by pretreatment with *Xanthomonas citri* subsp. *citri* (Xcc) DNA sequencing confirmed that the CsPDS gene was mutated at the target site with efficiency of approximately 3.2-3.9% and without any off-target mutagenesis, suggesting targeted genome modification in citrus using the Cas9/sgRNA system-a system holds considerable promise for the study of citrus gene function and for targeted genetic modification.

Advantages of CRISPR/Cas 9 Technology

The ease, simplicity, a relatively high degree of precision and accessibility of the CRISPR/Cas9 as a new gene editing technology platform offers substantial improvement and advantages over other genome editing methods, on a genomic scale. The main advantages of genome engineering using the CRISPR-Cas9 system can be summarized as:

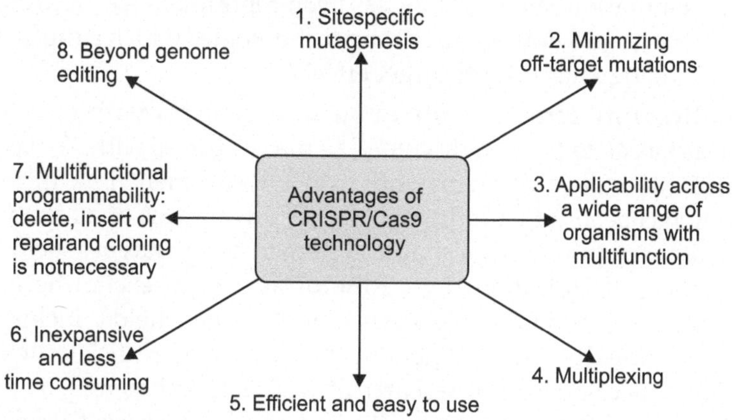

1. Site specific mutagenesis: The CRISPR/Cas 9 is a very versatile and comparatively precise approach to carry out strand-specific cleavage and modification of DNA at specific sites. In CRISPR, RNA-guided Cas9 nucleases use short RNAs to target and cleave DNA elements captured from foreign invaders (termed "spacers") in a sequence-specific manner. To achieve site-specific DNA recognition and cleavage, Cas9 must be complexed with both a CRISPR RNA (crRNA) and a separate trans-acting crRNA (tracrRNA). The specificity is determined by a 20-nucleiotide (nt) sequence within the crRNA, which can be altered to match any desired sequence in the endogenous DNA. Site-specific Cas9 nuclease also allow targeted molecular trait stacking, *i.e.,* the addition of several genes in close vicinity to an existing transgenic locus. Through CRISPR/Cas system it is now feasible to introduce multiple traits into crops with a low risk of segregation, which is difficult to achieve by classical breeding or even conventional genetic engineering. The insertion of large sequences by NHEJ or HR would allow the introduction of transgenes at defined loci that provide high-level transcription and do not hinder with the activity of endogenous genes.

2. Minimizing off-target mutations: To minimize off-target activity, a double nicking strategy can be employed to introduce DSBs at the target site of the genome. Cas9 nuclease is guided by a sgRNA to mediate a DSB at the target locus, e.g., the D10A mutant Cas9 nickase can be specified by a pair of appropriately spaced and oriented sgRNAs to simultaneously introduce single-stranded nicks on both strands of the target DNA. These DSBs from double nicking are then repaired via NHEJ and result in indel formation with similar levels of efficiency to that of WT Cas9. As single-stranded nicks are repaired without indel formation, DSBs would only occur if both sgRNAs are able to locate target sequences within a defined space. Thus, this strategy effectively doubles the number of bases that need to be specifically recognized at the target site and significantly increases the specificity of genome editing. In general, low mutation rate in plants has been reported in CRISPR/Cas system as comparation to previous gene editing technologies which simply indicated that this technology has less off-target effects.

3. Applicability across a wide range of organisms with multifunction: CRISPR/Cas has already been discussed in many species with 33–92% success rate, nutritional values or stress and crop improvement in which genome engineering has been difficult. Irrespective of advantages of a highly efficient mutation rate, it requires only a simple system to design target specific sgRNA. Precise genome modifications by CRISPR/Cas system excite the interest of scientists working in both basic science and applied fields, including gene therapy. Undoubtedly, targeted genome editing using artificial nucleases has the potential to accelerate basic research as well as plant breeding by providing the means to modify genomes rapidly in a precise and predictable manner improving a wide variety of agronomic traits in economically important plants. Particularly, success in genome modification has been noticed among several animal and plant species that are difficult to be modified by other techniques. Earlier, most of the studies have been conducted by using animal systems but during last few years, CRISPR-Cas9 mediated mutagenesis was performed successfully in arabidopsis, sorghum, tobacco, proving applicability of this technique to both dicot and monocot plants.

4. Multiplexing: The main practical advantage of CRISPR/Cas is that it can simultaneously introduce multiple gene disruptions, which allows researchers to edit multiple genes in one plant line through a single transformation without time-consuming which is otherwise difficult to achieve through other gene editing technologies. Multiplex editing induced by CRISPR helps to create allelic variation at quantitative trait loci to modify multiple agronomic traits (quality, yield, disease resistance and abiotic stress tolerance). Through other gene editing technologies like ZFNs and TALENs it is very difficult to obtain multiplexed genes as they needs separate dimeric proteins specific for each target.The simultaneous introduction of DSBs at multiple sites can be used to edit several genes at the same time and can be particularly useful to knock out unnecessary genes effectively. The similar strategy can also be used to engineer large genomic deletions or inversions by targeting two widely spaced cleavage sites on the same chromosome.

5. Efficient and easy to use: CRISPR/Cas9 technique is affordable, easy to use, and importantly it works for high throughput multi-gene experiments. CRISPR also give scientists a precise way to delete and edit specific bits of DNA-even by altering a single base pair. In CRISPR technology, Cas9 can be easily retargeted to new DNA sequences by simply purchasing a pair of oligos encoding the 20-nt guide sequence. Previous genome editing technologies ZFNs and TALEN requires separate dimeric proteins and construction of genes specific for each target which are on the other hand not essential in CRISPR technology. Moreover, Cas9 offers several potential advantages over conventional genome editing technologies, including the ease of customization, higher targeting efficiency and the ability to facilitate multiplex genome editing. Also in old gene editing techniques, cloning of gene is pre-requisitive step, which is not essentially required in CRISPR technology and may be therefore considered as best possible alternative to substitute conventional genome editing technology.

6. Inexpansive and less time consuming: Older genome editing tools, such as ZFNs and TALENs, are slow and expensive due to their use of proteins necessary for findng out the portion of DNA to be cut. Also these techniques are based on the protein-guided recognition mechanism, in which the targeting of a specific DNA sequence requires the modular assembly of pairs of recognition proteins units while the vector system is being constructed, which is time-consuming and tedious work. Due to expensive nature of ZFNs and TALENs, these have not been widely adopted by the plant research community until now. Any number of gRNAs can be produced by *in vitro* transcription using two complementary annealed oligonucleotides. Unlike its predecessors, the CRISPR/Cas9 system does not require any protein engineering steps, making it much more straightforward.This allows the inexpensive assembly of large gRNA libraries so that the CRISPR/Cas9 system can be used for high-throughput functional genomics applications, bringing genome editing within the budget of any molecular biology laboratory. These milestones confirmed that the CRISPR/Cas9 system was a simple, inexpensive and versatile tool for genome editing, which has rightly been become to known as the 'CRISPR craze'.

7. Multifunctional programmability: delete, insert or repair and cloning is not necessary: The advent of CRISPR has now made it feasible to rewrite host DNA by introducing some major modifications. These modifications include gene replacement, deletions, inversion, knockouts, and translocations. Double-strand breaks induced by a nuclease at a specific site can be repaired either by non-homologous end joining (NHEJ) or homologous recombination (HR). Repair by NHEJ typically results in the insertion or deletion of accidental base pairs, causing gene knockout by disruption. If a donor DNA is available, which is simultaneously cut by the same nuclease leaving compatible overhangs, gene insertion by NHEJ can also be achieved. HR with a donor DNA template can be exploited to modify a gene by introducing precise nucleotide substitutions or to achieve gene insertion. The same strategy can also be used to engineer large genomic deletions or inversions by targeting two widely spaced cleavage sites on the same chromosome by targeting both endogenous genes and transgenes and by exploiting both NHEJ and HR to generate small deletions, targeted insertions and multiplex genome modifications.

8. Beyond genome editing: Undoubtedly, the CRISPR/Cas 9 is currently emerging as the most ground-breaking technology for genome editing among scientific community worldwide. The application of CRISPR-Cas9 has now even made it possible to rewrite host DNA by introducing few major alterations in plant genome Regardless of its prospective role in genome editing, the CRISPR/Cas has also found to contribute largely in various field e.g., the ectopic regulation of gene expression, which can provide useful information about gene functions and can also be used to engineer novel genetic regulatory circuits for synthetic biology applications. The accessibility of the CRISPR/Cas9 technology will assist both forward and reverse genetics and will boost basic research even in model species such as Arabidopsis, which already boast extensive (yet incomplete) mutant libraries. Most information concerning the properties of the CRISPR/Cas9 system is currently derived from studies in mammals, and although it assumess that many of the findings can be generalized it is still necessary to conduct similar studies in plants to ensure that system properties are translatable to different species. This surely applies to extended applications such as orthogonal gene targeting, which have yet to be tested in plant systems.

Box 1

Common Terminologies Used in CRISPR/Cas9 Technology

CRISPR- Clustered Regularly Interspaced Short Palindromic Repeats
Cas9 -CRISPR associated protein 9
ZFN-Zinc Finger Nucleases
TALENs- transcription activator-like effector nucleases
PAM -Protospacer Adjacent Motif
crRNA- CRISPR RNA
tracrRNA- Trans acting crRNA
sgRNA- Single guide RNA
HR- Homologous recombination
HDR - Homology directed DNA repair
NHEJ - Non-homologous end-joining
DSBs- Double-strand DNA breaks
Indel - Insertion and/or deletion

Future Aspects

The CRISPR/Cas9 technology presents ***innovative molecular scissors*** for engineering biology and has recently become one the most versatile and dominant platforms. One of the most important aspect of this technology is to allow precisely and predictable multiple genetic changes simultaneously. Although the CRISPR/Cas9 system is an excellent tool for genome editing, but the extent of off-target mutation needs to be explored with high cleavage efficiency among different but perfectly matched targets. However, improvement in this technique could be deployed in the upcoming future to combat deadly phytopathogenic diseases. In this direction research works by various agricultural scientists are in progress and hopefully, we will get the best possible results soon.

Conclusion

The CRISPR/Cas system is an excellent promising tool for genome editing in plants due to its simplicity, efficiency, minimal off-target effects, and high specificity for targeted mutagenesis. It provides a novel platform for resistance activation through continous breeding in crops. Importantly this technique has now been evolved as principal technique that has made it possible to modify host genome by introducing some major modifications. These modifications include gene replacement, deletions, inversion, knockouts, and translocations. The most potential prospects of this technique for producing plants with mutations also contribute greatly to other disciplines of science, *i.e.*, synthetic biology, biofuel production, disease resistance, abiotic stress tolerance, phytoremediation etc. Undoubtedly, CRISPR/Cas9 system can facilitate potent research on genome modifications in crop plants but improvements in sequence specificity and reduction of off-target effects must be corrected, aspects needed to be considered for the design of the gRNA-Cas9 complex. Through this technology recessive resistance could be exploited with the aid of the CRISPR/Cas9 system to create novel resistance alleles in crop plants to protect them against problematic viruses using host translation initiation factors. Another significant attribute of this CRISPR/cas9 system is that it is by far the most user friendly system among all the currently available genome editing techniques. With this powerful and innovative technique, resistance in plants could be advanced which thereby contribute for sustainable agriculture in the future for maximizing yield by combating abiotic and biotic stresses.

REFERENCES

Acevedo-Garcia J, Kusch S, Panstruga R (2014) Magical Mystery Tour: mLO Proteins in Plant Immunity and Beyond. New Phytol 204:273–281.

Ainley WM, Sastry-Dent L, Welter ME, Murray MG, Zeitler B R, Amora *et al* (2013) Trait Stacking via Targeted Genome Editing Plant Biotechnol J 11:11261–134.

Ali Z, Abulfaraj A, Idris A, Ali S, Tashkandi M, Mahfouz MM (2015) CRISPR/Cas9-Mediated Viral Interference in Plants. Genome Biol 16:238.

Ali Z, Ali S, Tashkandi M, Zaidi SS, Mahfouz MM (2016) CRISPR/Cas9-mediated Immunity to Geminiviruses: Differential Interference and Evasion. Sci Rep 6:26912.

Baltes NJ, Hummel AW, Konecna E, Cegan C, Bruns AN, Bisaro DM, *et al* (2015) Conferring Resistance to Geminiviruses with the CRISPR-Cas Prokaryotic Immune System. Nat Plants 1:15145.

Barrangou R, Fremaux C, Deveau H, Richards M, Boyaval P, Moineau S, *et al* (2007) CRISPR Provides Acquired Resistance Against Viruses in Prokaryotes. Science 315:17091–2.

Belhaj K, Chaparro-Garcia, A, Kamoun S, Patron NJ, Nekrasov V (2015) Editing Plant Genomes with CRISPR/Cas9. Curr Opin Biotechnol 32:768–4.

Bolotin A, Quinquis B, Sorokin A, Ehrlich SD (2005) Clustered Regularly Interspaced Short Palindrome Repeats (CRISPRs) have Spacers of Extra Chromosomal Origin. Microbiology 151:25512–561.

Bortesi L, Fischer R (2015). The CRISPR/Cas9 System for Plant Genome Editing and Beyond. *Biotechnol Adv* 33:415–2.

Brouns SJ, Jore MM, Lundgren M, Westra ER, Slijkhuis RJ, Dickman MJ, *et al* (2008) Small CRISPR RNAs Guide Antiviral Defense in Prokaryotes. Science 321:960–964.

Chandrasekaran J, Brumin M, Wolf D, Leibman D, Klap C, Pearlsman M (2016) Development of Broad Virus Resistance in non-transgenic cucumber using CRISPR/Cas9 technology. Mol Plant Pathol 17:11401–153.

Chaparro-Garcia A, Kamoun S, Nekrasov V (2015) Boosting Plant Immunity with CRISPR/Cas. Genome Biol 16: 254.

Cho SW, Kim S, Kim JM, Kim JS (2013) Targeted Genome Engineering in Human Cells with the Cas9 RNA-guided Endonuclease. Nat Biotechnol 31:230–232.

Cong L, Ran FA, Cox D, Lin S, Barretto R, Habib N, Hsu PD, Wu X, Jiang W, Marraffini LA, Zhang F (2013) Multiplex Genome Engineering using CRISPR/Cas Systems. Science 339:8198–23.

Czosnek H, Eybishtz A, Sade D, Gorovits R, Sobol I, Bejarano E, *et al* (2013) Discovering Host Genes Involved in the Infection by the Tomato Yellow Leaf Curl Virus Complex and in the Establishment of Resistance to the virus using Tobaccorattle Virus-based Post Transcriptional Gene Silencing. Viruses 5:9981–022.

Deltcheva E, Chylinski K, Sharma CM, Gonzales K, Chao Y, Pirzada ZA, *et al* (2011) CRISPR RNA Maturation by Trans-Encoded Small RNA and Host Factor RNase III. Nature 1728–4.

Doudna JA, Charpentier E (2014) Genomeediting. The New Frontier of Genome Engineering with CRISPR-Cas9. Science 346:1258096.

Feng Z, Zhang B, Ding W, Liu X, Yang L Y, Wei P, *et al* (2013) Efficient Genome Editing in Plants Using a CRISPR/Cas System. Cell Res 23:12291–232.

Garneau JE, Dupuis ME, Villion M, Romero DA, Barrangou R, Boyaval P, *et al* (2010) The CRISPR/ Cas Bacterial Immune System Cleaves Bacteriophage and Plasmid DNA. Nature 468:6771.

Hale CR, Zhao P, Olson S, Duff MO, Graveley BR, Wells L, Terns RM, Terns MP (2009) RNA-Guided RNA Cleavage by a CRISPR RNA-Cas Protein Complex. Cell 139:9459–56.

Horii T, Hatada I (2014) Genome Engineering using the CRISPR/Cas System.World Journal of Medical Genetics 4(3): 697–6.

Hsu PD, Lander ES, Zhang F (2014) Development and Applications of CRISPR-Cas9 for Genome Engineering. Cell 157:1262–1278.

Iqbal Z, Sattar MN, Shafiq M (2016) CRISPR/Cas9: A Tool to Circumscribe Cotton Leaf Curl Disease. Front Plant Sci 7:475.

Ishino Y, Shinagawa H, Makino K, Amemura M, Nakata A (1987) Nucleotide Sequence of the iap gene, Responsible for Alkaline Phosphatase Isozyme Conversionin *Escherichia coli*, and Identification of the Gene Product. J Bacteriol 169:5429–5433

Jansen R, Embden JD, Gaastra W, Schouls LM (2002) Identification of Genes that are Associated with DNA Repeats in Prokaryotes. Mol Microbiol 43:15651–575.

Ji X, Zhang H, Zhang Y, Wang Y, Gao C (2015) Establishing a CRISPRCas-like Immune System Conferring DNA virus Resistance in Plants. Nat Plants 1:15144.

Jia H, Wang N (2014) Targeted Genome Editing of Sweet Orange Using Cas9/sgRNA. PLoS One 29:e93806.

Jinek M, Chylinski K, Fonfara I, Hauer M, Doudna JA, Charpentier E (2012) A Programmable Dual- RNA-guided DNA Endonuclease in Adaptive Bacterial Immunity. Science 337: 816–821.

Jinek M, Jiang F, Taylor DW, Sternberg SH, Kaya E, Ma E, *et al* (2014) Structures of Cas9 Endonucleases Reveal RNA-mediated Conformational Activation. Science 343(6176):1247997.

Kumar V, Jain M. (2014) The CRISPR–Cas System for Plant Genome Editing: Advances and Opportunities. *J Exp Bot* 66:47–57.

Lellis AD, Kasschau KD, Whitham SA, Carrington JC (2002) Loss-of-susceptibility Mutants of *Arabidopsis thaliana* reveal an Essential Role for eIF (iso) 4E During Potyvirus Infection. Curr Biol 12(02):1046–1051.

Li JF, Norville JE, Aach J, McCormack M, Zhang D, Bush J, *et al* (2013) Multiplex and Homologous Recombination-Mediated Genome Editing in *Arabidopsis* and *Nicotiana benthamiana* Using Guide RNA and Cas9. *Nat Biotechnol* 31:688–691.

Liu D, Chen X, Liu J, Ye J, Guo Z (2012) The rice ERF Transcription Factor OsERF922 Negatively Regulates Resistance to *Magnaporthe oryzae* and Salt Tolerance. J Exp Bot 63:3899–3911.

Mali P, Esvelt KM, Church GM (2013) Cas9 as a Versatile Tool for Engineering Biology. Nat Methods 10:957–963.

MaoY, Zhang, H, Xu N, ZhangB, Gou F, Zhu JK (2013) Application of the CRISPR-Cas System for Efficient Genome Engineering in Plants. Mol Plant 6:2008–2011.

Mojica FJ, Diez-Villasenor C, Garcia-Martinez J, Soria E (2005) Intervening Sequences of Regularly Spaced Prokaryotic Repeats Derive Fromforeign Genetic Elements. J Mol Evol 60(2):174-82.

Mojica FJ, Díez-Villaseñor C, Soria E, Juez G (2000) Biological Significance of a Family of Regularly Spaced Repeats in the Genomes of Archaea, Bacteria and Mitochondria. Mol Microbiol 36:2442–46.

Moose SP, Mumm RH (2008) Molecular Plant Breeding as the Foundation for 21st Century Crop Improvement. Plant Physiol 147: 9699–77.

Nishimasu H, Ran FA, Hsu PD, Konermann S, Shehata SI, Dohmae N, Ishitani R, Zhang F, Nureki O (2014) Crystal Structure of Cas9 in Complex With Guide RNA and Target DNA. Cell 156:935–949.

Noman A, Aqeel M, He S (2016) CRISPR-Cas9: Tool for Qualitative and Quantitative Plant Genome Editing. *Front. Plant Sci.* 7:1740.

Pennisi E (2013). The CRISPR Craze. Science 341:833–836.

Price AA, Sampson TR, Ratner HK, Grakoui A, Weiss DS (2015) Cas9-mediated Targeting of Viral RNA in Eukaryotic Cells. Proc Natl Acad Sci U S A 112:6164–6169.

Puchta H, Fauser F (2013) Gene Targeting in Plants: 25 Years Later. Int J Dev Biol 57:629–637.

Pyott DE, Sheehan E, Molnar A (2016) Engineering of CRISPR/Cas9-mediated Potyvirus Resistance in Transgene-free *Arabidopsis* Plants. Mol Plant Pathol 17:1276–1288.

Ran FA, Hsu PD, Wright J, Agarwala V, Scott DA, Zhang F (2013) Genome Engineering using the CRISPR-Cas9 System. Nat. Protoc. 8:2281–2308.

Richter C, Gristwood T, Clulow JS, Fineran PC (2012) *In vivo* Protein Interactions and Complex Formation in the *Pectobacterium atrosepticum* Subtype I-F CRISPR/Cas System. PLoS ONE 7:e49549.

Romay G, Bragard C (2017) Antiviral Defenses in Plants Through Genome Editing. Front Microbiol 8: p. 47.

Schaeffer SM, Nakata PA (2015) CRISPR-Mediated Genome Editing and Gene Replacement in Plants: Transitioning from Lab to Field. Plant Sci 240:130–142.

Schuster M, Schweizer G, Reissmann S, Kahmann R (2015) Genome Editing in *Ustilago maydis* Using the Crispr-cas System. Fungal Genet Biol 89:3–9.

Seo YS, Lim JY, Park J, Kim S, Lee HH, Cheong H, Kim SM, Moon JS, Hwang I (2015) Comparative Genome Analysis of Rice-Pathogenic Burkholderia Provides Insight into Capacity to Adapt to Different Environments and Hosts. BMC Genom 16:349.

Song J, Yang D, Xu J, Zhu T, Chen YE, Zhang J (2016) RS-1 Enhances CRISPR/Cas9- and TALEN-mediated Knock-in Efficiency. Nat Commun 7:10548.

Sorek R, Lawrence CM, Wiedenheft B (2013) CRISPR-mediated Adaptive Immune Systems in Bacteria and Archaea. Annu Rev Biochem 82:237–266.

Sternberg SH, Redding S, Jinek M, Greene EC, Doudna JA (2014) DNA Interrogation by the CRISPR RNA-Guided Endonuclease Cas9. Nature 507:62–67.

Sugano SS, Shirakawa M, Takagi J, Matsuda Y, Shimada T, Hara-Nishimura I, Kohchi T (2014) CRISPR/Cas9-mediated Targeted Mutagenesis in the Liverwort *Marchantia polymorpha* L. Plant Cell Physiol 55:475–481.

Upadhyay SK, Kumar J, Alok A, Tuli R (2013) RNA-Guided Genome Editing for Target Gene Mutations in Wheat. G 33: 2233–2238.

Wang F, Wang C, Liu P, Lei C, Hao W, Gao Y, Liu YG, Zhao K (2016) Enhanced Rice Blast Resistance by CRISPR/Cas9-targeted Mutagenesis of the ERF Transcription Factor Gene OsERF922.PLoS One 11: e0154027.

Wang Y, Cheng X, Shan Q, Zhang Y, Liu J, Gao C, Qiu JL (2014) Simultaneous Editing of Three Homoeoalleles in Hexaploid Bread Wheat Confers Heritable Resistance to Powdery Mildew. Nat Biotechnol 32:947–951.

Xing HL, Dong L, Wang Z P, Zhang HY, Han CY, Liu B (2014) A CRISPR/Cas9 Toolkit for Multiplex Genome Editing in Plants. BMC Plant Biol. 14:327.

Yang CF, Chen KC, Cheng YH, Raja JAJ, Huang YL, Chien WC, *et al* (2014) Generation of Marker-Free Transgenic Plants Concurrently Resistant to a DNA Geminivirus and a RNA Tospovirus. Sci Rep 4:5717.

Zetsche B, Gootenberg JS, Abudayyeh OO, Slaymaker, IM, Makarova KS, Essletzbichler P, *et al* (2015) Cpf1isasingleRNA-Guidedendonucleaseofa Class 2CRISPR-Cassystem. Cell 163:759–771

Zhou H, Liu B, Weeks DP, Spalding MH,Yang B (2014) Large Chromosomal Deletions and Heritable Small Genetic Changes Induced by CRISPR in Rice. Nucleic Acids Res 42:10903–10914.

Plant Physiology : *Stress, Diseases and Management* **Pages 143-191**
Edited by: **Mr. Prasann Kumar; Dr. Pawan Kumar 'Bharti'**
ISBN: 978-93-88854-00-9
Edition: **2019**
Published by: **Discovery Publishing House Pvt. Ltd., New Delhi (India)**

7 Potential and Existing Uses of Alternative Methods to Manage Post Harvest Diseases

[1]Madhu Prakash Srivastava

The world today is characterized by an exponential growth in population. The prospects are that the world population will increase to 8.3 billion in 2025. This rapid urbanization also leads to industrialization as well as pollution. Though, there are claims that food production has also increased but at the same time there are reports of depletion of our natural resources. If this trend continues unchanged, there is almost a unanimous consensus that the limits to growth on this planet will be reached sometime within the next one hundred years. The most probable result will be a rather a sudden and uncontrollable decline in both, population and industrial capacity, however, this doomsday scenario will materialize only if our present way of doing thing will not improve. Since there are ample evidence of mankind's ingenuity and social flexibility, we can safely assume that it is possible to alter these growth trends and to establish a condition of ecological and economic stability that is sustainable far into the future. To ensure sufficient food, both in quantity and in quality to every inhabitant, native ecosystems are being rapidly converted to human use, destroying forests, soil and native plants and animals. To produce sufficient food, commercial and subsistence farming systems must be highly productive, but sustainable and nonpolluting (Sharma and Prabha, 2012).

Time and money are required to cultivate food products, and unless the farmer is providing food only for his own household, he automatically becomes part of the market economy, he must sell his produce, he must recover his costs, and he must make a profit. Economics of crop production, economics of losses caused by a disease in a specific situation, and ease and cost of applying disease management methods determine the level of intervention that a farmer is willing to commit to realize gains from farming.

Losses due to post harvest diseases, a general phenomenon, are a matter of grave concern for agriculture sector. This is happening in almost every developing country. Approximately half of the population in the Third World

[1] Department of Botany, University of Lucknow, Lucknow-226 007, Uttar Pradesh, India

does not have access to adequate food supplies. There are many reasons for this, one of which is food losses occurring in the post-harvest and marketing system. It is estimated that over 25% of our harvested food in the United States is lost to postharvest spoilage. In developing countries these losses can run over 50%. A study was conducted by a committee of the United States National Research Council, on, *"Postharvest Food Losses in Developing Countries"*. The committee extrapolated from apparent loss-patterns and expected production trends and projected post-harvest food-losses to be at minimum, 47,000,000 metric tons of durable crops and 60,000,000 metric tons of perishable crops. The average minimum losses reported for roots and tubers and fruits and vegetables were 16 per cent and 21 per cent respectively; many more 'qualitative' references, not included here, indicate estimates of 40- 50 per cent and above. Globally, postharvest fruit and vegetable losses have been reported at 19% for the USA at an estimated annual loss of $ 18 billion. Higher losses have been reported for African countries ranging between 15%-30% of the harvested product. Both quantitative and qualitative food losses of extremely variable magnitude occur at all stages in the post-harvest system from harvesting, through handling, storage, processing and marketing to final delivery to the consumer. An additional constraint to improving this situation is that in most developing countries including India, the number of scientists concerned with post-harvest food losses is significantly lower than those involved in production research.

All fruits, vegetables and root crops are living plant parts containing 65 to 95 percent water, and they continue their living processes after harvest. Their post-harvest life depends on the rate at which they use up their stored food reserves and their rate of water loss. When food and water reserves are exhausted, the produce dies and decays. Factors affecting post-harvest food losses of perishables vary widely from place to place and become more and more complex as systems of marketing become more complicated. The principal causes of loss are *physiological deterioration*, insect infestations, unwanted microbial growth, injuries and blemishes due to improper handling or transportation and lack of technology and infrastructure.

Abnormal physiological deterioration occurs when fresh produce is subjected to extremes of temperature, of atmospheric modification or of contamination. This may cause unpalatable flavors, failure to ripen or other changes in the living processes of the produce, making it unfit for use. *Mechanical damage (physical injury)* due to careless handling of fresh produce causes internal bruising, which results in abnormal physiological damage or splitting and skin breaks, thus rapidly increasing water loss and the rate of normal physiological breakdown. Skin breaks also provide sites for infection by disease organisms causing decay.

Fresh produce can become infected before or after harvest by diseases widespread in the air, soil and water. Some diseases are able to penetrate the unbroken skin of produce; others require an injury in order to cause infection. Fruits due to their high sugar content are very susceptible to attack by microorganisms. Eckert and Ratnayake in 1983 estimated that out of 100,000 species of fungi, less than 10% are plant pathogens and more than 100 species of fungi are responsible for the majority of postharvest diseases.

Chemical pesticides are commonly used for the control of many such plant diseases and pests. The application of effective fungicides just prior to or shortly after harvest generally controls postharvest decay. About 23 million kg of fungicides are applied to fruits and vegetables annually, and it is generally accepted that production and marketing of these perishable products would not be possible without their use. Some of the problems associated with using pesticides include failure of pest control, contamination of the environment, and damage to human health However, use has also been restricted due to their carcinogenicity, teratogenicity, high and acute residual toxicity, long degradation period, environmental pollution, effects on food and on humans (Unnikrishnan and Nath, 2002).

Resistance to pesticides is the main cause in which pesticide use can lead to pest control failure. Resistance develops in pest populations through the differential survival of members of the pest population that best detoxify or avoid exposure to the pesticide. Over several generations, pest populations may develop that can no longer easily be killed by one or more pesticides. Since 1945, the number of insects, weeds, and, most recently, plant pathogens that have become resistant to pesticides has increased dramaticall. Another way in which pesticide use can foster outbreaks of pests is the destruction of the target pest's natural enemies. Most pesticides kill natural enemies, which often are more sensitive to the pesticide than is the pest itself. Concern over these issues has prompted some countries to seek to reduce pesticide use.

Food Quality Protection Act (FQPA) in the US; Food and Environment Protection Act (FEPA) 1985 and Control of Substances Hazardous to Health (COSHH) Regulations 1988, made under the Health and Safety at Work Act 1974 in the UK are the guiding force in the regulation of pesticides. Several countries have implemented their own specific policies to reduce pesticide use. Similarly, fruit industries worldwide have accepted the concept of integrated fruit production (IFP). IFP aims to produce high-quality fruit in harmony with the consumer and environment. This implies minimum usage of chemicals, especially after harvest (Sharma *et al.*, 2011).

Globally, greater restrictions on pesticides use in the developed nations have resulted in increasing trends for natural, non-chemical or organic approaches to disease control. Understandably, alternatives to chemical pesticides or products that allow reduced usage in terms of fewer or reduced rates of application are beginning to appear on the market. A part of the solution to this problem is biological control, the foundation on which sustainable, nonpolluting pest control for tomorrow's farms must be built.

Postharvest Treatments

"Market Pathology", a term given by Powell in 1906 has changed its emphasis in recent years. Food safety has emerged as a key element in decay control programs. Continued failure to effectively control certain postharvest disease and the need for more environmentally friendly crop control material is driving a new approach to disease control. Integrated postharvest decay control is the concept that offers the most promise for the future. Society can no longer rely on one or two control strategies but must enlist the entire spectrum of strategies to reduce postharvest losses. Products and methods used for postharvest decay control should only be used after the following critical points are considered:

- Type of pathogen involved in the decay.
- Location of the pathogen in the produce.
- Best time for application of the treatment.
- Maturity of the host.
- Environment during storage, transportation and marketing of produce.

Specific methods are selected based on these conditions. In general, these alternatives could be divided into physical, chemical and biological control. Some of them have direct effects on the pathogens but others may act indirectly by increasing fruit resistance to the pathogens or retarding senescence. In this review we discuss various combinations of these treatments with biological control on fruits after harvest.

PHYSICAL TREATMENT

Heat Treatments

Heat treatment before storage has been shown to beneficially affect fruit quality. Heat disinfection requires products to be heated to a specified core temperature for a defined period of time. The commodities are heated via energy transfer from a heating medium, which is either air or water. Water is the preferred medium for most applications since it is more efficient heat transfer medium than air. Heat may be applied to fruit and vegetables by hot water dips, hot water rinsing and brushing, hot dry air or by vapor heat (steam). Heat treatment eliminates incipient infections. Heat may also inhibit pathogen spread by inducing defense mechanisms in the outer layers of epicarp. Heat treatments can also be used to inhibit ripening processes, induce resistance to chilling injury (CI) and external skin damage during storage, thus extending storability and marketing (Paull and Chen, 2000). Natural openings and barely-visible cracks in the epidermis of treated fruit were partially or entirely sealed with rearranged natural wax components present on the cuticle, thus limiting sites of fungal penetration into the fruit (Porat *et al.*, 2000). This sealing of cracks or natural openings significantly reduced weight loss, thus maintained fruit firmness after prolonged storage (Hic *et al.*, 2001). Hot water treatments of fruits do not pose significant health risk as from chemical residues and as a result, are more appealing to consumers (Singh and Thakur, 2002). The primary obstacle to the widespread use of heat to control postharvest fruit diseases or insect infestation is the sensitivity of many fruit to the temperatures required for effective treatment.

Hot Water Dipping

The use of hot water treatments (HWT) was one of the earliest non-chemical methods of control investigated to reduce postharvest decay. Hot water treatments have several advantages which include relative ease of use, short treatment time; reliable easy monitoring leaves no chemical residue on the fruit surface and pathogens may be eradicated even after they have entered the fruit. Hot water treatment of fruits and vegetables to control postharvest pathogens are usually applied at temperatures above 40°C.

Research done in 1922 indicated that brown rot caused by *Phytophtora* spp. on lemons was prevented by dipping the fruit for 2 min in water at 46–49°C . Peaches inoculated with *Metschnikowia fructicola* to control *Rhizopus stolonifer* were dipped for 7 min at 49°C, 3 min at 54°C or 2 min at 60°C, either 1 or 24 h after inoculation, had approximately 70% less decay than non-treated peaches after 2–6 days.

Fig. 7.1: Effect of hot water treatment to control blue mold of apple (*in vivo*)

In addition, genetic differences among fungi result in a great deal of variation in their sensitivity to high temperature. *M. fructicola*, for instance, is more heat sensitive than *P. expansum*. In 'Spartan' and 'Golden Delicious' apples exposed to 38°C for 4–6 days and then stored at –1°C for 4–7 months, fruit softening was suppressed and naturally occurring decay, largely due to *Corticium* and *Penicillium* sp., was reduced. Similarly, exposure at 40°C for 2–4 days maintained firmness of stored 'Golden Delicious' fruits. In addition, Klein *et al.*(1990) found that the best heat treatment for 'Anna' and 'Granny Smith' apples was exposure to 38°C for 4 days. Later work indicated that heating 'Golden Delicious' apples inoculated with *Penicillium expansum* for 4 days at 38°C completely inhibited decay development. These workers concluded that the effect of heating on fruit decay caused by *P. expansum* is not only a result of direct inhibition of fungal germination and growth by high temperature, but the formation of an antifungal substance in the heated peel may also play a role. (Janisiewicz and Conway, 2010)

Hot Water Rinsing and Brushing

In addition to hot water dipping, a more recent technology, hot water brushing (HWRB) has shown promise (Fallik *et al.* 2008). This technique involves hot water rinsing and brushing to clean and disinfect freshly harvested produce. Treatment time is kept no longer than 30 s at temperatures between 48 and 53°C (Fallik, 2004). Fresh produce is rinsed with pressurized hot water by nozzles from above while rolling on brushes made from soft synthetic bristles, which tends to clean and disinfest the produce. Treating stone fruits with HWRB at 60°C for 20 s and then dipping them into a cell suspension of the antagonistic yeast *Candida* spp. (10^8 CFU/mL) 24 h after inoculation with *P. expansum* reduced decay development on stone fruits by 60% compared with the controls (Karabulut *et al.*, 2002).

Air

Forced hot air heating (FHAT) and vapor heat treatment (VHT) are the two methods where air becomes the medium for heat transfer. FHAT also known as non conditioning air heating, the heating of fruit is carried out by passing air held at specified temperature through a bed of fruit. The heat moves from the warm air to the cooler fruit by conduction via the skin. Heat rapidly transfers towards the center of the fruit. On the other side VHT involves heating air that is nearly saturated with moisture and passing the air stream across the product. The difference between VHT and FHAT is that the fruit surfaces remain dry during forced air treatment compared to condensation on the fruit surface during VHT. Early work with strawberries revealed that exposure to hot air at 43°C for 30 min at a relative humidity of 98% or 60 min at 90% relative humidity effectively reduced postharvest decay during 4 subsequent days at 16°C.

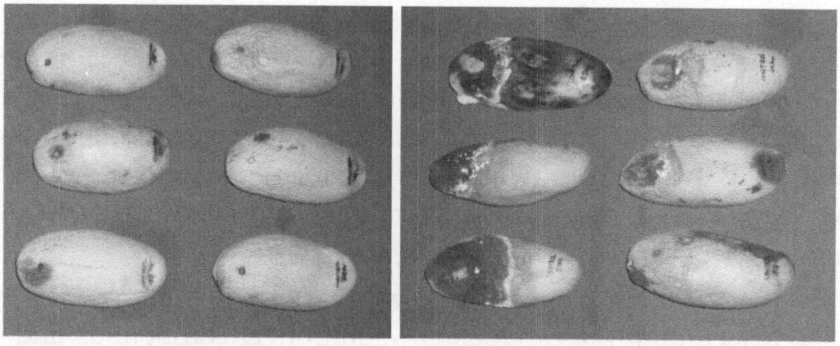

Fig. 7.2. Effect of hot air heating (FHAT) and vapor heat treatment (VHT) on mango against *Aspergillus* niger. (Sharma *et al.*, 2011)

Vapor (steam)

A strategy for postharvest control of black root rot (BRR) of mango caused by *Theilaviopsis basicola,* combined steam heat using a steam pressure of 4 bar (maximal produce surface temperature was measured at 85°C. (Eshel *et al.*, 2009). After treatment, the mango were stored for 1 month at 0.5°C and then transferred to a shelf-life simulation room at 20°C for 8 days.

Treatment of mango with Shemer before storage did not affect BRR disease incidence but steam reduced the incidence of decay by approximately 47% during the shelf-life period after cold storage. Applying *M. fructicola* after a 3 s exposure of the mango to steam resulted in a synergistic effect that reduced BRR decay by 86%. It was concluded that the improved efficacy of *M. fructicola* might be the result of either pathogen weakening or induced resistance in heat-treated mango tissue (Karabulut *et al.*, 2002).

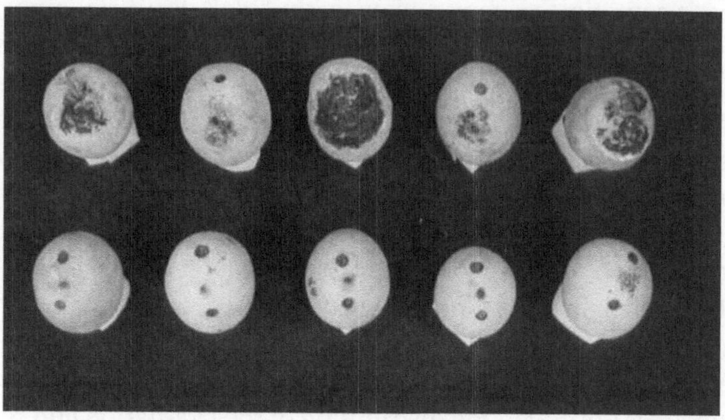

Fig. 7.3: Effect of stream on the mango fruits to control black rot

Ultraviolet Light

Fungi, like all organisms are exposed to the natural radiation of environment. These radiations may be damaging, beneficial or innocuous depending the nature of the fungus and the nature of the radiation. Radiation has lethal effects on spore germination in several fungi. More recently, low doses of ultraviolet light irradiation (254 nm UV-C) reduced postharvest brown rot of peaches and Penicillium rot of Indian Gooseberry (personal communication). In this case, the low dose ultraviolet light treatments had two effects on brown rot development; reduction in the inoculum of the pathogen and induced resistance in the host.

When the fruits are exposed to low doses of UV a number of changes are induced including the production of antifungal compounds and delays ripening. A new terminology called 'hormesis' was introduced, which is the application of potentially harmful agents at low doses to living organisms in order to induce stress responses. Non-ionizing UV irradiation, although low in energy and lacking penetrating power, affects a wide range of biological processes and has been reported to stimulate numerous plant responses. There are two possible explanations by which storage rot of fruits and vegetables could be reduced following treatment with UV -C light: first being the germicidal effect on pathogens found on the surface of fruits and vegetables, second, low dose UV-C hornesis was shown to induce resistance in post-harvest commodities to harvest decay and to extend shelf life of fruits by delaying the ripening and senescence process (Sharma and Alderson, 2005). Because the UV wave lengths employed to elicit hermetic effects are strongly absorbed by the DNA of living organisms, consideration must be given to the possibility that the UV doses delivered to fruit can directly inactivate fungi or fungal spores that may be present at the surface of the fruit. Indeed the wavelength range in question is sometimes referred to as 'germicidal'. Fruit ripening, like other development processes, is under the control of plant growth regulators of which ethylene plays a key role, however polyamines have also been implicated in the control of ripening. Delay of ripening by UV treatment has been reported in peaches (Stevens *et al.*, 1998) and this was associated with enhanced activity of phenyalanine ammnia layase (PAL) and suppression of ethylene production. The induced resistance appears to be stronger and longer lasting in plant storage organs such as sweet potatoes, carrots or potatoes (Stevens *et al.*, 2004) than in fruits such as apple, peach, citrus fruits, grapes or tomato, although significant reductions in postharvest decay have been observed among these fruits after UV treatment (Stevens *et al.*, 2005). Using UV-C lamps above and below a conveyer improved the distribution of the irradiation and reduced the variation in fruit response to the treatment (Stevens *et al.*, 2006).

However, maximum UV doses are limited ultimately by induction of undesirable changes like skin discoloration, increasing susceptibility to rot and premature ripening.

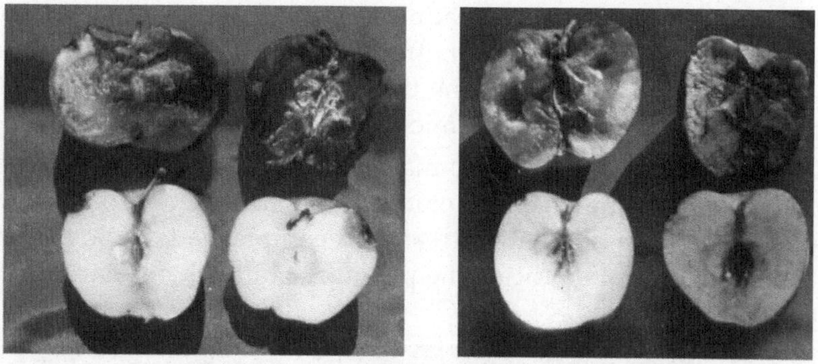

Fig. 7.4. Effect of UV-C treatment to control Penicillium rot of apple

Gamma Radiation

Gamma radiation has been studied for controlling decay, disinfestations, and extending the storage and shelf-life of fresh fruits and vegetables. Commercial application of gamma radiation is limited due to the cost and size of equipment needed for the treatment and to uncertainty about the acceptability of irradiated foods to the consumer. Gamma irradiation may be used more in the future once methyl bromide is no longer available to control insect infestation in stored products. All uses of methyl bromide are being phased out to avoid any further damage to the protective layer of ozone surrounding the earth.

Microwaves

The feasibility of using microwaves to kill different pests on harvested commodities has been explored for almost two decades. It was shown to be promising for the eradication of a quarantine pest, codling moth, on sweet cherry. The larvae of this pest reside and feed in the centre of the fruit and microwaves can raise the temperature to the desired level in the centre of the fruit quickly. The quality of fruits treated with the microwaves was comparable to untreated controls or fruits treated with methyl bromide.

Two microwave frequencies have been approved by the United States Federal Communication Commission for heating application, 915 and 2,450 MHz. The 915 MHz microwaves have higher energy and penetrate more deeply in fruits and vegetables than 2,450 MHz (Janisiewicz and Conway, 2010) The 2,450 MHz microwave (used in kitchen type microwave ovens) has been successfully used to control postharvest grey mould and blue mould of peaches caused by *B. cinerea* and *P. expansum,* respectively, under laboratory conditions (Karabulut and Baykal, 2002). Treatment of peaches with 2,450 MHz microwave for 2 min followed by the application of an antagonist, *C. laurentii,* reduced decay incidence caused by *R. stolonifer* to 23.7% compared with 95% decay in the control, to 75% when using the antagonist alone, and to 42.1% after microwave treatments alone (Zhang *et al.*, 2004). Microwave treatments did not harm the fruits. Similar treatments on pears reduced the incidence of blue mould, caused by *P. expansum*, from 100% in the control to 72.6% after microwave treatment, to 65.5% using the antagonist only, and 20.2% after the combination of the antagonist and microwave treatments.

The treatments did not impair major fruit quality indices (Zhang *et al.*, 2006). Microwave treatments have eradicative activity but impart no residual protection. Again, the alternative treatment complements biological control, which generally cannot eradicate the pathogens but has persistent protective activity.

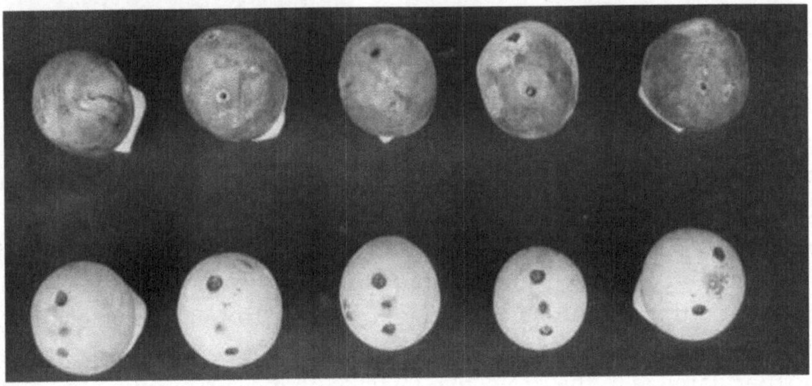

Fig. 7.5: Effect of microwave treatment to control rot of mango

Controlled or Modified Atmosphere

Generally, harvested produce has more resistance to infection by potential pathogens earlier in their postharvest life, and as fruits and vegetables ripen and senesce, they become more susceptible. Therefore, delaying ripening also delays the time at which produce becomes more susceptible to decay, thus prolonging their storage life. CA or modified atmosphere (MA) has been found to be effective in delaying the onset of ripening and senescence in stored fruits and vegetables, with much of the initial research done on apples

Majority of research work is related to low temperature storage with combination of coatings and packaged in polyethylene or carton having ethylene absorbents had a very positive. Effect on not only external appearance of these fruits but also help to reduce weight loss and respiration rate resulting in considerable extension in shelf life of fruit. The low temperature and controlled atmosphere storage technique have no doubt to increase the shelf life of fruits but these are cosdy one and out of reach of common farmer or producer.

Alterations in ozone and carbon-di-oxide concentrations are sometimes provided around fruit and vegetables. With close control of these gases, the synthetic atmosphere is commonly called a controlled atmosphere; the term modified atmosphere is used when there is little possibility of adjusting composition during storage or transportation. Because the pathogen respires as does produce, lowering the O_2 or raising the CO_2 above 5% can suppress pathogenic growth in the host. In crops such as stone fruits, a direct suppression occurs when fungal respiration and growth are reduced by the high CO_2 of the modified atmosphere. Other technologies that have been tested for lowering postharvest decay with limited success have been storage and transport under low O_2 and the use of carbon monoxide.

Ozone

Ozone has traditionally been used as a water disinfectant throughout the world. It can also be used to reduce fungal spore contamination in water used for handling fruits and vegetables in packinghouses, and therefore reduce new infections (Smilanick *et al.*, 2002). Ozonated water, however, is not effective in controlling infections from wounds on pears or citrus fruits inoculated before ozone treatment (Smilanick, 2003). An ozone atmosphere causes abnormal development of fungal colonies and greatly reduces germination of the detached spores depending on the species. Ozone at 0.3–1.0 ppm in air retarded production of fungal spores and slightly reduced the rate of decay by major fruit pathogens such as *B. cinerea, Mucor piriformis, P. expansum, Penicillium digitatum and Penicillium italicum* on strawberries, grapes, peaches, and citrus fruits (Palou *et al.*, 2002). By inhibiting spore production ozone can reduce the number of spores in the packinghouse atmosphere and thereby effectively reduces the number of infection cycles, especially on citrus fruits (Smilanick, 2003). Ozone treatment at 0.1 mg/g significantly reduced populations of filamentous fungi, yeasts and bacteria on the berry surface of table grapes after exposure for 1 min, and by more than 90% after 10 min in most cases. This could negatively affect biocontrol agents applied to the surface of the fruit. However, the application of the biocontrol agent *Muscodor albus,* which produces inhibitory volatiles, in tea bags placed in grape cluster bags, reduced decay incidence on berries artificially infected with *B. cinerea* from 91.7% (control) to 21.2%. The ozone treatment alone or in combination with *M. albus* reduced incidence of decay to 19.3% or 10.1%, respectively (Micota *et al.*, 2010). A rye culture of *M. albus* in the tea bags survived the ozone treatment, indicating that this treatment can be applied before or after ozone treatment. This makes integration of ozone and *M. albus* easily achievable. On organically grown grapes, where the natural incidence of grey mould was 31%, treatment with a combination of *M. albus* and ozone reduced decay incidence to 3.4%, which was a greater reduction than either treatment alone, after 1 month of storage at 0.5ºC. In this combination of treatments, ozone effectively sanitised grapes and reduced the amount of inoculum residing on the fruit surface, while *M. albus* provided long lasting suppression of grey mould that developed from incipient infections which resided inside the berries and were protected from the killing action of ozone, but the durability of this induction was not investigated. Ozone treatment also reduced decay on mango inoculated with *R. stolonifer* before or after treatment with ozone, indicating a possible induction of resistance in berries.

CHEMICAL TREATMENTS

Bicarbonate and Carbonate Salts

SBC ($NaHCO_3$, baking soda) and sodium carbonate (SC) (Na_2CO_3, soda ash) are common food additives allowed with no restrictions and are generally regarded as safe (GRAS) by the United States Food and Drug Administration. They have also been found to be useful in controlling plant pathogens, and for many years have been especially useful in the citrus industry (Porat *et al.*, 2003). A 90% reduction in blue mould caused by *P. italicum* in oranges occurred when fruits were treated with a 3 or 4% SC solution at 45°C. SBC applied at room temperature at 2–4% reduced decay caused by *P. italicum* by more than 50% (Palou *et al.*, 2001). The effect of the SBC and SC treatments is primarily fungistatic because the fungal spores were not killed and spore germination was only delayed. Germinating spores seem to be more readily killed by SBC than nongerminating spores. A 2% SBC solution killed germinating *P. digitatum* spores in citrus wounds. Control of green mould caused by *P. digitatum* was significantly improved by following treatment with a 3% SBC or SC solution with applications of the antagonist *Pseudomonas syringae* strain ESC 10 (the active ingredient in BioSave 10; Jet Harvest Solution, Longwood, FL). Several isolates of *Bacillus subtilis* were evaluated for control of green mould and blue mould on citrus fruits. While one of the antagonist isolates or SBC alone reduced decay to 10–20%, the combination resulted in complete control of both diseases (Obagwu *et al.*, 2002).

Control of *P. expansum* and *Alternaria alternata* on pears was significantly increased when the antagonist's *C. laurentii* or *Trichosporon pullulans* were combined with 2% SBC (Yao *et al.*, 2004). *C. laurentii*, with and without SBC, provided more effective control of both pathogens than *T. pullulans*, and in combination with SBC, completely eliminated *A. alternate* decay on pears. The antagonist *Pantoea agglomerans* CPA-2 combined with SC and SBC reduced incidence of green mould from approximately 90% among control oranges to 55% and 25%, respectively after treatment with SC and SC + the antagonist, and 60% and 40%, respectively after treatment SBC and SBC + the antagonist (Usall *et al.*, 2008). A 2% solution of SBC combined with *M. pulcherrima* significantly reduced blue mould of apple fruits caused by *P. expansum*. However, there was no significant effect when SBC was combined with *C. laurentii* although the combination tended to result in smaller lesions (Conway *et al.*, 2005). In a pilot test, 'Golden Delicious" apples were wound-inoculated with *P. expansum* and treated with various combinations of SBC and two antagonists (*M. pulcherrima*,

C. laurentii) and stored in CA (1.5% O_2 and 2.0% CO_2) (Janisiewicz *et al.*, 2010). SBC alone reduced decay but was much more effective when combined with the antagonists. In combining SBC or SC with any antagonist, it is important that the antagonist is compatible with the carbonate solution and able to proliferate in fruit wounds in their presence.

Fig. 7.6: Effect of Bicarbonate and carbonate salts to control decay on apple

Calcium

Postharvest decay caused by fungal pathogens in apples was reduced by applications of calcium solutions. This early work involved active infiltration, either by pressure or vacuum infiltration, of $CaCl_2$ solutions directly into apple fruits. In this case, the mechanism by which increased tissue calcium reduces decay and maintains firmness may be related to calcium ions in the cell wall. Calcium-induced resistance to fungal pathogens is attributed to a process making the cell wall less accessible to fruit-softening enzymes or to cell wall degrading enzymes produced by fungal pathogens. Therefore; calcium reduces decay mainly by increasing resistance of the fruit rather than any direct effect on the pathogen. In a study emphasising this type of resistance mechanism and showing the beneficial effect of combining calcium solutions and biocontrol, apple fruits were pressure infiltrated (10^3 kPa, 3 min) with a 4% solution of $CaCl_2$, stored for 6 months at 1°C, and then wound inoculated with *P. expansum* or with *P. expansum* plus the antagonist *P. syringae*. The antagonist alone reduced the incidence of decay by approximately 40% while fruits treated with calcium alone had 53% less decay. Fruits treated with both the antagonist and the calcium solution had 88% less decay than the untreated apples. More recently, research has emphasized the direct effect of calcium solutions by inhibiting spore germination and growth study was conducted to determine the effect of salt solutions combined with yeast antagonists (*Candida* sp.) in reducing postharvest decay of apples caused by *B. cinerea* and *P. expansum*. Fruit wounds were treated with a suspension of *Candida* sp. in

0–2% solutions of $CaCl_2$ and then inoculated with either of the two pathogens. Biological control of both pathogens was enhanced when wounds were treated with the antagonist in a 2% solution of $CaCl_2$. The effect of calcium on the biocontrol effectiveness of these strains of *Candida* sp. was thought to result from an interaction by the pathogen with the yeast or its metabolic products in the wound site. Another study, also indicating that calcium reduces fungal infection through direct inhibition of fungal spore germination and growth, was conducted using 2% calcium solution, two antagonistic yeasts, *Candida guilliermondii* and *Pichia membranefaciens,* and *R. stolonifer* causing decay on peach and nectarine fruits (Tian *et al.*, 2002). The addition of calcium resulted in lower spore germination rates and slower growth of germ tubes *in vitro,* as well as in lower disease incidence and smaller lesion diameters compared with the yeast antagonists alone. The addition of the calcium solution also allowed the use of lower concentrations of the antagonist without reducing control achieved with the antagonist alone at the higher concentration. Similarly, the two antagonistic yeasts, *Candida guilliermondii* and *Pichia membranefaciens,* in combination with a 2% calcium solution were evaluated for the control of apple decay caused by *P. expansum* (Gholamnejad *et al.*, 2009). Results were similar to the previous study (Tian *et al.*, 2002) in that the addition of the calcium solution resulted in lower spore germination rates and slower germ tube growth *in vitro,* as well as in lower disease incidences and severity compared with the yeast treatment alone.

An investigation was undertaken to evaluate the antagonist *C. laurentii* for its activity in reducing postharvest grey mould of pear caused by *B. cinerea* (Zhang *et al.*, 2005). Suspensions of *C. laurentii* at concentrations of 10^6–10^9 CFU/mL were prepared in distilled water or in 2% $CaCl_2$ solutions. The suspensions were applied into fruit wounds followed by inoculation with *B. cinerea.* The efficacy of *C. laurentii* was significantly enhanced by the addition of the calcium solution which allowed a reduction in the antagonist concentration from 10^9 CFU/mL to 10^8 CFU/mL without reducing control of the decay (Tian *et al.*, 2002). Another study was designed to evaluate the feasibility of the combined application of an antagonist, *Aureobasidium pullulans,* and 1% $CaCl_2$ in controlling naturally occurring postharvest decay of sweet cherry (Ippolito *et al.*, 2005). These naturally occurring decays were mainly caused by *B. cinerea, A. alternata* and *Monilinia laxa.* Using postharvest dips of cherry in a calcium solution or the antagonist, the calcium treatment reduced decay incidence by up to 33%, the antagonist alone by up to 44% and the combination of the calcium solution and the antagonist reduced decay incidence by up to 70%. Once again, it was concluded that the addition of the calcium solution directly inhibited the pathogens and enabled the antagonist to better compete with the pathogens. The biocontrol activity of *P. membranifaciens* against anthracnose rot caused by *C. acutatum* on loquat fruits was enhanced by the addition of the 2% calcium solution and resulted in significantly improved decay control compared with treatment by the antagonist or calcium alone (Cao *et al.*, 2008). In addition, a combination of the antagonist with the 2% $CaCl_2$ solution induced higher activities of two defence related enzymes, chitinase and β-1,3-glucanase, and inhibited spore germination and germ tube elongation of *C. acutatum* more than the antagonist or $CaCl_2$ alone. The addition of $CaCl_2$ also enhanced the efficacy of a series of antagonists in controlling postharvest decay of table grapes (Ligorio *et al.*, 2008). In all of the above studies, the calcium solution had no negative effects on the antagonist's populations.

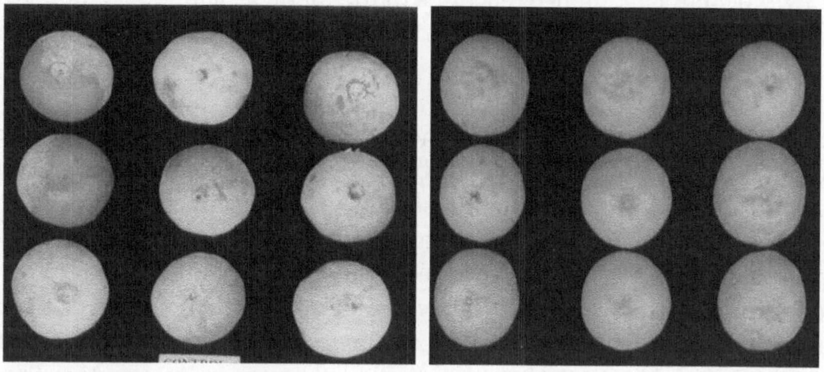

Fig. 7.7: Effect of calcium coating on citrus fruits control rot caused by *P. expansum*

Ethanol

Ethanol occurs naturally in many foods and is considered an approved preservative for many. Its efficacy in reducing fungal decay by postharvest pathogens is probably the result of protein denaturation, especially those of mitochondrial membranes. On lemons inoculated with *P. digitatum,* immersion in solutions of 10–20% ethanol at 32, 38 and 44°C effectively controlled decay on fruits stored at 20°C for 3 weeks. At 50°C, all treatments, including water, reduced incidence of decay to less than 5%. Little additional enhancement occurred when ethanol concentrations exceeded 10%. In a second study, a combination of hot water and ethanol (10%) at immersion temperatures of 46 or 50°C for 2.5 min. reduced the postharvest decay of naturally inoculated peaches and nectarines caused by *M. fructicola* and *R. stolonifer* from 82.8% to 33.8% and 24.5%, respectively Ethanol (50%) applied before harvest to organically grown strawberries significantly reduced the incidence of postharvest grey mould caused by *B. cinerea* (Karabulut *et al.*, 2004). The antagonist *Saccharomyces cerevisiae* combined with ethanol controlled grey mould caused by *B. cinerea* on apples and pear. Biocontrol activity of *S. cerevisiae* was strongly affected by the addition of ethanol. Ethanol at a concentration of 22% was toxic to the antagonist but completely inhibited spore germination of *B. cinerea*. On the other hand, ethanol at 16% enhanced antagonistic activity against the pathogen. On lemons, immersion of fruits inoculated with *P. digitatum* in 10% ethanol at 45°C followed by an application of the biocontrol yeast *Candida oleophila* reduced the incidence of green mould by 95% (equivalent an imazalil treatment) compared with a 50% reduction by the yeast alone.

Silicon

Silicon is a major inorganic constituent of plants and its exogenous application has been shown to reduce disease severity of fungal infections (Rodrigues *et al.*, 2003). The mechanism by which silicon reduces disease is thought to involve eliciting biochemical defence reactions in the plant. *C. laurentii* combined with silicon (2%) was more effective in controlling decay caused by *A. alternata* or *P. expansum* on jujube fruits than silicon alone or silicon combined with the yeast *Rhodotorula glutinis* (Tian *et al.*, 2004). After 7 days at 20°C, the only treatment that eliminated the incidence of decay caused by *P. expansum* and reduced decay caused by *A. alternata* by 80% was a combination of silicon and *C. laurentii*. Silicon or either antagonist alone or silicon in combination with *R. glutinis* reduced the incidence of decay by no more than approximately 20%. There was no effect of silicon on the populations of either antagonist. In a more thorough study on sweet cherry, fruits treated with silicon (1% sodium metasilicate) alone had 63.4% and 86.6% lower incidence of decay caused by *P. expansum* and *M. fructicola*, respectively, and was more effective than the antagonist (*C. laurentii*) alone, which reduced incidence of decay by either pathogen by about 50% after incubation at 20°C for 3 days (Tian *et al.*, 2008).

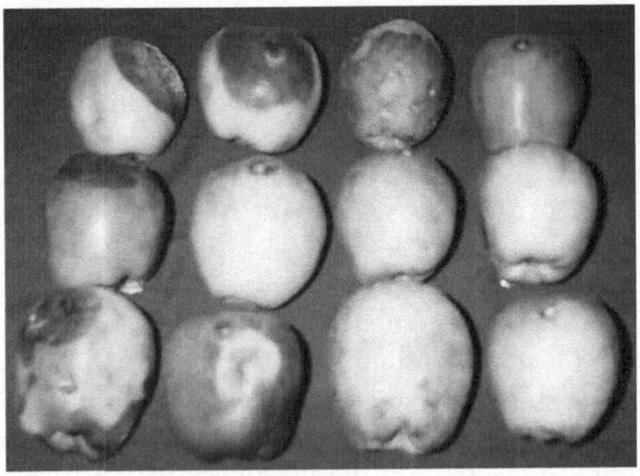

Fig. 7.8: Effect of silicon on to reduction of *P. expansum* in apple

Nisin

Nisin, a broad spectrum pore-forming bacteriocin, is produced by lactic acid bacteria that are often found on produce (Li *et al.*, 2002). It is active against many gram-positive bacteria. Nisin is the only commercially available bacteriocin recognized as a safe and legal biological food preservative by the

United States Food and Drug Administration. The addition of 4% nisin to the antagonist *C. oleophila* suspension, used for treating apples, eliminated grey mould and reduced blue mould decay by 93%, while the antagonist alone reduced decay by 68% and 67%, respectively. Nisin enhanced the antagonistic activity of *C. oleophila* in the wounds of apples by inhibiting spore germination and restriction of the growth of germ tubes of both pathogens, which favoured the antagonist and therefore enhanced biocontrol.

Chitosan and Harpin

Chitosan (poly β-(1→4)*N*-acetyl-D-glucosamine) is a deacetylated form of chitin, which is commonly obtained by a chemical process from crustacean shells (Devlieghere *et al.*, 2005). It has widespread applications in agriculture, food, medicine and environmental remediation. In addition to its antimicrobial activity it can induce resistance in plants (De Capdeville *et al.*, 2002). The antimicrobial activity of chitosan and its derivatives (e.g., glycolchitosan or carboxy-methyl chitosan) depends mainly on the degree of deacetylation, pH of the medium, temperature and the presence of food components. Yeasts appear to be more sensitive than bacteria, but reductions in bacterial populations as high as 5 log were reported. Chitosan and its derivatives can be used as an antimicrobial film on strawberries, raspberries, peach, kiwifruit, Japanese pear, cucumber, bell papers, longan fruit, banana and mango to extend the shelf-life of these produce (Kittur *et al.*, 2001). Because of its antimicrobial activity, chitosan and its derivatives must be screened for their effect on biocontrol agents and the most appropriate concentrations determined before they can be used as a combined treatment (El-Ghaouth *et al.*, 2001). Combining glycochitosan at 0.2% with the antagonist *Candida saitoana* resulted in control of green mould of oranges and lemons equivalent to an imazalil treatment (El-Ghaouth *et al.*, 2001). Pretreatment of lemon with SC prior to application of the yeast with glycolchitosan further improved control of green mould. The glycolchitosan/ antagonist treatment reduced the incidence of grey mould and blue mould of apple from 100% in controls to 23% and 25%, respectively. On both apple and citrus fruits, the combined treatment was always superior to the individual treatments. Chitosan at a concentration of 0.1% reduced germination of *P. expasum* conidia by 50% but did not inhibit populations of the antagonist *C. laurentii* in apple wounds (Yu *et al.*, 2007). Combining chitosan with *C. laurentii* reduced incidence of blue mould of apples from 100% to 14.0%, while treatments with chitosan or the antagonist alone reduced decay incidence by 87.5% and 48.4%, respectively (Yu *et al.*, 2007). The antagonistic activity of this yeast against *P. expansum* on pear was enhanced greatly (from 40% to 6% decay) when the yeast was grown in culture media supplemented with 1% chitin powder (De Capdeville *et al.*, 2003). Similarly grown yeast grew better in pear fruit wounds and had much higher chitinase activity compared with the yeast grown in unamended media. The culture filtrate also had higher chitinase activity and significantly reduced severity of blue mould. Chitosan at 1% induced resistance in 'Red Delicious' apple (De Capdeville *et al.*, 2003). The effects were strongest 96 h after treatment, and higher on fresh than on CA-stored fruits. The reduction of decay by the combination of chitosan with *C. saitoana* was greater than either treatment alone. In the same study, combining the yeast with harpin treatment also resulted in superior control of blue mould (De Capdeville *et al.*, 2003).

Despite its antimicrobial activity, chitosan and its derivatives can be combined with yeast biocontrol agents to improve control of fruit decay. The dual action of antimicrobial activity and induced resistance necessitates the careful selection of the optimal concentrations for each antagonist/pathogen/host system. The coating properties of chitosan can provide a venue for good distribution of a biocontrol agent and has already resulted in the development of a product "Bio-Coat" that showed promise in commercial trials (Schena *et al.*, 2005). Tripathi and Dubey, (2004) reviewed the exploitation of some natural products such as flavor compounds, acetic acid, jasmonates, glucosinolates. propoils. fusapyrone. chitdsan, essential oils etc. and plant extracts for the management of fungal rotting of fruits and vegetables. Chitosan is a soluble form of chitin. Chitosan and its derivatives have plant protective and antifungal properties. They can trigger defensive mechanism in plants against pathogenic attacks at very low concentrations. Recently Sharma *et al.*, (2006) reported chitosan as a soft fungicide that successfully inhibited spore germination of *Aspergillus niger* on mango.

Control Pre Treatment Pre Treatment

Fig. 7.9: Treatment of different concentration of Chitosan pre and post harvest in tomato.

Methyl Jasmonate and Salicylic Acid

Jasmonic acid (JA), its methyl ester methyl jasmonate (MeJA) and salicylic acid (SA) are signalling molecules occurring in a wide variety of plants and play important roles in plant growth, development and responses to environmental stresses, including defence reactions against pathogen invasion

(Terry and Joyce, 2004). As applications of SA primes cells for rapid expression of defence genes upon invasion by pathogens, the activity of applied JA and MeJA depends on the subsequent action of ethylene (Walling 2001). There can be signal cross-talk between SA- and JA-induced pathways resulting in additive or synergistic effects (Bostock, 2005). Activity of the key enzymes, such as chitinase, ß-1,3-glucanase, phenylalanine ammonia-lyase, peroxidase or super oxide dismutase, involved in defence reactions, was often stimulated in fruits following application of these growth regulators (Yao and Tia, 2005). Application of MeJA or SA induced resistance to various pathogens in different fruits, including resistance to brown rot (caused by *M. fructicola*) and blue mould (caused by *P. expansum*) in sweet cherry (Chan *et al.*, 2008) fungal decay in papaya, anthracnose (caused by *Colletotrichum cocodes*) in tomatoes (Tzotzakis, 2007) anthracnose (caused by *C. acutatum*) in loquat fruits (Cao *et al.*, 2008) green mould (caused by *P. digitatum*) in grapefruits, and apple decay. The application of MeJA and SA in combination with various antagonists resulted in control of fruit decay that was superior to individual treatments on a variety of fruits. On pears, combining the antagonist *R. glutinis* with MeJA (200 μM) resulted in a 4.2% incidence of blue mould compared with 7.5%, 14.6% and 20.8% for *R. glutinis*, MeJA and control treatments, respectively, on naturally-infected fruits stored for 2 months at 4°C followed by 15 days at 20°C (Zhang *et al.*, 2005). On peach, combining *C. laurentii* with MeJA (200 μM) allowed a reduction in antagonist concentration from 1×10^8 CFU/mL to 5×10^7 CFU/mL without a resulting reduction in control of brown rot (caused by *M. fructicola*) or blue mould (caused by *P. expansum*) (Yao and Tian, 2005). This could significantly lower the cost of the antagonist treatment. MeJa (10 μM) reduced germination of *C. accutatum* spores from 96% to 29%, and growth of germ tubes from 6.1 to 2.3 μm *in vitro*; however, it did not reduce anthracnose lesions on loquat fruits when used alone and when used in combination with the yeast antagonist, *P. membranifaciens,* reduced decay incidence from 100% to only 84% after 6 days at 20°C (Cao *et al.*, 2009).

A combination of SA (10 μg/mL) with *C. laurentii* significantly improved control of blue mould on apple (Yu and Zheng, 2006) and blue and grey mould on pears (Yu *et al.*, 2007). The effect of SA was most pronounced when fruits were inoculated 48 or 72 h after the treatment, again indicating induction of resistance in fruits. SA (0.5 mM) combined with *C. laurentii* or *R. glutinis* improved control of blue mould on sweet cherry, and combined with *P. membranefaciens* or *R. glutinis* improved control of brown rot and grey mould, respectively, on peach (Zhang *et al.*, 2008). Proteome analysis of peach exposed to SA and *P. membranefaciens* suggests that antioxidant and pathogenesis related proteins, and enzymes associated with sugar metabolism were involved in the induction of resistance by these treatments (Chan *et al.*, 2007).

Although the efficacy of many of these combined treatments in reducing fruit decay is still below commercially acceptable levels, the fact that MeJA and SA induced resistance in fruits and sometimes had a direct effect on various pathogens, indicates their potential for use together with biocontrol treatments. Additional tests, with more effective antagonists on a larger scale, are needed to reveal the full potential of these treatment combinations.

Botanicals

Many workers have investigated the antifungal and antibacterial efficiency of botanicals. Several plant extracts and essential oils have been found to he effective in inhibiting the growth of several fungi and bacteria (Delespaul *et al.*, 2000, Sharma and Tripathi, 2008). The advantage of essential oil is their bioactivity in vapour phase, a characteristic that makes them attractive as possible fumigants for stored product protection (Delespaul *et al.*, 2000). Recent studies have shown that especially vapor extracted essential oils of many different tropical and temperate plant species are highly potent biocides that in very low concentrations can control or kill fungi and/or bacteria by at least the same efficiency as synthetic anti-microbial compounds (Sharma and Tripathi, 2006). Aqueous extract from the leaves of garlic creeper (*Adenocalymma alliaceum* Miers.) was investigated for their antifungal activity

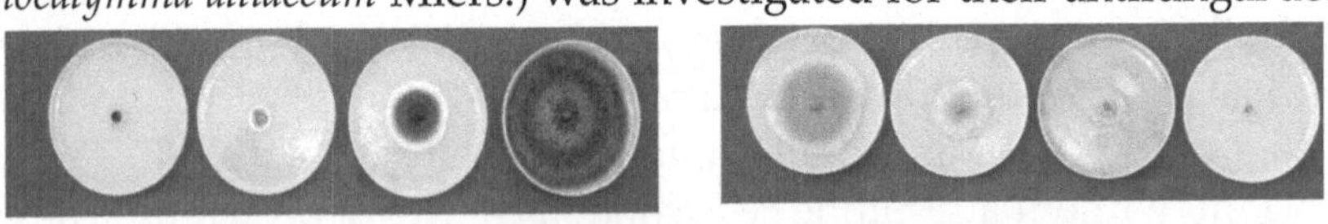

Fig. 7.10: Effect of essential oil from Citrus on *Alernaria*

Fig. 7.11: Effects of essential oil on the reduction of Aspergillus rot apple

against these pathogens by seed treatment. The extract demonstrated wide spectrum fungitoxicty. The seed were treated with Aqueous extract of leaf for

5 mit to 2 h. it is evident that the treatment of leaf extract for 1.30 h inhibited the growth of dominant fungi as *Aspergillus nige,r Penicillium itaclicum, Rhozoctonia solani,* and *Sclerotium rolfsii* The result indicated that the longer duration of seed treatments with plants extracts was effective in controlling the growth of the entire surface borne seed mycoflora.(Sharma and Srivastava, 2008) The antimicrobial activity expressed by various herbs is due to their essential oil fractions. There have been some studies on the effects of essential oils on post-harvest pathogens. Some of the essential oils have been reported to inhibit post-harvest fungi in *in vitro* conditions in Soybean (Sharma and Srivastava, 2012).

Flavour Compounds

Fruits and vegetables have a number of constitutive and inducible compounds that are antimicrobial. The flavor compounds are secondary metabolites having unique properties of volatility and fat and low water solubility. Being volatile not very water soluble, and easily absorbed, they arc very useful in post harvest protection. Many volatiles express their effects at very low concentration. As potential fungicides, their natural occurrence as part of human diet, their ephemeral nature, and their biodegradability suggest low toxic residue problems. Some plant volatiles, e.g. acetaldehyde, benzeldehyde, cinnamaldehyde, ethanol, benzyl alcohol, nerolidol-nonanone have also been found to have antifungal activity against fruits and vegetable pathogens (Utama *et al.*, 2002).

Acetic acid fumigation offers promise as a method for surface- sterilizing a wide range of fruit and possibly vegetables. Acetic acid is a metabolic .intermediate that occurs naturally in many fruit. The inhibitory effect of acetic acid on microorganisms is greater due to pH alone and un-dissociated acetic acid can penetrate the microbial cells to exert its toxic effect. Jasmonates Gasmonic acid and methyl jasmonates) are naturally occurring plant growth regulators belong to a class of olypines derived from oxygenase-dependent oxidation of fatty acids. Several jasmonates have been shown to activate genes encoding anti-fungal proteins such as osmotin, a novel ribosome inactivating protein RIP and several other genes involved in phytolexin biosynthesis. Propolis is a natural resinous substance obtained from leaf buds and bark of poplar and conifer trees. It has antibiotic activity, antibacterial and anti-fungal Activity.

Biological Treatments

The introductions of new alternative technologies hold the promise to raise the limits to growth. One of the main approaches has been using biological control alone or in combination with other physical and chemical alternatives to conventional fungicide control. Dr. C.L. Wilson is rightly considered the "Father of biological control of fruits and vegetables" for the first time gave this concept. This was further highlighted and grew into a new field of research.

Cook and Baker 1983 in their book on biological control cited only one example of the biocontrol of postharvest disease of a fruit or vegetable. Subsequently in 1985, Wilson and Pusey presented their initial research on using a strain of *Bacillus subtilis* to control brown rot on peach, caused by *Monilinia fructicol*a and the organism was patented. This seminal work provided the initial ideas and principles that, over the ensuing twenty years, fostered a wealth of research and product development around the world. In the past 25 years, research on biological control of postharvest diseases has moved from laboratory to practical applications (Korsten, 2006). A number of microorganisms (bacteria, yeasts and fungi), which effectively control postharvest pathogens, have been identified for postharvest control of diseases and some of these have been patented and registered (El Ghaouth and Wilson, 2002, Sharma *et al.*, 2011).

Fig. 7.12: Effects of antagonist on the development of Penicilium soft rot in citrus

Isolation of Antagonist

Yeasts are effective colonizers of plant surfaces, even under adverse environmental conditions. Often carposphere, phylloplane, flowers and stems have provided the major source for antagonists (Sharma, 1999). A basic understanding of the ecological succession of microorganisms on the surface of fruits and vegetables tells a different story. Undiluted fruit washings when plated on agar plates exhibited a dense population of yeast and bacteria and upon dilution of these washings filamentous fungi were isolated. This suggests that bacteria and yeast, naturally present on the surface may inhibit the growth of other microorganisms, including plant pathogenic fungi (Sharma, 2002). Later it was observed that citrus fruits when washed and stored rotted faster than the unwashed ones suggesting that these bacteria and yeast provide protection to fruits against pathogens. (Sharma *et al.*, 2012)

Most antagonistic yeasts are efficient colonizers as they utilize nutrients rapidly, produce extracellular materials that enhance their survival on fruit surfaces and have the ability to adapt to environment. Members of the genus *Cryptococcus* are easily isolated from the surface of leaves, stems, fruit and buds of apple, pear and other economically important crop plants. It was observed that fruit orchards with marginal insect control provided rich source of epiphytic yeast effective in postharvest biocontrol, both in quantity and in diversity. The sugar rich honydew from insects' coats the leaves and fruits and is probably responsible for the high populations of yeasts on them In few cases potential yeast antagonists have also been isolated from other matrixes.

Rather than *in vitro* screening of organisms in Petriplates, which favored the identification of antibiotic-producing organisms, a selection strategy was developed to identify suitable yeast antagonists. The method involved placing washing fluids obtained from the surface of fruit into fruit wounds that were subsequently inoculated with a rot pathogen. Organisms were then isolated from the surface of wounds that did not develop infections. These were plated out and isolated. Yeast antagonists can from freshly made wounds on fruits in the orchard that were exposed to colonization by fruit-associated microbiota from one to four weeks before harvest.

Yeast genera thus isolated were identified, pure cultures of potential antagonists were produced, and then each organism was screened individually in fruit wounds to assess its potential as a biocontrol agent. This method identified a number of antagonists that were studied more intensely and measured against the criteria set for suitability for commercial production as outlined by Wilson and Wisniewski (1989) and Hofstein *et al.*, (1994).

- Genetically stable.
- Effective at low concentrations.
- Not fastidious in its nutrient requirements.
- Ability to survive adverse environmental conditions (including low temperature and controlled atmosphere storage).
- Effective against a wide range of pathogens on a variety of fruits and vegetables.
- Amenable to production on an inexpensive growth medium.
- Amenable to a formulation with a long shelf life.
- Easy to dispense.
- Does not produce metabolites that are deleterious to human health.
- Resistant to pesticides.

- Compatible with commercial processing procedures.
- Does not grow at 37 °C and is not associated with infections in humans.
- Non-pathogenic to host commodity. Biocontrol activity.

The antagonist activity can be expressed in a number of ways: the most common are production of metabolites, competition and direct parasitism, but other mechanisms are also involved, for example induced resistance sometimes associated with reduction of pathogen enzyme activity. In recent years the use of antibiotic-producing bacteria has been abandoned, in order to prevent the appearance of resistance in pathogen strains for man or animal. In addition, it is extremely difficult precisely to explain the antagonist mechanisms involved, even when they seem to be clear, as for the antibiotic-producing strains. This is the case of pyrrolnitrin produced by *Pseudomonas cepacia*, which can control strains of *Penicillium digitatum* resistant to this antibiotic. The use of yeasts as antagonists appears to be quite promising, although the mechanism has not yet been fully elucidated. However, competition for nutrients and space is the major mechanism involved for *Pichia guilliermondii*, *Cryptococcus laurentii, Candida utilis, Candida oleophila, Debaryomyces hansenii* and other yeasts employed as bioagents. In the studies conducted in our lab we have observed that the concentration of antagonist had significant effects on biocontrol effectiveness: the higher the concentrations of the antagonist lower the disease incidence that is in agreement with several other studies (Zhang *et al.*, 2005). Droby *et al.* (1989) reported that an increase of *Debaryomyces hansenii* concentration resulted in more effective control while it was found that 10^8 CFU per ml of yeast cell concentration completely limited rot development in case of *Pichia guilliermondii*, *Cryptococcus laurentii, Metschnikowia pulcherrima* and lower concentrations were found ineffective. Application of yeast simultaneously or prior to pathogen inoculation always provided better control of the pathogen. The results indicated the ability of the yeast to utilize available nutrients and that when saturation of the wound sites with yeast cells is achieved there is no difference between different applied concentrations.

Studies with various sugars occurring in apple showed greater uptake and utilization of $_{14}$C fructose and stronger inhibition of conidia germination in diluted apple juice by the antagonists other than *Saccharomyces cerevisiae,* suggesting that competition for nutrients may play an important role. Janisiewiez *et al.,* (2000) have developed a non-destructive method using tissue culture plates having a defusing membrane at the lower end of cylindrical inserts to study competition for nutrients separated from the competition for space.

While early studies indicated that nutrient competition and the fast growth rate of antagonists played a major role in biocontrol activity, subsequent studies indicated a much more complex interaction between the antagonist, pathogen, and commodity. Some of antagonists adhere to and parasitize pathogen hyphae. For example *Pichia guilliermondii* US-7 exhibits nutrient competition along with direct parasitism as antagonist of *P. digitatum* in grapefruit, and of *B. cinerea* in apples and so does *Metschnikowia pulcherrima* (Spadaro *et al.*, 2002). Zhang *et al.*, (2005) reported that *Pichia membranefaciens* and *Cryptococcus albidus* exhibited tenacious attachement with pathogen hyphae along with secretion of extracelluluar lytic enzymes. Ultrastructural and cytochemical studies on yeast *Candida saitoana*, when cocultivated with *Botrytis cinerea* showed cytological damage as papillae and protuberances in the cell wall and degeneration of the cytoplasm It also stimulated structural defense response in the host. Host cell walls were well preserved and displayed an intense and regular cellulose-labeling pattern.

Yeast cells are able to produce hydrolytic enzymes capable of attacking the cell walls of pathogens, and extracellular polymers that appear to have antifungal activity. Yeast *Pichia anomala* strain K, effective in the control of gray mold of apple, increased production of exo-β-1, 3-glucanase threefold in the presence of cell wall preparations of *B. cinerea* in apple wounds, reducing lesion size by more than half compared to the antagonist alone. This strengthens the hypothesis that exo- β -1,3-glucanase is involved in the biocontrol of gray mold by this antagonist. Higher β -1,3-glucanase and chitinase activity was also detected in apple wounds treated with strains of an antagonist, *A. pullulans*, effective in controlling various decays on apple, table grape, and other fruits (Castoria *et al.*, 2001).

Recent studies report the ability of the yeast to form a biofilm and prevent germination cues and/or nutrients from reaching the pathogen. Yeast like *Candida famata* are reported to control green mold due to induction of phytoalexins scoparone and scopolectin. *A. pullulans* can cause a transient increase in glucanase, chitinase and peroxidase activities on apple fruit, starting 24 h after treatment. However, the role of enzymes and phytoalexins in biocontrol activity warrants further investigations.

More recently, molecular approaches to examine the mode of action have been studied on the yeast biocontrol agent, *Candida oleophila*. A transformation system for this yeast, produced yeast lines with either higher or lower levels of a 1, 3- ß-glucanase gene/enzyme expression compared to the wild type. Biocontrol activity did not differ between the different yeast lines but the results did not rule out a role for this gene in biocontrol activity (Yehuda *et al.*, 2003). It was also demonstrated that overexpression of a lytic peptide belonging to the defensin family of antimicrobial peptides in yeast can enhance biocontrol activity.

Low Doses of Fungicides

Application of low doses of fungicides with biocontrol agents may serve several purposes. It may: broaden the spectrum of activity of the treatment (e.g., fungicide may provide eradicative effect); manage fungicide resistance (e.g., rotation with fungicides with different modes of action to which pathogens did not develop resistance); bring the efficacy of the biocontrol treatment to commercially acceptable levels; and reduce the amount of biocontrol agent applied without compromising decay control, making biocontrol treatment more economical. Yeast antagonists vary in sensitivity to fungicides and generally are very sensitive to triazoles and dithiocarbamates (Lima *et al.*, 2006). Their tolerance to low doses of fungicides must be established not only *in vitro* but also on fruits as the MIC may not be the same in both tests. Combining *Pichia guilliermondii* (US-7) with 200 pm of thiabendazole (TBZ) reduced the incidence of citrus decay equivalent to the commercial treatment of 2,000 ppm TBZ. The decay control in the combined treatment was more consistent than with TBZ treatment alone. Similarly, application of the commercial product Aspire, based on the antagonistic yeast *C. oleophila,* in combination with 200 ppm TBZ, resulted in a reduction of blue and green mould incidence of citrus equivalent to the conventional fungicide treatment. The combined treatment also controlled sour rot (*Geotrichum candidum*) a disease that cannot be controlled with the fungicide alone. *C. infirmo-miniatus* (YY6) and *C. laurentii* (HRA5) in combination with 15 ppm TBZ reduced blue mould of apples as effectively as a conventional treatment with TBZ at 525 ppm. The same antagonists in combination with 20 ppm iprodione controlled brown rot (caused by *M. fructicola*) of cherries equivalent to the full dose, 525 ppm, of the fungicide. Similarly, integrating *C. laurentii* with 104 ppm of TBZ improved control of grey mould (caused by *B. cinerea*) on apples (Lima *et al.*, 2006), and the application of *C. laurentii* in combination with 25 ppm imazalil or 50 ppm kresoxim-methyl resulted in less decay caused by *A. alternata* and *M. fructicola* than when the treatments were applied separately on jujube fruits stored in a CA of 10% O_2 + 0% CO_2 at 0°C (Qin and Tian 2004). Blue mould of pears caused by a TBZ-sensitive *P. expansum* isolate was also completely controlled by a combination of TBZ at 100 ppm with either *C. infirmo-miniatus* (YY6), *R. glutinis* (HRB6) or *C. laurentii* (HRA5), and blue mould control by *Pseudomonas syringae* (BioSave 110) or *C. oleophila* (Aspire) combined with 100 ppm of TBZ was equal to control with 569 ppm of TBZ, the highest allowed rate, in packinghouse trials Sequential application of TBZ immediately after harvest followed 6 weeks later by BioSave 110 provided excellent decay control after 5 months of cold storage on nonwounded pears containing natural inoculum (Sugar and Basile, 2008). This approach may contribute to the suppression of the development of resistance to fungicides in pathogens. The addition of the fungicide cyprodinil at 20 ppm to *P. syringae* (used in BioSave 100) treatment allowed a reduction in the concentration of the antagonist from 1×10^8 CFU/mL to 6×10^7 CFU/mL without reducing the effectiveness of blue mould control on 'Empire' and 'McIntosh' apples. This greatly reduced the cost of the treatment and may be helpful in the development of a management strategy for benzimidazole (TBZ)-resistant populations of *P. expansum* (Errampalli and Brubacher, 2006).

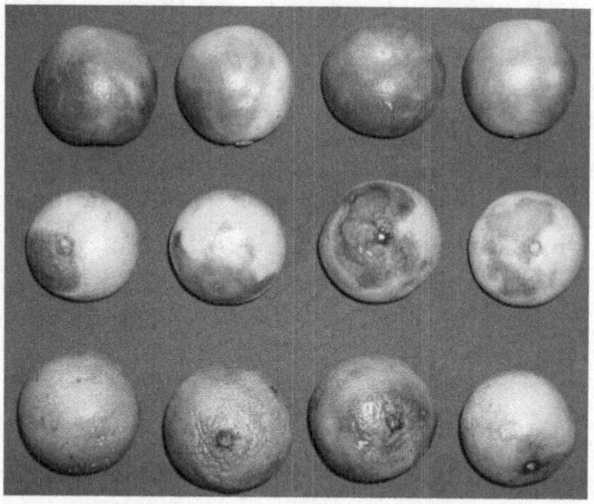

Fig. 7.13: Effects of Low doses of fungicides on the development of Penicilium rot in citrus

Nutrients and Nutrient Analogues

The effectiveness of biocontrol on fruits depends on the balance between the antagonist and the pathogen. This balance could be easily tilted to the antagonist's advantage if higher populations of the antagonist are applied to the fruit, if antagonist populations or the mechanism of biocontrol on fruits are boosted by addition of nutrients, or growth of the pathogen is inhibited by exogenously applied substances. Although applying higher populations of the antagonist is the simplest way to achieve this, it is also the most expensive. Thus, various attempts have been made to use nutrients to stimulate antagonist populations or increase the mechanism of biocontrol, or nutrient analogs have been employed to inhibit pathogen growth. To enhance decay control activity, applied nutrients must benefit the antagonist to a much greater extent than the pathogen. Fruits are rich in carbon but poor in nitrogen sources, therefore, applications of nitrogenous substances with antagonists were very effective in improving biocontrol (Nunes *et al.*, 2001). Combining L-asparagine and L-proline (80 mM) with *P. syringae* increased populations of the antagonist by as much as 1 log unit in the wounds of mature 'Golden Delicious' apples, and resulted in an additional reduction of the incidence of blue mould of apples from 41% to 0% and from 75% to 20%, respectively (Janisiewicz *et al.*, 2008). L-serine and L-aspartic acid at a concentration of 4 mM combined with *Candida sake* reduced lesion size of blue mould decay on apples from 9 mm to 0 mm and from 4 mm to 0 mm, respectively (Nunes *et al.*, 2001).

Interestingly, 5 mM ammonium molybdate reduced the growth of *C. sake* in apple and pear wounds and at the same time improved control of blue mould, grey mould, and Rhizopus rot (Nunes et a ., 2002). Apparently the beneficial effect of this compound comes from its ability to inhibit pathogen growth, as it alone significantly reduced fruit decay. Interest in using this compound to enhance biocontrol on fruit is expanding and the beneficial effects were also reported in other systems on pear, cherry and jujube fruits (Qin *et al.*, 2006). At a concentration of 1 mM it reduced growth of the antagonist *R. glutinis* in a media but not in pear fruit wounds, and enhanced control of blue mould by reducing disease incidence from 52% when using the antagonist alone to 11% in the combined treatment (Wan and Tian, 2005). On jujube fruit, at a concentration of 15 mM, in combination with *C. laurentii* and *R. glutinis,* it reduced incidence of blue mould by from 40% to 2% and from 57% to 20%, respectively (Wan *et al.*, 2003). Also on cherry fruit, at a concentration 5 mM combined with *C. laurenti* and *P. membranefaciens,* it significantly improved control of brown rot, and the incidence of decay was less on fruits in CA than in the air storage (Qin *et al.*, 2006).

The nutrient analog 2-deoxy-D-glucose (2-DOG) can be absorbed by yeast and filamentous fungi but they cannot metabolise it, so it accumulates in cells, and retards growth. The degree of inhibition depends on the intracellular concentration. A combined treatment of 2-DOG at 2 mg/mL with the antagonist *Sporbolomyces roseus* allowed more than a 10-fold reduction in the concentration of the antagonist applied to fruits without diminishing the level of control of blue mould on apples and pears. A combination of 2- DOG with *P. syringae* was also very effective; no lesions developed on apples and only small lesions on pears. A concentration of 1 mg/mL 2-DOG combined with *C. sake* enhanced biocontrol of blue mould on pears by 64% (Nunes *et al.*, 2001). A 2 mg/mL concentration of 2-DOG combined with *C. saitoana* improved control of decay on apples and various citrus fruits, often to the level obtained with commercially used fungicides (El-Ghaouth, 2001).

Both nutrients and nutrient analogs can be very useful in enhancing biocontrol of fruit decay. Their application, however, could be more suitable as a part of a developed antagonist formulation than as a separate treatment.

Integrated Control

Since biocontrol of postharvest diseases has little eradicative activity, a combination of various other treatments can prove to be more effective.

Heat Treatments and Antagonist

Hot water treatment followed by biocontrol would be effective in providing both eradicant and protectant activities. Research as conducted to determine the effects of hot water treatment 55°C for 30 s and an antagonist, *C. laurentii,* alone and in combination, in reducing black rot of strawberries caused by *R. stolonifer*. As stand-alone treatments, hot water dips and the antagonistic yeast reduced the percentage of infected wounds from 96.7% to 65% and 63.3%, respectively. However, in fruits treated with the combination of hot water dips followed by *C. laurentii,* the percentage of infected wounds as only 43%.

To develop an integrated method to control postharvest diseases of banana, an antagonist (a member of the *Murkholderia cepacia* complex) and hot water dips, alone and in combination, were tested for their efficacy in reducing anthracnose, crown rot and blossom end rot of bananas caused by *Colletotrichum musae* (De Costa and HRUT, 2005). The optimum temperature and exposure time were determined to be 50°C for min. The most effective concentration of *B. cepacia* was 10^{10} CFU/mL and the addition of 2% Tween 20 to the bacterial suspension increased its efficacy. While either treatment alone reduced decay severity by approximately 50%, the combination of a hot water dip with the antagonist resulted in almost complete control of the fungus. The combination of HWRB and *Candida* spp. had no significant additional effect against *M. fructicola* compared with HWRB alone. The antagonistic yeast might be able to colonise the carrot wounds more effectively due to reduced competition from other microflora that are killed by the heat treatment.

Combining heat treatment of 'Gala' apples after harvest (38°C, 4 days) with pressure infiltration of a 2% $CaCl_2$ solution, and antagonist treatment (*Pseudomonas syringae*) reduced blue mould decay caused by *P. expansum* more than the treatments applied alone After 6 months in storage at 1°C, no decay lesions developed on fruit that were heated after inoculation with *P. expansum* or any combination of *P. expansum,* the antagonist or $CaCl_2$. Heat treatment had little effect on lesion size when the fruit were inoculated with *P. expansum* after heat treatment in the parallel lots. $CaCl_2$ alone, the antagonist alone and heat plus $CaCl_2$ all reduced the incidence of decay by approximately 25%, whereas heat plus the antagonist reduced it by 70%. $CaCl_2$ plus the antagonist or $CaCl_2$ plus the antagonist and heat reduced decay incidence by 89% and 91%, respectively. Similar decay reduction occurred when $CaCl_2$-treated 'Golden Delicious' fruits were inoculated with *Botrytis cinerea* prior to heat treatment. It is important to treat fruit with calcium prior to rather than following heat treatment. An electron microscope study revealed that epicuticular wax on the surface of non-heated fruits exhibited numerous deep surface cracks that formed an interconnected network on the fruit surface. The epicuticular wax of heat-treated fruits did not exhibit a similar network of deep cracks. This apparent obstruction or elimination of deep cracks may limit penetration of the $CaCl_2$ into fruits. The addition of any of the antagonists before heat treatment also reduced lesion size and incidence of decay (Leverentz *et al.,* 2000). Heat treatment was shown to be effective in sanitising the fruit and enhancing the wound healing process. Factors other than wound healing may be involved in this process. Enhanced production of phenolic substances near wounded tissue is known to be a common response to wounding. These phenolics may be incorporated into lignified cell walls during wound healing or may be directly toxic to the pathogen. On apples, heat treatment has the added benefit of improving fruit colour, especially in 'Golden Delicious' fruits, but does not lead to softening, since it inhibits the synthesis of cell wall hydrolytic enzymes .In another study, heat and 1-methylcyclopropene (MCP) treatment were combined with biocontrol to reduce postharvest decay of 'Golden Delicious' apples (Leverentz *et al.*, 2003). Fruits were treated with MCP, wounded and inoculated with *P. expansum* alone or with a heat tolerant yeast antagonist, the same one as used in the previous study (Leverentz *et al.*, 2000). After incubation at room temperature for up to 48 h, the apples were heated at 38°C for 4 days or moved to cold storage for 5 months. The combinations of heat treatment with the yeast antagonist were more effective than either treatment alone, with a resulting reduction in decay incidence of 96–100%. The addition of MCP had no beneficial effect on decay reduction and even slightly increased lesion diameter. On heat treated apples the antagonist population increase was greater than on non-heated fruits. Because the heat treatment reduces the population pressure and competition of other microorganisms in the apple wounds, it is likely that the heat tolerant yeast had an advantage in colonising the surface and competing with the pathogen. Similarly, in other work, biocontrol of green mould of citrus (caused by *P. digitatum*) by a bacterial strain *Pseudomonas glathei* was significantly improved when the inoculated fruits were incubated at 30°C for 24 h before being moved to 25°C. The incubation conditions prevented the fungal spores from germinating, but the bacterial populations increased greatly in the wounds. In another study,

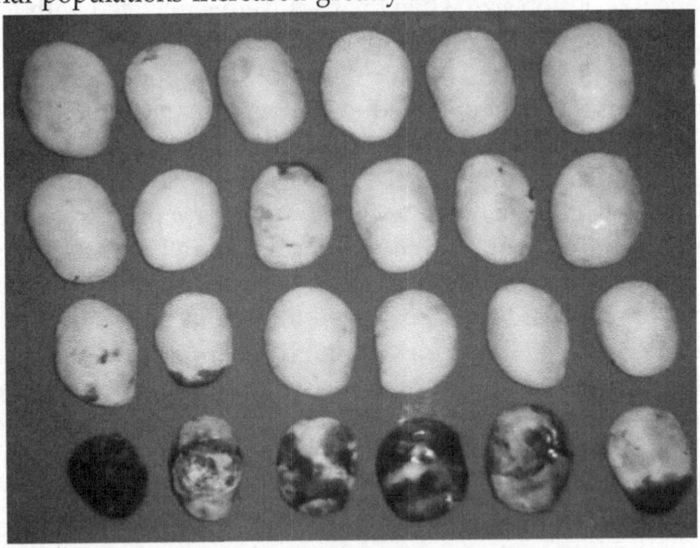

Fig. 7.14: Effects of Heat treatments and antagonist to reduce soft rot of mango

an antagonist, *Metchnikowia pulcherrima* (Janisiewicz, 2001), was integrated with MCP, heat treatment and stored in controlled atmosphere (CA; 1.1% O_2,

1.8% CO_2) to control bitter rot and blue mould decay on apples caused by *Colletotrichum acutatum* and *P. expansum,* respectively (Janisiewicz *et al.*, 2003). MCP treatment increased decay caused by *C. acutatum* and *P. expansum* but these decays were controlled on MCP-treated apples by a combination of the antagonist and heat treatments. The antagonist controlled *C. acutatum* more effectively than *P. expansum,* while *P. expansum* was more effectively controlled by heat treatment.

Low Temperature and Antagonist

On 'Gala' apples, less decay developed on fruits treated with heat (38°C, 4 days) or cold storage (1°C, 4 days) before wound inoculation with *P. expansum* and the antagonist *P. syringae* or one of the two yeast antagonists than on fruits not treated with these temperatures, after storage for 7 days at 20°C or 3 months at 1°C. On 'd'Anjou' pears stored for 4 days at –1°C after wounding, compounds such as callose, gums, pectic substances, starch, suberin and phenolics increased in wound tissue. The accumulation of these compounds appears to coincide or precede the increase in resistance to decay. Prestorage heat treatment at 26.5°C for 2 days is recommended for 'Anjou' and 'Bosc' pears prior to rapid cooling to –1 to 0°C in cold storage. The same wound healing response was accelerated and occurred after 1 day when fruits were heated at 28°C.

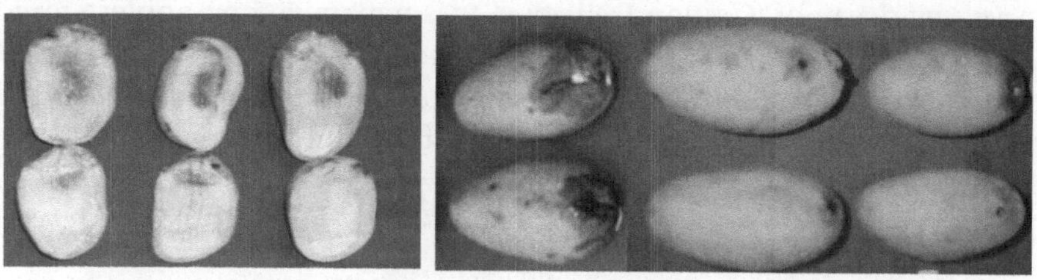

Fig. 7.15: Effects of low temperatures and antagonist to reduce soft rot of mango

Salt and Antagonist

In a subsequent study, the addition of sodium bicarbonate (SBC) to heat treatment and two yeast strains further reduced decay caused by these pathogens on 'Golden Delicious' apples (Conway *et al.*, 2004). Both yeast antagonists reduced decay caused by *P. expansum,* whereas heat or heat in combination with either antagonist eliminated decay. Either heat or the antagonists alone reduced decay caused by *C. acutatum*, but a combination of the two was required to eliminate decay caused by this pathogen. Adding SBC to heated or antagonist-treated fruits had little effect on decay caused by either pathogen but when used on non-heated fruits it significantly reduced decay caused by *P. expansum* after 4 months at 0°C. A similar study with 'Golden Delicious' apples that used heat treatment (38°C, 4 days) and one strain of *M. pulcherrima* from the previous study (Conway *et al.*, 2004), alone or in combination with a different antagonist (*Cryptococcus laurentii*), had similar results (Conway *et al.*, 2005).

'Golden Delicious' apples wound-inoculated with *P. expansum* and treated with various combinations of SBC and two antagonists (*M. pulcherrima, C. laurenti*) had 30% smaller lesions when stored in CA (1.4% O_2 and 3% CO_2) than in the air after 2 months storage at 1°C (Conway *et al.*, 2007). Combining SBC with either or both of the antagonists in air storage reduced lesion diameters by 95 to 98%, but the best control was achieved with the combinations of *C. laurentii* plus SBC and the two antagonists plus SBC stored in CA, where no decay developed. After 4 months in storage, all of the control fruits stored in air or CA were totally decayed, and while either antagonist alone in both air and CA storage significantly reduced decay, the only combination that completely controlled blue mould was the two antagonists plus SBC stored in CA.

The CA conditions had no adverse affect on antagonist populations. Similar results were obtained in a subsequent pilot trial under commercial storage conditions, using the same treatments except the CA regime, which was 1.5% O_2 and 2.0% CO_2 , showing that the combination of antagonists and SBC under CA conditions would be a viable alternative to chemical control (Janisiewicz *et al.*, 2008).

The biocontrol potential of the yeast *Candida sake* (CPA-1) against *P. expansum* decay of 'Golden Delicious' was maximized on apples stored in CA (3% O_2 and 3% CO_2) at 1°C where reduction in decay incidence was 97% compared with only about 40% in ambient or air storage (Usall *et al.*, 2000). The antagonist growth was compatible with all of the atmospheres tested.

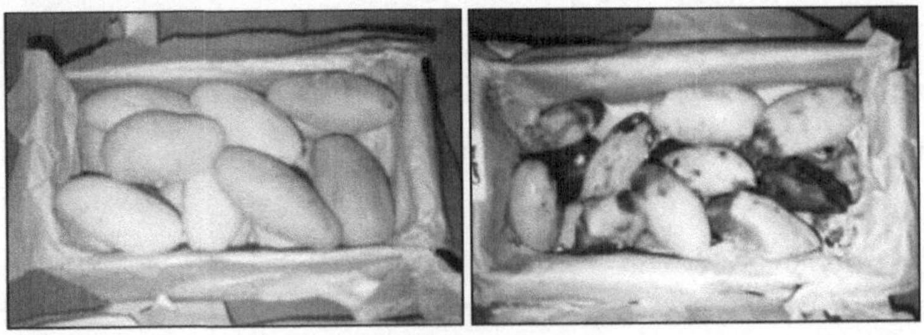

Fig. 7.16: Effects of salt with antagonist on the reduction of Aspergillus rot on mango

The biocontrol capability of the yeasts *Trichosporon* sp and *Cryptococcus albidus* against *B. cinerea* and *P. expansum* was evaluated in 'Golden Delicious' apples and 'Jingbai' pears at 1°C in air and under CA (3% O_2 and 3% CO_2 or 3% O_2 and 8% CO_2) conditions (Tian *et al.*, 2002). The application of the antagonists controlled decay caused by both pathogens better on apples than on pears, and more effectively in CA than in air. *Trichosporon* sp. was a more effective antagonist than *C. albidus*. In another study, the combined effect of modified atmosphere packaging (MAP) (polyethylene bags; O_2 levels = 1 to 15%; CO_2

levels = 0 to 15% and ambient conditions as well) and the application of a bacterial antagonist (*Erwinia* sp.) to control grey mould caused by *B. cinerea* on 'Golden Delicious' apples was investigated. Grey mould on fruits stored under these MA conditions was not affected by O_2 levels but it was controlled when CO_2 was increased from 0–15%, and when the bacterial antagonist (*Erwinia* sp) was added. How ever, the antagonist was most effective under ambient conditions.

Some exogenous substances, such as chitosan, amino acids, antibiotics, calcium salts and carbohydrates have been studied to enhance biocontrol capability of antagonists against fungal pathogens. Calcium chloride improved biological control of the yeast *P. guilliermondii,* while 2-deoxy-D-glucose, in combination with a mutant strain of *Sporobolomyces roseus*, produced a tenfold reduction in the concentration of the antagonist required for biocontrol of blue mold on apples . Combining 0.2% glycolchitosan with the antagonist *C. saitoana* was more effective in controlling green mold of oranges and lemons, caused by *P. digitatum*, and gray and blue molds of apples than either treatment alone (El Ghaouth *et al.*, 2000). In recent study by the author, a combination of chitosan and yeast *Candida utilis* was found effective in controlling postharvest pathogens on tomato (Sharma *et al.*, 2006), mango and apple. The studies also showed that several yeast genera were compatible with low concentrations of chitosan and the protection afforded by this combination was superior to the stand-alone treatments. Applying a 2% solution of calcium chloride together with the yeast antagonist *Candida* spp. enhanced biocontrol of gray and blue molds on apples, but calcium chloride solution alone did not reduce decays GRAS substances such as sodium carbonate, sodium bicarbonate, and ethanol reduced conidial germination of *P. digitatum*, the causal agent of green mold of citrus. Ethanol at 10%, in combination with ethanol-resistant *S. cerevisiae* strains 1440 and 1749, reduced the incidence of gray mold decay on apples from more than 90% to close to 0% respectively, whereas either treatment alone did not reduce decay.

UV-C and Antagonist

Low doses of ultraviolet light C have been used to control storage rots of fruits and vegetables. Stevens *et al.*, 1998 reported that when applying UV-C to peaches, it stimulated the yeast population by two to three folds compared to the control. However, when yeast was placed on paper disk and irradiated there was germicidal reduction of the yeast population. It appears that UV-C, the host and antagonist may play some role in plant-mediated resistance to pathogens.

Combining UV-C treatment with the biocontrol agent *Debaromyces hansenii* improved control of brown rot (caused by *M. fructicola*) of peach, green mould (caused by *P. digitatum*) on tangerines, and Rhizopus rot (caused by *R. stolonifer*) on tomato and sweet potato (Stevens *et al.*1997). The efficacy of the combined treatments, which also included $CaCl_2$, was equivalent to benomyl treatment of peaches, and even superior to dichloran treatment of sweet potatoes. Implementation of the UV-C irradiation treatment to complement biocontrol should not be difficult. In fact, some apple packinghouses already use UV irradiation boxes with the intention of reducing fungal inoculum on fruits. However, to achieve more consistent control, the UV-C treatment procedure will have to be developed for each commodity, and even then significant variation in efficacy of the UV-C treatment can be expected. The efficacy of the UV-C treatment is affected by a variety of factors including, positioning of the fruit in relation to the irradiation source, type of fruit, cultivar or fruit maturity, which can cause significant variations in efficacy. The induction of resistance in table grapes was greatly enhanced when UV-C irradiation was combined with a preharvest chitosan treatment (Ramanazzi *et al.*, 2006).

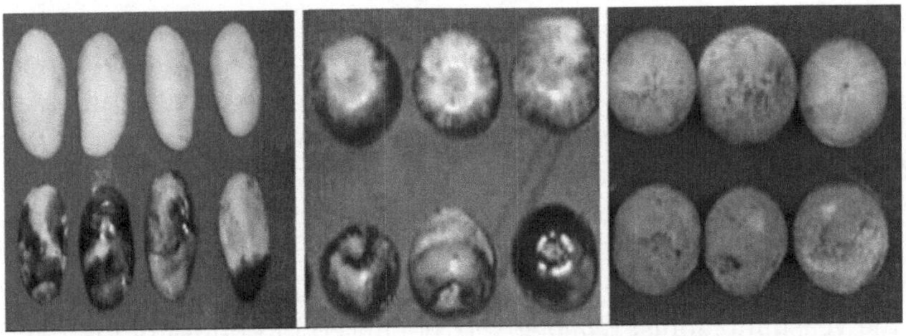

Fig. 3.17: Biocontrol as shown by yeasts in different fruits. Treated fruits with bioagents are in the *upper line* while infected fruits can be seen on the *bottom side*

Constraints in Product Development and Registration

In the early years several yeast antagonists that had commercial potential were misidentified. This caused some confusion in the patenting process and emphasized the need to have at least two conforming identifications by reputable yeast taxonomic services. It also emphasized the weakness of using physiological tests as the basis for making taxonomic determinations. Another shortcoming with the use of postharvest biocontrol products has been inconsistency in performance and their inability to control previously established and latent infections because they exhibit protective rather then eradicative properties.

For commercialization, it is essential that the antagonist is consistent in its performance, and for that several semi-commercial and commercial trials have to be conducted for which large volumes of antagonist is required. The mass production by rapid, efficient and inexpensive fermentation of the antagonist is a key issue. Therefore it is fundamental to find carbon and nitrogen sources that provide maximum biomass production at minimum cost, whilst maintaining biocontrol efficacy. Cheap industrial waste materials such as cottonseed meal, corn steep liquor, partially digested peptones, yeast extract, dry brewer's yeast, sucrose and molasses have been used as growth media for multiplication of cells.

A major obstacle to the commercialization of biocontrol products is the development of a shelf stable product that retains bioactivity similar to that of fresh cells. Formulations can influence the survival and activity of biocontrol agents. An accurate formulation has a profound effect on efficacy of biocontrol agent, including its shelf life, ability to grow and survive after application, effectiveness in disease control, ease of operation and application, and cost. A biofungicide should be effective for at least 6 months and preferably for 2 years .This can be achieved by supplementing the yeast with protectants, carriers or additives. Alternatively, yeast can be conditioned during fermentation by using an emulsifier.

Drying the product and maintenance in a dry environment or suspension in oil are common approaches. Products are available as wettable powder, as frozen cell concentrated pellets or as liquid formulations. It was found that freeze dried cells were Products are available as wettable powder, as frozen cell concentrated pellets or as liquid formulations. It was found that freeze dried cells were significantly less effective than fresh cells. Certain freeze-drying protective agents and rehydration media enhanced the viability of the antagonist *Pantoea agglomerans* strain CPA-2, effective against blue mold and gray mold of pome fruits (Costa *et al.*, 2000). Survival of cells of the antagonistic yeast *C. sake* was improved from 0.2% to 30–40%, by using freeze-drying protective media consisting of skim milk and other protectants, such as 10% lactose or glucose, and 10% fructose or sucrose. The presence of trehalose in liquid formulations appeared to help preserve the viability of *C. sake* during storage. It is known that intracellular trehalose exerts a protective effect on yeast under extreme environmental conditions such as dessication, freezing, osmotic stress and heat shock and it also provides thermal stability to the cells.

Formulations may include wetters (humectants) to facilitate reabsorption of moisture from air. Wetter not only makes water spray stay on plants but, like oil carriers, they also enable organisms to reach otherwise inaccessible places such as depressions, stomata, and lenticels, thereby improving the chances of establishing antagonists for disease control. Oil carriers are expensive, but formulations containing oils can enhance the reliability of biological control agents. Research is needed to determine the value of each additive alone and also in the presence of other ingredients as well as ensure the requirements for ecological safety.

One of the major limitations with biological disease control is the inconsistency in efficacy which is often observed when useful antagonists" reach the stage of large-scale testing, and can arise from a variety of causes reflecting the biological nature of the control microorganism. Essentially the organism must first survive application and then retain activity in the environment of use throughout the period when active control is required, which may be several months for some pathogens. During this time, it must survive fluctuations in the physical environment and the action of the indigenous and competitive microbiota. The use of appropriate inoculum production, formulation and application technologies together with quality control checks should also help in this process. Nevertheless, even if reliable BCAs can be produced, they must still be easy to use and cost-effective, or they will either never reach the market place or not be used by By early 2000, there were two yeast based postharvest biological products available on the market: Aspire^{TM} containing *Candida oleophila* I-182 and YieldPlus^{TM} containing yeast *Cryptococcus albidus* (Wilson and El Ghaouth, 2002). The commercial development of Aspire by Ecogen-Israel Partnership, Ltd. focussed on the biocontrol of postharvest decays of citrus, mainly blue mold and green mold caused by *P. italicum* and *P. digitatum*, respectively, which invade through wounds after harvest. YieldPlus was developed for use on pome fruits especially apples and pears. Throughout the course of developing Aspire^{TM}, considerable research went into finding methods to enhance the reliability and efficacy of the product and other selected antagonists as well.

As a result, second generation of biocontrol products were developed using a combination of natural products along with a yeast antagonist to address the poor ability. Research efforts led to the development of two new products whose main components consisted of the yeast antagonist, *Candida saitoana*, and either a derivative of chitosan (Biocoat) or lysozyme (Biocure) (El Ghaouth *et al.*, 2000). Both compounds have been tested worldwide and shown to have strong eradicant activity. Both products contain additional additives, such as sodium bicarbonate, to enhance efficacy and perform as well as currently available postharvest fungicides. While this research was initially conducted under a CRADA with American Cyanamid and then MicroFlo (a subsidiary of BASF), the technology has now been licensed to Memphis Associates and is awaiting registration by the U.S. Environmental Protection Agency.

Another constraint concerns registration. Currently there are no fungal biocontrol products registered and sold worldwide. Some of the products are available in several countries while others are sold in their respective countries. Most of the others appear to be sold only in the country of development. This reflects the problems associated with registration requirements in different countries, and includes concerns about releasing non-indigenous microorganisms. Authorities in USA and Europe are also aware that legislation drafted essentially for chemical pesticides is not always applicable to biological pesticides, and the requirements for registration of biological pesticides are currently under discussion for appropriate review.

Thirdly, the position of the biocontrol product in the market governs its future. For example if the products enter the agrochemical market, it competes against synthetic fungicides that can kill pathogenic organisms while yeast alone based products cannot do so, neither do they have systemic action. They mainly act as protectants that may also induce resistance in the hosts. Thus, it will require a new generation of "BCA' that include other natural fungicides. The other option is to position the product in 'all green' category, in markets such as those of perishables where no other option is available thus, eliminating any competition and fulfilling the principal objective of consumer and environmental safety.

Two products containing this BCA are available: Contans WG, in Germany and Switzerland, and KONI, in Hungary. Both are granular formulations, but Contans WG is sprayed and incorporated into soil after dispersal in water whereas KONI is incorporated into soil directly. Application must be made several weeks prior to planting crops to allow time for the sclerotia to be destroyed. Currently, although use is restricted to glasshouses and polyethylene tunnels for a range of high-value crops use on field crops and amenity areas is planned. *C. minitans* strain CON/M/91-08 in Contans WG is undergoing consideration for full European registration under the European Union (EU) Council Directive 91/414 and in spring 2001 received approval from the US-EPA and Austria.

The BCA *Gliocladium virens* has appeared on the market in two formulations, GlioGard™, an alginate pill formulation, and SoilGard™, a granular fluid-bed formulation. These products target damping-off diseases of vegetable and ornamental plant seedlings caused by *Rhizoctonia solani* and *Pythium* spp. Application was confined to greenhouse or interior container use. Only the product SoilGard is now produced and is marketed by Thermo Trilogy Corp., Columbia, Maryland, USA.

A commercial formulation of *Trichoderma harzianum* strain 1295-22 (T-22) is manufactured by BioWorks, Inc., Geneva, New York, USA, and sold through several distributors as T-22 Planter Box™. This conidial formulation is designed for application to large-seeded crops such as maize, beans, cotton and soybeans, and in most cases can be applied to seeds already treated with fungicides (Harman and Bjorkman, 1998). *Trichoderma viride* is available as a BCA in India from Hoechst Schering AgrEvo Ltd in a product named Ecofit. It is a talc-based powder sold for the control of root rot, seedling rot, damping-off; collar rot and Fusarium wilt in cotton, chick-pea, pigeonpea, Bengal gram, groundnut, sunflower, soybean, tobacco and vegetables. Depending on the plant and disease of interest, Ecofit can be applied before sowing as a dry powder or slurry seed treatment, before planting as a rhizome, tuber or set dip, or as a soil drench for soil incorporation following a preliminary scale-up procedure involving prior inoculation on to farmyard manure.

Many naturally occurring microorganisms have been used to control diseases on the aerial surfaces of plants. The most common bacterial species that have been used for the control of diseases in the phylloshpere include *Pseudomonas syringae, P. fluorescens, P. cepacia, Erwinia herbicola,* and *Bacillus subtilis*. Fungal genera that have been used for the control of air borne diseases include *Trichoderma* spp., *Ampelomyces* spp., and the yeasts *Tilletiopsis* and *Sporobolomyces*.

Ampelomyces quisqualis, formulation AQ 10, is the first biocontrol fungus developed specifically for controlling powdery mildew. AQ 10 is water-dispersible and acts as a mycoparasite on powdery mildews affecting leaves, stems or fruits of plants. The range of plants protected includes strawberry, tomato, grape, tree fruit and ornamentals (Dik *et al.,* 1998).Strain T39 of *T. harzianum* has been used for greenhouse control of *Botrytis cinerea*. It is produced by Makhteshim Chemical Works and is marketed as Trichodex TM in Europe and Israel. The strategy for best control involves alternating chemical and biological control treatments.

A combination of strains IMI 206040 and IMI 206039 of *T. harzianum* and *T. polysporum*, respectively, sold as BINAB-T, is one of the oldest commercial biopesticide preparations still available. Produced by Bio-lnnovation Eftr AB in Sweden it has been used for over 20 years. BINAB-T has been registered and used in the past for control of numerous diseases, but currently, in Sweden and Denmark, is used largely for the control of grey mould (*B. cinerea*) on strawberries, with some minor use in glasshouse crops to control soil-borne pathogens. The other main market is Chile, where it is used for the suppression of silver-leaf disease (*Chondrostereum purpureum*) and chlorotic leaf curl in stone fruit and grapes, respectively.

Future Line of Research

Future line of research should be directed to find methods to enhance the reliability and efficacy of selected antagonists and the field is gaining momentum. It should aim at finding additives or physical control methods that would act synergistically with the antagonist. This involves combining the product with a low-level of postharvest fungicide or GRAS substances. It has been reported that physical treatments such as hot air, curing, hot water brushing, and combinations of the above with pressure infiltration of calcium could also increase the efficacy of antagonists. Means of inducing host resistance to decay in harvested commodities, also demonstrate that this approach could enhance the performance of yeast antagonists. Using mixtures of antagonists, or combining antagonists with specific nutrients or sugar analogs is also suggested as an approach to increase efficacy.

Genetic manipulation of antagonists is a field in its infancy. Current efforts are focused on developing efficient transformation procedures for yeast antagonists and inserting genes for tracking the antagonist in the environment rather than enhancing biocontrol (Yehuda *et al.*, 2003). However, attempts to over express genes involved in biocontrol, e.g., lytic enzymes, or engineering strains with desired biocontrol traits may soon yield positive results. Since one mechanism involved in the biocontrol of postharvest fruit pathogens is mycoparasitism, cell wall degrading enzymes, such as chitinases, proteases and glucanases produced by bacterial and fungal microorganisms, could be inserted into the potential antagonists to improve the degradation of the pathogen cell walls, resulting in death or growth inhibition of the antagonised fungus.

Other approaches could be the insertion of the gene for amylase under constitutive promoter in some BCAs to allow an effective utilisation of the fruit carposphere starch; biocontrol strains with a higher capability of exploitation of the nitrogen compounds present, or with a higher transport or metabolism rate of the limiting factor could be developed, because nitrogen is often a limiting substance when the biocontrol mechanism of action is competition for nutrients; use of mutants that use new substrates, not metabolised by the pathogen, to provide a nutritional advantage or attempt to obtain strains resistant to phenolic compounds

Early experiments of transformation for marker genes have been successful: *M. pulcherrima* was transformed with the green fluorescent protein gene, *C. oleophila* was transformed with the glucuronidase geneand histidine auxotrophs of *C. oleophila* were transformed with *HIS3, HIS4* and *HIS5* genes In all cases the transformed antagonists maintained their biocontrol capability and there were no detectable differences between the wild type and the transformants. All these studies were accomplished only to obtain variants of the antagonistic strains with a genetically stable marker to expedite studies on the ecology of the yeast antagonists on the fruit surface, but are highly effective for subsequent insertions of useful genes. Jones and Prusky (2002) have investigated the possibility of expressing a DNA sequence in *Saccharomyces cerevisiae* to allow the production of a cecropin A-based antifungal peptide. Yeast transformants inhibited the growth of germinated *Colletotrichum coccoides* spores and inhibited decay developments caused by the pathogen in tomato fruit. The lack of activity toward non-target organisms by the peptide and the use of *S. cerevisiae* as a delivery system suggest that this method could provide a safe alternative for postharvest disease control. However, attempts to overexpress genes involved in biocontrol, e.g., lytic enzymes, or engineering strains with desired biocontrol traits may soon yield positive results.

Conclusion

Harvested fruit and vegetables are agricultural produce that require stringent control of post-harvest handling, to avoid disease and to preserve the quality of the produce (Prusky and Lichter, 2008).

Now it is clear that the stage is set for fungal biological disease control agents to play a greater part in agriculture and horticulture. The need for alternatives to chemical fungicides, when viewed against a groundswell of feeling by the public for more natural or organic food production systems, makes this a priority. This would require researchers and extension scientists, government, producers, grower organizations and levy boards, retailers and agrochemical companies to collaborate for successful implementation. It will open job and wealth creation opportunities because of numerous niche markets that it will create. Importantly, low cost production, corporate commitment, good management and market research will provide rapid success to small-medium-size enterprises and also benefit the end users. This approach would undoubtedly encourage environmentally desirable products that are wanted by the public to reach the market place rapidly.

It has been 25 years since research first showed that biological control could be successfully used on harvested fruits when brown rot of peach was effectively controlled using the soil isolated bacterium *Bacillus subtilis* B3 Since then, the development of biological control of postharvest disease (BCPD) has gone through various phases, including the search for bacterial and yeast antagonists naturally occurring on fruit, upscale tests under semi-commercial conditions, pilot tests, toxicology tests, and registration of the first commercial products (Janisiewicz and Korsten, 2002). Currently there are more than two dozen programs world-wide workings on various aspects of BCPD, and new products are being registered for postharvest application in various countries (Janisiewicz, 2010). As the commercial use of BCPD increased, originally perceived limitations of this approach become a reality. This spurred significant interest into research on addressing the limitations of the registered products, as well as antagonists in the developmental stage.

One of the main approaches has been combining biological control with alternatives to conventional fungicide control, which by themselves may not provide commercially acceptable control but may complement the limitations of the biological control treatment (Janisiewicz, 2008). In general, these alternatives could be divided into physical and chemical methods. Some of them have direct effects on the pathogens but others may act indirectly by increasing fruit resistance to the pathogens or retarding senescence. In this review we discuss various combinations of these treatments with biological control on fruits after harvest.

Biological control of plant diseases in general and on fruit after harvest in particular is a niche market, with a relatively small profit potential. However, it is clear that the stage is set for biological control agents to play a greater part in agriculture and horticulture. It will open job and wealth creation opportunities because of numerous niche markets that it will create. Low cost production, corporate commitment, good management and market research will provide rapid success to small-medium-size enterprises and also benefit the end users. This approach would undoubtedly encourage environmentally desirable products that are wanted by the public to reach the market place rapidly.

Table 7.1: Commercial Products Currently on the Open Market or Under Registration Include

Product	Biocontrol agent	Effective against	Manufacturer/ distributor
Anti-fungus	*Trichoderma spp*		Grondortsmettigen De Cuester, Belgium
Bas-derma	*T.viride Basarass*		Biocontrol Res. Lab., India
Binab	*T.harzianum (ATCC20476) and T. polysporum (ATCC 20475)*	Control of wound decay and wood rot	Bio-innovation AB, UK
Bioderma	*T .harzianum, T. viride*		Biotech International Ltd., India
Biofungus	*Trichoderma spp.*	*Sclerotinia, Phytophthora, Rhizoctonia solani,Pythium spp.,Fusarium, Verticillium.*	Grondortsmettigen De Cuester n.v., Belgium
Bio-trek 22G	*T. harzianum*		Bioworks, Inc. of Geneva, NY
Ecofit	*T.viride*		Hoechst Schering Afgro Evo Ltd., India
Root pro, Root Potato	*T. harzianum*	*R. solani, Pythium spp.,Fusarium spp.,* and *Sclerotium rolfsii*	Efal Agr, Israel
Root shield, Plant shield, T -22 Planter Box	*T.harzianum Rifai strain* KRL-AG (T- 22)	*Pythium spp., R-solani, Fusarium spp.*	Bioworks Inc., USA
RUTOPIA	*Trichoderma spp.*	Organic Soil Amendment. Turfgrass Biostimulant	NaEx Corp/Poulenger USA, Inc
SoilGard (formerly. SlioGard).	*Trichoderma spp.*	Damping-off diseases caused by *Pythium* and *Rhizoctonia spp.*	USA

Supresivit	*T.harzianum*	Various fungi	Borregaard and Reitzel, Czech Republic
T -22 G, T -22 HB	*T.harzianum* starin *KRL-AG2*		THT Inc., USA
Trichoderma 2000	*Trichoderma spp.*	*R. solani, S. rolfsii Pythium spp., Fusarium spp.*	Myocontrol Ltd., Israel
Trichodex Trichophel	*T.harzianum*	Botrytis of vegetables and , grapevines	Makhteshim Chemical Works Ltd., USA
Trihcophel, Trichoject, Trichodowels Trichoseal	*T.harzianum* and *T. viride*	*Armillaria,Botryosphaeria, Chondrosternum, Fusarium, Nectria,Phytopht hora,Pythium,Rhizoctonia,*	Agrimm Technologies Ltd., New Zealand.
Tri-control	*Trichoderma spp.*		Je ee Biotechs, India
Trieco	*Trichoderma viride*	*Rhizoctonia spp., Pythium spp., Fusarium spp.*, root rot, seedling rot, collar rot, red rot, damping-off Fusarium wilt	Ecosense Labs Pvt. Ltd., Mumbai,India
TV	*Trichoderma*		Myocontrol, Israel
Tusal	*Trichoderma spp.*	Damping-off diseases caused by *Pythium, Phoma* and *Rhizoctonia species,* rhizomania disease of sugar beet and drop of lettuce	Spain

REFERANCES

Bostock RM. 2005. Signal Crosstalk and Induced Resistance: Straddling the Line Between Cost and Benefit. *Annual Review in Phytopathology* 43: 545–580.

Cao S, Zheng Y, Tang S and Wang K. 2008. Improved Control of Anthracnose Rot by Loquat Fruit by Combination Treatment of *Pichia membranifaciens* with $CaCl_2$. *International Journal of Food Microbiology* 126: 216–22.

Cao S, Zheng Y, Wang K, Tang S and Rui H. 2009. Effect of Yeast Antagonist in Combination with Methyl Jasmonate Treatment on Postharvest Anthracnose Rot of Loquat Fruit. *Biological Control* 50: 73–77.

Castoria R, De Curtis F, Lima G, Caputo L, Pacifico S. and De Cicco V. 2001. *Aureobasidium pullulans* (LS-30) an Antagonist of Postharvest Pathogens of Fruits: Study on Its Modes of Action. *Postharvest Biol Technol* 22:7-17.

Chan Z, Qin G, Xu X, Li B and Tian S. 2007. Proteome Approach to Characterize Proteins Induced by Antagonist Yeast and Salicylic Acid in Peach Fruit. *Journal of Proteome Research* 6: 1677–1688.

Chan Z, Wang Q, Xu X, Meng X, Qin G, Li B and Tian S.2008. Functions of Defense-Related Proteins and Dehydrogenases in Resistance Response Induced by Salicylic Acid in Sweet Cherry Fruits at Different Maturity Stages. *Proteomics* 8: 4791–4807.

Conway WS, Janisiewicz WJ, Leverentz B, Saftner RA and Camp MJ. 2007. Control of Blue Mold of Apple by Combining Controlled Atmosphere, An Antagonist Mixture, and Sodium Bicarbonate. *Postharvest Biology and Technology* 45: 326–333.

Conway WS, Leverentz B, Janisiewicz WJ, Blodgett AB, Saftner RA and Camp MJ. 2004. Integrating Heat Treatment, Biocontrol and Sodium Bicarbonate to Reduce Postharvest Decay of Apple Caused by *Colletotrichum acutatum* and *P. expansum*. *Postharvest Biology and Technology* 34: 11–20.

Conway WS, Leverentz B, Janisiewicz WJ, Saftner RA and Camp MJ. 2005. Improving Biocontrol Using Antagonist Mixtures with Heat and/or Sodium Bicarbonate to Control Postharvest Decay of Apple Fruit. *Postharvest Biology and Technology*: 36: 235–244.

De Capdeville G, Wilson CL, Beer SV and Aist JR. 2002. Alternative Disease Control Agents Induce Resistance to Blue Mold in Harvested "Red Delicious" Apple Fruit. *Phytopathology* 92: 900–908.

De Capdeville, Beer SV, Watkins CB, Wilson CL, Tedeschi LO and Aist JR.2003. Pre- and Post-harvest Harpin Treatments of Apples Induce Resistance to Blue Mold. *Plant Disease* 87: 39–44.

De Costa DM and HRUT. Erabadupitiya 2005. An Integrated Method to Control Postharvest Diseases of Banana Using a Member of the *Burkholder cepacia* Complex. *Postharvest Biology and Technology* 36: 31–39.

Delespaul Q, de Billebeck VG and Roques EG 2000. The Antifungal Activity of Essential Oils as Determined by Different Screening Methods. *Journal of Essential Oil Research.* 12: 256-266.

Devlieghere F, Vermeulen A and Debever J. 2004. Chitosan: Antimicrobial Activity, Interaction with Food Components and Applicability as a Coating on Fruit and Vegetables. *Food Microbiology* 21: 703–714.

Dik AJ, Verhaar MA and Belanger RR. 1998. Comparison of Three Biological Control Agents Against Cucumber Powdery Mildew (*Sphaerotheca fuliginea*) in Semi-commercial-scale Glasshouse Trials. *European Journal of Plant Pathology* 104: 413-423.

Droby S, Chalutz E, Wilson E and Wisniewski M. 1989. Characterization of the Biocontrol Activity of *Debaryonryce shansenii* in the Control of *Penicillium digitatum* on Grapfruit. *Canadian Journal of Microbiology*. 3.5: 794-800.

El Ghaouth A and Wilson CL 2002. *Candida saitoana* Compositions for Biocontrol of Plant Postharvest Decay. U. S. Patent No. 6,419,922.

El Ghaouth A., Smilanick J, Brown E, Ippolito A. and Wilson CL 2000. Application of *Candida saitoana* and Glycolchitosan for the Control of Posthrvest Diseases of Apple and Citrus Fruit Under Semi-commercial Conditions. *Plant Dis.* 84: 243-248.

El-Ghaouth A, Smilanick JL, Brown G, Ippolito A and Wilson CL. 2001. Control of Decay of Apple and Citrus Fruits in Semicommercial Tests with *Candida saitoana* and 2-deoxy-D-glucose. *Biological Control:* 20: 96–105.

Errampalli D and Brubacher NR. 2006. Biological and Integrated Control of Postharvest Blue Mold (*Penicillium expansum*) of Apples by *Pseudomonas syringae* and Cyprodinil. *Biological Control*: 36: 49–56.

Eshel D, Regev, R, Orenstein J, Droby S and Gan-Mor S 2009. Combining Physical, Chemical and Biological Methods for Synergistic Control of Postharvest Diseases: A Case Study of Black Root Rot of Carrot. *Postharvest Biology and Technology* 54: 48–52.

Fallik E 2004. Prestorage Hot Water Treatments (Immersion, Rinsing and Brushing). *Postharvest Biology and Technology* 2004: 32: 125–134.

Fallik E, Alkalai-Tuvia S and Perzelan Y. 2008. Prestorage Hot Water Rinsing and Brushing Technology to Reduce Decay Development in Fresh Produce. In: Proceedings of COST Action 924 International Congress, Novel Approaches for the Control of Postharvest Diseases and Disorders. Bologna, Italy: CRIOF, University of Bologna, 141–148.

Gholamnejad J and Ebabarian HR. 2009. Effect of Calcium Chloride on the Biocontrol Efficacy of Two Antagonistic Yeasts against *Penicillium expansum* on Apple Fruit. *Phytoparasitica* 37: 255–261.

Harman GE & Bjorkman T 1998. Potential and Existing Uses of *Trichoderma* and *Gliocladium* for Plant Disease Control and Plant Growth Enhancement. In: Harman, G.E. and Kubicek, C.P. (eds) *Trichoderma* and *Gliocladium*: Enzymes, Biological Control and Commercial Applications, Vol. 2. Taylor & Francis, London, pp. 229-265.

Hic Z, Polevaya Y, Tuvia-Alkalai S, Copel A and Fallik E. 2001. A Short Prestorage Hot Water Rinse and Brushing Reduces Decay Development in Tomato, While Maintaining Its Quality. *Trop. Agric. Res. Ext.* 4: 1-6

Hofstein R, Fridlender B, Chautz E, Wisnewski M. and Wilson Cl. 1994. Large-scale Production and Pilot Testing of Biological Control Agents for Postharvest Diseases. In: Wtlson, C. and Wisniewski, M. Eds. Biological Control of Postharvest Diseases of Fruits and Vegetables -Theory and Practice. CRC Press, Boca Raton, FL.USA, pp. 89-100.

Ippolito A, Schena L, Pentimone I and Nigro F. 2005. Control of Postharvest Rots of Sweet Cherries by pre- and Postharvest Applications of *Aureobasidium pullulans* in Combination with Calcium Chloride ore Sodium Bicarbonate. *Postharvest Biology and Technology* 36: 245–252.

Janisiewicz WJ and Conway WS 2010. Combining Biological Control with Physical and Chemical Treatments to Control Fruit Decay After Harvest. *Stewart Postharvest Review.* 2010, 1: 3 doi: 10.2212/spr.2010.1.3

Janisiewicz WJ and Korsten L. 2002. Biological Control of Postharvest Diseases of Fruits. *Annual Review of Phytopathology* 40: 411– 441.

Janisiewicz WJ, Leverentz B, Conway WS, Saftner RA, Reed AN and Camp MJ. 2003. Control of Bitter Rot and Blue Mold of Apples by Integrating Heat and Antagonist Treatments on 1-MCP Treated Fruit Stored Under Controlled Atmosphere Conditions. *Postharvest Biology and Technology* 29: 129–143.

Janisiewicz WJ, Saftner RA, Conway WS and Yoder KS. 2008. Control of Blue Mold Decay of Apple during Commercial Controlled Atmosphere Storage with Yeast Antagonists and Sodium Bicarbonate. *Postharvest Biology and Technology* 49: 374–378.

Janisiewicz WJ, Tworkowski TJ and Kurtzman CP. 2001. Biocontrol Potential of *Metchnikowia pulcherrima* Strains against Blue Mold of Apple. *Phytopathology* 91: 1098–108.

Janisiewicz WJ. 2008. Commercial Applications and Future Prospects for the Use of Biological Control After Harvest. In: Proceedings of the COST 924 International Congress on Novel Approaches for the Control of Postharvest Diseases and Disorders. P. Bertolini (ed.), CRIOF – University of Bologna, Italy; pp. 9–18.

Janisiewicz WJ. 2010.*Quo Vadis* of Biological Control of Postharvest Diseases. In: Post-harvest Pathology, Plant Pathology in the 21st Century, Prusky D and Gullino ML (eds), Vol.2. Springer: pp. 137–148

Janisiewiez WJ, Tworkoski TJ and Sharer C 2000. Characterizing the Mechanism of Biological Control of Postharvest Diseases on Fruits with a Simple Method to Study Competition for Nutrients. *Phytopathology.* 90: 1196-2000.

Jones RW and Prusky D 2002. Expression of an Antifungal Peptide in *Saccharomyces*: A New Approach for Biological Control of the Postharvest Disease Caused by *Colletotrichum coccodes*. *Phytopathology* 92: 33-37.

Karabulut OA and Baykal N 2002 Evaluation of the Use of Microwave Power for the Control of Postharvest Diseases of Peaches. *Postharvest Biology and Technology* 2002: 26: 237–240.

Karabulut OA, Arslan U and Kuruoglu G. 2004.Control of Postharvest Diseases of Organically Grown Strawberry with Preharvest Applications of Some Food Additives and Postharvest Hot Dips. *Journal of Phytopathology* 152: 224–228.

Karabulut OA, Cohen L, Wiess B, Daus A, Lurie S and Droby S. 2002. Control of Brown Rot and Blue Mold of Peach and Nectarine by Short Hot Water Brushing and Yeast Antagonists. *Postharvest Biology and Technology:* 24: 103–111.

Kittur FS, Saroja N, Habibunnisa and Tharanathan RN. 2001. Polysaccharidebased Composite Coating Formulations for Shelf-life Extension of Fresh Banana and Mango. *European Food Research and Technology* .213: 306–311.

Klein J D and Lurie S 1990. Prestorage Heat Treatment as a Means of Improving Poststorage Quality of Apples. *Journal of the American Society for Horticultural Science*: 115: 265–269.

Korsten L.2006. Advance in Control of Post Harvest Diseases in Tropical Fresh Produces. *Int. j. Post Harvest Technol and Innov.*1 (1):48-61.

Leverentz B, Conway WS, Janisiewicz WJ, Saftner RA and Camp MJ. 2003. Effect of Combining MCP Treatment, Heat Treatment, and Biocontrol on the Reduction of Postharvest Decay of 'Golden Delicious' Apples. *Postharvest Biology and Technology* 27: 221–233.

Leverentz B, Janisiewicz WJ, Conway WS, Saftner RA, Fuchs Y, Sams CE and Camp MJ. 2000. Combining Yeasts or a Bacterial Biocontrol Agent and Heat Treatment to Reduce Postharvest Decay of 'Gala' Apples. *Postharvest Biology and Technology* 21: 87–94.

Li J, Chikindas ML, Ludescher RD and Montville TJ.2002. Temperature- and Surfactant Induced Membrane Modifications that alter *Listeria monocytogenes* Nisin Sensitivity by Different Mechanisms. *Applied and Environmental Microbiology* 68: 5904–5910.

Ligorio A, Platania G, Schena L, Castiglione V, Pentimone I, Nigro F, Di Silvestro I and Ippolito A. 2008. Control of table grape Storage Rots by Combined Applications of Antagonistic Yeasts, Salts, and Natural Substances. In: Proceedings of COST Action 924 International Congress, Novel Approaches for the Control of Postharvest Diseases and Disorders. Bologna, Italy: CRIOF, University of Bologna, 124–128.

Lima G, De Curtis F, Piedimonte D, Spina AM and De Cicco V. 2006.Integration of Biocontrol Yeast and Thiabendazole Protects Stored Apples from Fungicide Sensitive and Resistant Isolates of *Botrytis cinerea. Postharvest Biology and Technology* 40: 301–307.

Micota Gabler F, Mercier J, Jimenez JI and Smilanick JL 2010. Integration of Continuous Biofumigation with *Muscodor albus* with Pre-cooling Fumifation Woth Ozone or Sulfur Dioxide to Control Postharvest Gray Mold of Table Grapes. *Postharvest Biology and Technology* 55: 78–84.

Nunes C, Usall J, Teixido N, Abadias M and Vinas I.2002. Improved Control of Postharvest Decay of Pears by the Combination of *Candida sake* (CPA- 1) and Ammonium Molybdate. *Phytopathology* 92: 281–287.

Nunes C, Usall J, Teixido N, Miro M and Vinas I. 2001. Nutritional Enhancement of Biocontrol Activity of *Candida sake* (CPA-1) against *Penicillium expansum* on Apples and Pears. *European Journal of Plant Pathology* .107: 543–551.

Obagwu J and Korsten L.2002. Integrated Control of Citrus Green and Blue Molds using *Bacillus subtilis* in Combination with Sodium Bicarbonate or Hot Water. *Postharvest Biology and Technology* 28: 187–194.

Palou, L, Smilanick JL, Usall J and Vinas I. 2001 Control of Postharvest Blue and Green Molds of Oranges by Hot Water, Sodium Carbonate, and Sodium Bicarbonate. *Plant Disease* 85: 371–376.

Paull RE and Chen NJ 2000. Heat Treatment and Fruit Ripening. *Postharvest BioL Technol.* 21: 21-38.

Porat R, Pavoncello D, 'Peretz Y, Weiss B, Cohen L, Ben-Yehoshua S, Fallik E, Droby S. and Lurie S. 2000. Induction of Resistance against *Penicillium digitatum* and Chilling Injury in Star Ruby Grapefruit by a Short Hot Water Brushing Treatment. *J. Hort. Sci. Biotech.* 75: 428-432.

Porat, R., Daus, A., Weiss, B., Cohen, L and Droby, S. 2003. Effects of Combining Hot Water, Sodium Bicarbonate and Biocontrol on Postharvest Decay of Citrus Fruit. *Journal of Horticultural Science and Biotechnology* 77: 441–445.

Prusky D and Lichter A 2008. Mechanisms Modulating Fungal Attack in Post Harvest Pathogens Interaction and their Control. *Eur j Plant Pathol* 121:281-289.

Qin GZ and Tian SP. 2004. Biocontrol of Postharvest Diseases of Jujube Fruit by *Cryptococcus laurentii* Combined with a Low Dosage of Fungicides under Different Storage Conditions. *Plant Disease* 88: 497–501.

Qin GZ, Tian SP, Xu Y, Chan ZL and Li BQ. 2006. Combination of Antagonistic Yeast with Two Food Additives for Control of Brown Rot Caused by *Monilinia fructicola* on Sweet Cherry Fruit. *Journal of Applied Microbiology* 100: 508–515.

Ramanazzi G, Mlikota Grabler F and Smilanick JL. 2006. Preharvest Chitosan and Postharvest UV Irradiation Treatments Suppress Gray Mold of Table Grapes. *Plant Disease* 90: 445–450.

Rodrigues FA, Vale FXR, Datnoff LE, Prabhu AS and Korndorfer GH. 2003. Effect of Rice Growth Stages and Silicon on Sheath Blight Development. *Phytopathology* 93: 256–261.

Schena L, Nigro F, Soleti Ligorio, V, Yaseen T, Ippolito A and El Ghaouth A. 2005. Biocontrol Activity of Bio-coat and Biocure against Postharvest Rots of Table Grapes and Sweet Cherries. *Acta Horticulturae* (ISHS) 682: 2115–2120.

Sharma N 1999. Newer Strategies to Control Post-harvest Diseases of Perishables. In: "*Plant Pest Management,*" Eds. P.C. Trevedi, Published by: Avishkar Publishers, Distributors, Jaipur, pp. 57-74.

Sharma G and Alderson PA 2005. UV Hormesis in Fruits: A Concept Ripe for Commercialization. *Trends in Food Sci. Technol.* 16: 128-136.

Sharma N 2002. Effect of Neem and Its Derivatives in Insect-pest Management. In "*Plant Protection-A Biocontrol Approach*". Eds. P.C. Trivedi., Published by: Avishkar Publishers, Distributors, Jaipur, pp. 163-179.

Sharma N. and Prabha B 2012. Recent Trends in Management of Post Harvest Diseases. In: "*Advances in Botany*", Indian Botanical Society Commemoration Volume. Eds. Y. Vimala, P.C.Trivedi and C.M. Govil, Published by Pointer Publishers, Jaipur, pp. 36-57.

Sharma N and Srivastava MP 2008. Integrated Management of Seed Borne Fungi of Soybean by *Adenocalymma alliaceum* Miers." *Journal of Natural Resource and Development*.3 (2):91-96.

Sharma N and Srivastava MP 2012. Integrated Management of Soybean (*Glycine × max L. Merr.)* by Essential Oil of *Citrus sinensis (L)* Osbeck Epicarp in Post Harvest. *Journal of Ornamental and Horticulture Plants.* 2(1)33-44.

Sharma N and Tripathi A 2006. Fungitoxicity of the Essential Oil of *Citrus sinensis* on Post-harvest Pathogens. *World Journal of Microbiology & Biotechnology* 22(6): 587-593.

Sharma N and Tripathi A 2008. Integrated Management of Postharvest *Fusarium* Rot of Gladiolus Corms Using Hot Water, UV -C and *Ffyptis suaveolens* (L.) Poit. Essential oil. *Postharvest Biol Technol* 47: 246-254.

Sharma N, Awasthi P, Tripathi A, Sharma S, Prabha B and Agnihotri S. 2006. Control of *Aspergillus niger* (L.)Van Tieghem in Mango Fruits Utilizing Combination of Yeast and Chitosan, a Soft Fungicide. *Indian J. Plant Pathol* 24 (1 & 2):74-77.

Sharma N, Sharma S and Prabha B 2012. Post Harvest Biocontrol-New Concept and Application. B. venkateshwarulu *et al.* (eds), Crop Stress and Its Management: Perspectives and Strategies, doi 10.10007/978-94-007-2220-0_15 Springer Science + Business Media B. V.

Sharma N, Sharma S and Prabha B 2012. Postharvest Biocontrol - New Concepts and Application. In: *"Crop Stress and Its Management: Perspective and Prospects".* Ed.Venkateshwarulu *et al.*, DOI 10.1007/978-94-007-2220-0_15, Published by Springer Science Business Media B.V.

Sharma N, Tewari A, Srivastava MP and Bhanderi AS. 2011. Using Fungi and Yeast to Mange Post Harvest Disease of Perishables. *In 'Plant Health amd their Mangement"* (P.C. Trivedi Eds) Agrobios (India) pp. 407-420.

Sharma, N, Awasthi P, Tripathi A, Sharma S, Prabha B and Agnihotri S 2006. Control of *Aspergillus niger* (L.)Van Tieghem in Mango Fruits Utilizing Combination of Yeast and Chitosan, a Soft Fungicide. *Indian J. Plant Pathol* 24 (1 & 2):74-77.

Singh D. and Thakur AK 2002. Suppression of Green Mold Rot Caused by *Penicillium digitatum* in Kinnow Fruits by Hot Water Immersion Treatment. *Indian Pathopathol* 55(3): 282-285.

Smilanick JL 20003. Use of Ozone in Storage and Packing Facilities. Proceedings: Organic *Certification in the United States and Europe.* pp. 1–10. http: //postharvest.tfrec.wsu.edu/PC2003E.pdf.

Smilanick JL, Margosan DM and Mlikota Gabler F 2002. Impact of Ozonated Water on the Quality and Shelf-Life of Fresh Citrus, Stone Fruits, and Table Grapes. *Ozone Science and Engineering*: 24 (5): 343–356.

Spadaro D, Vola R, Piano S and Gullino ML 2002. Mechanisms of Action and Efficacy of Four Isolates of the Yeast *Metschnikowia pulcherrima* Active against Postharvest Pathogens on Apples. *Postharvest Biology and Technology* 24: 123-134.

Stevens C, Khan V, Lu JY, Wilson CL, Pusey PL, Igwegbe ECK, Kabwe MK, Mafolo Y, Liu J, Chalutz E and Droby S.1997. Integration of Ultraviolet (UV-C) Light with Yeast Treatment for Control of postharvest Storage Rots of Fruits and Vegetables. *Biological Control* 10: 98–103.

Stevens C, Khan VA, Wilson CL, Lu JY, Chalutz E and Droby S 2005. The Effect of Fruit Orientation of Postharvest Commodities Following Low Dose Ultraviolet Light-C Treatment on Host Induced Resistance to Decay. *Crop Protection*: 24: 756–759.

Stevens C, Khan VA, Wilson CL, Lu JY, Pusey L, Bassett CL, Igwegbe ECK, Wisniewski M, Chalutz E, Droby S and El Ghaouth A 2006. The Use of Low Dose UV-C Light Technology to Control Postharvest Storage Decay and Delayed Ripening and Senescence of Fruits and Vegetables. In: Advances in Postharvest Technologies for Horticultural Crops. Noureddine B and Norio S (Eds.); pp. 195–237.

Stevens C, Liu J, Khan V, Lu JY, Kabwe MK, Wilson CL Igwegbe ECK, Chalutz E and Droby S 2004. The Effect of Low-Dose Ultraviolet Light-C Treatment on Polygalacturonase Activity, Delay Ripening and Rhizopus Soft Rot Development of Tomatoes. *Crop Protection*: 23: 551–554.

Sugar D and Basile SR. 2008. Timing and Sequence of Postharvest Fungicide and Biocontrol Agent Applications for Control of Pear Decay. *Postharvest Biology and Technology* 49: 107–112.

Terry LA and Joyce DC 2004. Elicitors of Induced Resistance in Postharvest Horticultural Crops: A Brief Review. *Postharvest Biology and Technology* 32: 1–13.

Tian S, Fan Q, Yong X and Liu HB 2002. Biocontrol Efficacy of Antagonist Yeasts to Gray Mold and Blue Mold on Apples and Pears in Controlled Atmospheres. *Plant Disease* 2002: 86: 848–853.

Tian S, Qin G and Xu Y.2004. Synergistic Effects of Combining Biocontrol Agents with Silicon Against Postharvest Diseases of Jujube Fruit. *Journal of Food Protection* 68: 544–550.

Tian S, Qin G, Li B and Wang Q. 2008. Synergistic Effects of Combining Microbial Biocontrol Agents with Silicon Against Postharvest Diseases of Fruits. In: Proceedings of COST Action 924 International Congress, Novel Approaches for the Control of Postharvest Diseases and Disorders. Bologna, Italy: CRIOF, University of Bologna, 38–46.

Tian SP, Fan Q, Xu Y and Jiang AL. 2002. Effects of Calcium on Biocontrol Activity of Yeast Antagonists against the Postharvest Decay Fungal Pathogen *Rhizopus stolonifer*. *Plant Pathology* 2002: 51: 352–358.

Tripathi P and Dubey NK 2004. Exploitation of Natural Products as an Alternative Strategy to Control Postharvest Fungal Rotting of Fruits and Vegetables. *Postharvest Biol Technol* 32: 235-245.

Tzotzakis NG. 2007. Methyl jasmonate-induced Suppression of Anthracnose Rot in Tomato Fruit. *Crop Protection* 26: 1507–1513.

Unnikrishnan V and Nath BS 2002. Hazardous Chemicals in Foods. *Indian Journal of Dairy Bioscience* 11: 155–158.

Usall J, Smilanick J, Palou L, Denis-Arrue N, Teixido N, Torres R and Vinas I. 2008. Preventative and Curative Activity of Combined Treatments of Sodium Carbonates and *Pantoea agglomerans* CPA-2 to Control Postharvest Green Mold of Citrus fruit. *Postharvest Biology and Technology* 50: 1–7.

Usall J, Teixido N, Fons E and Vinas I. 2000. Biological Control of Blue Mould on Apple by a Strain of *Candida sake* Under Several Controlled Atmosphere Conditions. *International Journal of Food Microbiology* 58: 83–92.

Utama, 1M.S., Wills, R.B.H., Ben-Ye-Hoshua, S. and Kuck, C. 2002. *In vitro* Efficacy of Plant Volatiles for Inhibiting the Growth of Fruit and Vegetable Decay Microorganisms. J. *Agric. Food Chem.* 50: 6371-6377.

Walling LL. 2001. Induced Resistance: From the Basic to the Applied. *Trends in Plant Science* 6: 445–447.

Wilson C L and El Ghaouth A 2002. Biological Coating with a Protective and Curative Effect for the Control of Postharvest Decay. U.S. Patent No. 6,423,310.

Wilson Cl and Wisniewski ME 1989. Biocontrol of Postharvest Diseases of Fruits and Vegetables: An Emerging Technology. *Annual Review of Pythopathology,* 27: 425.

Yao H and Tian S 2005. Effects of Biocontrol Agent and Methyl Jasmonate on Postharvest Diseases of Peach Fruit and the Possible Mechanism Involved. *Journal Applied Microbiology* 98: 941–950.

Yao H, Tian S and Wang Y 2004. Sodium Bicarbonate Enhances Biocontrol Efficacy of Yeasts on Fungal Spoilage of Pears. *International Journal of Food Microbiology* 93: 297–304.

Yu T and Zheng XD 2006. Salicylic Acid Enhances Biocontrol Efficacy of the Antagonist *Cryptococcus laurentii* in Apple Fruit. *Journal of Plant Growth Regulation* 25: 166–174.

Yu T, Chen J, Chen R, Huang B, Liu D and Zheng X. 2007. Biocontrol of Blue and Gray Mold Diseases of Pear Fruit by Integration of Antagonistic Yeast with Salicylic Acid. *International Journal of Food Microbiology* 116: 339–345.

Zhang H, Fu C, Zheng X and Su D 2006 Postharvest Control of Blue Mold Rot of Pear by Microwave Treatment and *Cryptococcus laurentii. Journal of Food Engineering* 77: 539–544.

Zhang H, Fu C, Zheng X, Xi Y, Jiang W and Wang Y 2004. Control of Post Harvest *Rhizopus Rot of Peach by Microwave Treatment and Yeast Antagonist. European Food Research and Technology 218: 568–572.*

Zhang H, Zheng X and Xi Y 2005. Biological Control of Postharvest Blue Mold of Oranges by Cryptococcus laurentii (Kufferath) Skinner. BioControl 50: 331-342.

Index